CONSTRUCTING
DANGER

CONSTRUCTING
DANGER

Emotions and the Mis/Representation of Crime in the News

Second Edition

CHRIS McCORMICK

Fernwood Publishing • Halifax & Winnipeg

Editing and text design: Brenda Conroy
Cover design: John van der Woude
Cover artwork: Detail from *Deadlier than the Male* by Gary Panter
Printed and bound in Canada by Hignell Book Printing

Mixed Sources
Product group from well-managed
forests and other controlled sources
www.fsc.org Cert no. SW-COC-003438
© 1996 Forest Stewardship Council

Published in Canada by Fernwood Publishing
32 Oceanvista Lane
Black Point, Nova Scotia, B0J 1B0
and 748 Broadway Avenue, Winnipeg, Manitoba, R3G 0X3
www.fernwoodpublishing.ca

Fernwood Publishing Company Limited gratefully acknowledges the financial support of the
Government of Canada through the Canada Book Fund, the Canada Council for the Arts, the
Nova Scotia Department of Tourism and Culture and the Province of Manitoba, through the
Book Publishing Tax Credit, for our publishing program.

Library and Archives Canada Cataloguing in Publication

McCormick, Christopher Ray, 1956-
Constructing danger: emotions and the mis/representation of crime in the news / Chris
McCormick. — 2nd ed.

Includes bibliographical references.
ISBN 978-1-55266-382-0 (pbk.) — ISBN 978-1-55266-387-5 (bound)

1. Crime and the press—Canada. 2. Crime in mass media—Canada. 3. Journalism—
Objectivity—Canada. I. Title.

PN4914.C74M33 2010   070.4'49364971   C2010-902870-8

Contents

Preface to the Second Edition

I have long been interested in how crime is reported in the news, and I have often used newspaper articles as examples to present current affairs topics in my criminology classes. However, I came to see that crime is more than simply reported in the news; it is also constructed, and sometimes distorted, exaggerated and manipulated as well. So what started out as a teaching aid expanded to become a topic of analysis, and I now teach advanced courses devoted solely to the topic of how crime is presented in the news.

I have never found the perfect book for that course, although some come close, and so I decided to write my own. I suspect many books stem from similar beginnings. What I wanted in particular was a book that showed how analysis was done rather than one that summarized the results of research after the fact. So the pedagogy of this book is designed to draw the reader to and through an analysis of crime in the news.

In 1991, I organized a symposium at Dalhousie University called Crime, Social Problems and Moral Panics: How the Media Deals with Social Issues. I had applied for a research grant from the Atlantic Institute of Criminology to study the way newspapers report crime, and the director, Don Clairmont, asked me if I was interested in organizing a conference on the topic and offered to sponsor it. The result was a day-long symposium with thirteen presenters — university academics, lawyers, police, civil servants, journalists and broadcasters. Each was local and worked in some way that put them in contact with the media. The conference provided a chance to look at common issues from different points of view. There were two workshops in the morning, "The Media and the Legal System" and "Inquiries and Commissions," and a roundtable on "Social Issues" in the afternoon.

This book retains the flavour of the conference in scope and organization. With the gracious permission of the speakers, I edited and condensed the presentations, and use them in each chapter to introduce a crime and the media topic from that professional's point of view. For example, one speaker pointed out that the media is male-centred, that women are not in the news except when they are crime victims or beauty contest winners; another presenter pointed out the difficulty of dealing with the press when reporters are not trained to understand how the criminal justice system works.

Following each synopsis, a section called Reading the News examines news articles that embody the points made by the speaker. This provides an overview of typical news reports on the crime, and a new section to this edition, Sample Study, discusses news coverage in more depth, such as how sexual assault is covered over a full year in a national newspaper.

Each chapter also builds on a certain theme, such as sensationalism or inadequate reporting, which is developed in the third part of each chapter, Analyzing the News. For example, in the chapter on the misrepresentation of AIDS in the media, newspaper stories are used to show how in the early 1980s AIDS was often linked to deviant groups. Such coverage reflected homophobia in society and contributed to its reproduction. This misrepresentation meant that more people were exposed to risk of contracting the disease.

This book challenges the reader to develop a more analytical view of the news by looking at a specific topic, such as how fear of crime is increased by newspaper reporting, and also a deeper theme, such as how fear of crime causes the law to become tougher. The analyses come from my own research and are meant to be used in an everyday reading of the news. In the process of understanding how crime is presented in the media we gain more control over our lives, because we begin to see how the ideology, or ideas people have about the world, are not owned by them and can be distorted by others. For example, the crimes reported in the media are often of the most violent or salacious sort, which doesn't accurately reflect reality. However, people come to believe what they read, watch and hear, and whether their beliefs are true or not, their ideas affect how they live their lives. Many people develop an exaggerated and distorted fear of crime in the world through exposure to violent crime in the media.

Much of what we learn about the world comes from television, newspapers, magazines and so on. However, what we know about the world is third-hand, not experienced directly or even indirectly through others. So my contention is that we need to question the view of the world we get from the media. For that job we need some measuring tools and concepts.

Living in a mediated world we formulate virtual images of danger that are moving signifiers: serial killers, school shooters, muggers, terrorists and carjackers. Living in relative safety from disaster, disease or danger, we nonetheless have become obsessed with risk. If we came face to face with a bear in the woods, we would know fear, and why, and what to do; but our fears in modern society are based in mediated, extralocal accounts of events we haven't seen, written by people we haven't met, of events we can't control. Exaggerating our perceived danger and our ability to deal with it is culture's outrageous lurid imagery of war and sexual extremity. The painting *Deadlier than the Male* by Gary Panter on the cover satirizes 1950s men's action magazine covers, in the artist's words, by pointing up the "bizarre self definitions that represent the sexes, emotion, repression, powers of state, victimization and boneheadedness of the human race."

Introduction

Thinking about the News

Crime, deviance, delinquency and other social problems have always been a staple of newspaper accounts, television news shows and crime dramas. As the saying goes, sex and violence sells. Although such knowledge is third-hand, it appears immediate, shocking, entertaining and informative, filtered through the media graphically and textually. The media has replaced first-hand experience and second-hand gossip as our source of information, opinion and news about the world. The pervasiveness and assumed facticity of the news are rarely questioned, and sometimes it's a jolt to realize that knowledge of events can be created.

The media can make it seem as if we are at the scene of a crime down the street or seeing events half a world away. The media presents us with stories about events created by people we will never meet of places we will never see. We accept the objective character of the news, and only when a source is misquoted or an issue receives inadequate coverage is the media questioned or criticized on how it does its job. But what exactly is that job, and is it usually done well enough? When crime news is sometimes criticized as biased, does that mean it usually is not?

The media does not merely report the news. First, it has to construct and assemble it, and in this way the perceptions of crime created by the news media are organized. When reading or watching the news, we are getting reports about events in the world, built from the work of reporters in the field and influenced by the perspective of editors, who are anticipating the reactions of consumers. Consumers are getting more than passively conveyed social facts because the news actively creates impressions and opinions about the world. For example, crime news trades upon and re/creates certain sub-texts — law and order, discipline, danger, fear, authority. These underlying themes implicitly define the boundaries of society and have an effect on how people think and live their lives.

The power of the media is evident in how it affects a whole range of attitudes about public and personal safety. For example, television crime can influence public anxiety, leading people to a mean world view, where they think that the world is more dangerous than it really is. The media can also play a reactive role, trivializing violent crimes such as sexual assault, so people

9

become desensitized, misconstruing violence and blaming the victim. The media can sensationalize crimes, exacerbated by interest groups that have something to gain by creating moral panic around issues such as child abuse, thereby inflaming public anger. On the other hand, the media can also be proactive in dispelling crime myths. Criminologists who try to use the media to educate the public engage in news-making criminology.

The media can influence our perceptions about everything from break-and-enter to terrorism. Media images of deviance and criminality can fuel the fear of crime and result in a tough law-and-order approach and calls for stiffer penalties against people convicted of crimes. The media has an incredible power to set agendas and reflect political points of view, a fact recognized and often exploited by politicians. It has the power to rock the foundations of a community when it reports on crimes that appear to threaten the very fabric of social life. It has the power to create a fear of crime that is not based in first-hand experience and thus it drives our cognitive and emotional views of the world.

Crime waves as well as individual crimes are subject to social construction as accounts created by journalists, fed by competition and coherence of opinion among newspapers, who rely on a restricted pool of experts and authorities for opinions. As the anecdote goes, early-twentieth-century journalist Lincoln Steffens said he could create a crime wave by writing about all the crime that normally occurs in a large city and that he could end the crime wave just as easily. If crime waves can be manufactured by journalists, what does this say about the social construction of crime?

Consumers, that is, readers and viewers of the news, are not often in a good position to judge the veracity of crime news because they do not know the background of the stories reported, their editorship or the priorities assigned in their production. The production of news is not open to view, even though the news is relied upon increasingly as a source of facts about the world. The world is experienced through the lens of the media, and our understanding of the world is mediated through the abstraction of the news, which stands in for experientially based knowledge. Once we start to realize that knowledge of the world is the sum total of opinions, attitudes, fears and desires produced in the consumption of the news, we begin to have a different attitude toward what we consume. Otherwise we remain alienated in our knowledge of the world.

Comprehending how knowledge is re/produced (and mis/represented) enables us to be more critical in an increasingly complicated, alienating and technologically dominated society, amid all the noise, babble and chaos of the information age. We don't want to be cynical but rather examine how even mis/perceptions are consequential in people's lives. For example, if the media reports that most sexual assaults are committed by strangers jumping out from behind bushes in parks, then that stereotype is more likely to be believed, reported to the police and taken seriously by the public. This stereotype distorts the reality of acquaintance assault.

Or, if the media portrays drug crime as narcotics handled in washrooms, then people will not worry about medicines their doctor prescribes them. If a crime wave is constructed around kids who swarm or muggers in dark alleys with knives, then people will not worry about bid-rigging, insider trading and environmental pollution. A steady diet of sensationalistic crimes hides more mundane and harder-to-detect crimes, just as a focus on street crime hides corporate crime.

The depiction of crime in the news affects people's perception of safety and danger in society with subsequent consequences. The news is an endless torrent of chatter and gossip about ephemera, issues that capture one's attention momentarily but are gone tomorrow. The chatter might contain truth, lies, distortions or half-truths and constitute the facts society lives by. But while people are drawn together through consuming the same news, they are also fractured. The media brings us together in a global village yet alienates us from control in the world.

The news media fills our days with information from everywhere about everything, and we do not have time to reflect on its meaning or to know what weight or value to assign to any of it. We are information junkies, demanding more and more but without any notion of what to do with it. It is just information. And the ubiquity of it has created what Marshall McLuhan called a global village, in which everything has become a commodity. This information does not usually directly affect our lives, as would news of a dam collapse upriver or an oncoming forest fire. Our relation to information is quite different. For us, information is a commodity that is bought and sold, but most of it has little to do with our lives.

An estimated that 95 million American viewers watched O.J. Simpson flee from police down the freeway on June 17, 1994. Mass viewership in itself is not surprising. The 2008 Superbowl drew 98 million viewers, and the final episode of M*A*S*H in 1983 drew 106 million viewers. However, a grand jury probing possible murder charges against Simpson had to be dissolved on the grounds that it had been tainted by pretrial publicity. Watching that chase it seemed there was little doubt he was guilty, and during the two hours viewers heard about the suicide note, wife abuse, divorce, stalking and jealousy, even though this was for most an event thousands of miles away of which they had no direct knowledge, described by people they would never meet about an event they could not control.

To watch, read and hear about such spectacles is to rely less on direct experience of the world and more on extra-locally produced knowledge. Subsequent gossip about crime is based on information brought by others via these stories, texts and pictures. And the technological fact of production and delivery gives these stories added weight. The construction of an arena of public discourse creates a form of social consciousness that is extra-local and externalized in relation to ourselves. Paradoxically, we can place ourselves in the experiences of others we will never meet, at the same time as we can distance ourselves from the emotional pain they feel. More subtly, in the process, certain images of crime and criminal justice are normalized.

In watching, listening to or reading the media, we become a news subject ourself, receiving a constructed knowledge of the world bounded in a discourse that has a beginning, middle and end. This standard, uniform knowledge does not always have a context or history, and it is not always apparent who wrote the news or from what perspective they wrote it. However, these atemporal events without context and author structure our understanding of the world. In some ways, authorless information has the most authority because it cannot easily be dismissed as idiosyncratic. News, as opposed to personal experience, is objective information because it does not have the taint of subjectivity. Even seeing bias in the news presumes knowing what unbiased news supposedly looks like, and ironically this tends to be news that is authorized, broadcast and copyrighted by the news organization that produced it.

The consequence of learning about crime from a media that constructs stories extra-locally is that misunderstanding and fear of crime may be increased. The world portrayed in the media can be disembodied, sensationalistic and stereotypical. When a crime is portrayed as an isolated event, nothing is learned about its underlying causes and the context that surrounds it, the decisions that motivate it, the actions that result in its detection, the search for suspects and the actions of the police. Moreover, crime is not seen as mediated by the news and the justice system. When crimes are not seen realistically, people become increasingly afraid to walk in their own neighbourhoods, they become more desensitized to crime and they think the criminal justice system treats offenders too leniently.

Some criticize the tabloid media and true crime shows of sensationalism, of blurring the line between entertainment and reality. But the sin is not left only to them. Sensationalism can easily feed into the perception of increasing crime and that social order will crumble unless there is a crackdown on gun-toting punks who commit brutal, senseless murders.

Even though there is evidence that crime was not on the increase in the 1990s, major western countries all introduced measures to get tough on crime. And now, we have similar get-tough measures being introduced by the Conservative government, such as sentencing reform, tighter parole restrictions and more severe criminal sanctions. Where do these ideas come from? Is it as simple as examining the media to see how crime becomes constructed as a social fact, some of it distorted and sensationalized while other crimes are underplayed? Are symbolic issues the motor of social change? Here we look at some of the ways researchers have turned to the media as an important site of analysis.

Studying the News

Canadian and international newspaper articles are used to illustrate certain points in this book. In many cases, these articles are taken from clippings files developed for teaching and research purposes and supplemented with news articles from various sources. For the first edition, the *Canadian News Index (CNI)*, was useful; while in the second, the *Canadian Business and Current Affairs (CBCA)*, *FP Infomart*, and public archives and newspapers were used more. Many major newspapers such as the *Globe and Mail*, the *Toronto Star*, and the *New York Times* have online searchable archives, and articles from international news agencies can also be accessed via the Internet.

The *Canadian News Index* listed stories since 1977 by subject from seven major Canadian dailies: *Halifax Chronicle-Herald*, *Montreal Gazette*, *Toronto Star*, *Winnipeg Free Press*, *Edmonton Journal*, *Calgary Herald* and *Vancouver Sun*. The *CNI* provided enough information to get the article from microfilm or interlibrary loan. Since 1993 the *CNI* has been called the *Canadian Index*, and newspaper citations have been amalgamated with those for magazines and other periodicals. The *Index* did not list all stories on crime that had been published because only items of major interest were selected and compiled. The advantage of using the *Canadian Newspapers Fultext FP Infomart* is that this database offers full-text access to more than fifty Canadian newspapers; coverage dates vary by title but for New Brunswick, papers goes back to at least 1998.

Historical research can also be done with primary documents found in libraries and archives. A provincial depository usually has local community and provincial newspapers from the 1800s onwards on microfilm and can be used to research events such as the Oka standoff in Quebec of 1990, the 1991 Halifax riot in Nova Scotia, the debate on the *Juvenile Delinquents Act* of 1908, the Winnipeg General Strike or Riel Rebellion, or the imposition of the federal *War Measures Act* during the FLQ crisis. In my course on the historical development of criminal justice in Canada, the news has become an important source of information and insight into then current events and a resource for studying the construction of public opinion, for example, the editorial influence on attitudes toward the abolition of capital punishment in the *Globe* in the 1970s.

Daily newspapers are a good source of information on events that were not always important enough to be included in history books or academic journals. Local newspapers are usually easily available, and university and public libraries receive national and international newspapers. Reading international newspapers can take less time if one is looking for specific topics, and it is also a good way to search for topics seldom covered, such as police deviance and political corruption.

Researching the news is something anyone can do, but it requires some time and organization. Once samples are collected, one can begin to see patterns in the length, placement and discourse of the articles that wouldn't have been immediately apparent. For example, why are there so few stories about wife abuse in the news, yet so many stories about youth crime? Why do community papers have a court report section, but national papers do not? Why are corporate crimes reported in the *Globe and Mail* often found only in the business section? What crime stories make the front page?

A basic assumption in this book is that news constitutes a textual re/ presentation of crime, and analyzing the media involves examining discursive themes and patterns. For example, in articles on youth violence, what is of interest is whether the problem is characterized as widespread, how new it is said to be and the degree of violence reported. This characterization of youth violence can then be compared with official statistics on youth crime to see if there is any consistency between them.

Comparing the patterns found in the news with the official incidence of crime is one way of obtaining a standpoint on the news. This is called context analysis. The following sources of official information are used throughout to create context: crime statistics collected by police departments across the country and published by Statistics Canada, special statistical reports published by the Canadian Centre for Justice Statistics and analyses of victimization data obtained through the General Social Survey. These and other secondary sources of information are used in part to compare what is officially known about crime with how crime is presented in the news, but there is no assumption that these official sources of information are perfect or that news accounts should necessarily match them.

The textual characterizations in the news can also be examined internally to reconstruct the claims made about youth crime, to see which point of view is represented and thus analyze why the public has become more concerned with youth crime as an issue even though it does not appear that it has actually increased. This is called content analysis, and it is especially useful in teasing out political themes and ideological messages.

Specific devices are useful in doing a content analysis, such as analysis of metaphors, tropes, elisions and misrepresentations. An example of a metaphor is the use of a descriptive term in a way that is not intended literally, as in "crazed serial killer," where it is not really known whether the killer has a mental illness or not. Such metaphors easily lead to sensationalism and contribute to social panics. A trope is a figure of speech, as in speaking of prostitutes as "ladies of the night," that is also both metaphorical and ironic.

Tropes can contribute to misperceptions and distortions of crime, such as viewing prostitution as women's deviance. An elision is an absence, a failing to include something essential in the account, as in omitting that most sexual assault is violent exploitation between acquaintances rather than a crime between strangers. Elisions contribute to ideological misunderstandings about crime that can actually increase their likelihood.

There are clearly some overlaps in these textual devices, but they provide a connecting thread that links the topics of the chapters with a deeper underlying theme of social construction. Ordinary misrepresentations, stereotypes and distortions are identified as well. To see how these textual devices work requires an especially close reading in some cases.

The analysis developed here is not based on how people are affected by what they read in the news. Although that is important, this book is primarily concerned with an analysis of how reading is ideological, how the news takes possible interpretations of events in the world and constructs a dominant point of view. Crime news is ideological because through the media we acquire systematic misperceptions about the world, for example, that youth gangs are rampant. But news is not simply exaggerated or unreal, it has real consequences. Thus, the pertinent question is not simply how well the news represents a crime but how the crime is represented. News is part of the ideological apparatus of our society. It supports the status quo and represents the point of view of the powerful. The distortion in the news might convince readers that the world is a violent place but this is not an analysis of how people read, it is an analysis of how the news could possibly be read to (re)create social order.

The analysis in this book draws from various ideas in criminology but is based generally on a social constructionist approach: the idea that our news about the world does not necessarily reflect reality and that crime topics are as much constructed as reported. This approach comprises a variety of research and is best known for its ability to deflate moral panics. For example, crime news is often sensationalized and largely reflects the perspectives of the police and the criminal justice system. Crime waves can occur like fads, reflecting the fear of the day.

The moral panics model, developed first in the 1970s, drew heavily on symbolic interaction and labelling theory. It was used to great advantage in unpacking exaggerated fears around narcotics, pornography, prostitution and child abuse. The original model assumed that there were folk devils, so-called, who symbolized a moral threat to society. Society itself was assumed to be homogeneous and monolithic and subject to moral panics contained in speeches, sermons, law-and-order agendas, crime legislation and so on.

As an example of how we can begin to do an analysis of crime in the news, consider a recent attempt to introduce anti-crime legislation in Canada.

In February 2009, the Conservative government introduced stiffer penalties for certain offences. If we were to construct an exemplary discourse on the topic it might look like: "Prime Minister Stephen Harper visited Vancouver, what his public safety minister calls Canada's gang capital… and met with police chiefs and the families of gang-violence victims who've become lobbyists for a crackdown… 'We've had a terrible wave of violence in British Columbia, and quite frankly the public is sick and tired of what's going on,' said the police chief, while an opposition politician said, 'more jail time will not cure the violence.'"

The attempt to create unanimity of opinion around the need to do something about violent crime represents an orthodox ideology, while the difference of opinion illustrates the difficulty in doing same, an uneasy heterodoxy. The way in which these opinions are expressed, and debated, is through words, and we can use many techniques to analyze them.

Overview of the Book

The research this book represents is organized by topics: sexual assault, prostitution, domestic violence, the Mount Cashel orphanage scandal, AIDS, crime fear, Crime Stoppers, serial homicide and the Westray tragedy. Each chapter also has an underlying theme, such as sensationalism, invisibility, orthodoxy and community.

The first part of the book is called Gender and Crime. In Chapter 1, Sharon Fraser, a freelance journalist and broadcaster, speaks about working as a columnist writing about feminist issues and how issues that affect women are either not discussed in the media or not presented from a woman's point of view. Branching off from there, the chapter looks at how sexual assault is reported in the news media, how the police dominate as the authority on crime and how the media provides readers with an orthodox version of events that can actually misinform women, and men, about sexual assault. A sample study is created using all articles on sexual assault in the *National Post* during 2007.

In Chapter 2, Anne Derrick, then a noted criminal attorney and now a youth court judge, focuses on women who work as prostitutes and how they are narrowly stereotyped as hookers in the media. This label becomes their main identity and much less attention is paid to the organization of the sex trade, their poverty and the ways in which they are abused. Examples of how the media labels such women are reproduced, and it is argued that the characterization of prostitutes is part of the crime itself. By focusing too little on the roles of men as johns and pimps, the media and the criminal justice system end up revictimizing these women. A special case study on how women went missing in Vancouver's downtown eastside and also went missing from the media is discussed. The result was tragic.

In Chapter 3, Debi Forsyth-Smith, politician and civil servant, introduces the topic of violence against women in relationships. In analyzing news accounts of violence against women, certain features are important, such as article size, whether the violence is portrayed as unusual or normal and whether the article points to the larger context within which individual incidents of violence take place. As domestic violence is invisible in the media compared to its incidence, the analysis takes up the problem of how to account for invisibility and how some topics get taken up in the media while others do not.

The second part of the book, Distortion in the Media, deals with specific ways crime is misrepresented in the news. In Chapter 4, Gary Kinsman, an activist and sociology professor, looks at the Hughes Commission of Inquiry into child abuse at Mount Cashel in St. John's, Newfoundland. Kinsman describes how the media inscribes deviant categories by creating a link between homosexuality and child sexual abuse. The media does not invent this convergence but reproduces a pre-existing social idea. In the process of inscription, certain voices are presented while others are silenced. An orthodox view replaces a heterodox one. A sample study using articles from the *Ottawa Citizen* on the Cornwall pedophile ring is used to illustrate how blame is assigned.

In Chapter 5, Eric Smith, a former teacher and AIDS activist, talks about how AIDS is (mis)represented in the news media. While having AIDS is not a crime, in a process called convergence, it is distorted in the media and associated with drug users, prostitutes and other deviant groups. The signification of AIDS in the media as a problem of marginal groups makes it easier for authorities to call for quarantining infected people. Articles that exhibit this alarmist characterization of AIDS have an obvious tendency to scapegoat the problem, blame it on marginalized social groups and associate it only with them. The consequence of this misrepresentation is that many people still do not feel themselves to be at risk. This topic is taken up in the recent concern over swine flu.

In Chapter 6, Joy Mannette, activist and teacher, takes up the issue of ethnocentrism in the news, showing how race relations issues are portrayed in ways that reinforce ethnic bias. She recounts three cases of lack of ethnic sensitivity in the news. The theme of extra-locality, or distance from events, is discussed, using the example of the 1991 Halifax race riot, where Blacks rampaged through the streets committing random violence, finally leading to a confrontation with the police. This analysis illustrates how crime news comes to stand in for direct experience and shows the power of a mediated world. A more recent example of coverage in the Montreal *Gazette* of a race riot following a police shooting in 2008 is used for analysis.

The third part of the book, Law and Media, looks at the relationship between the news media and the criminal justice system. In Chapter 7, a retired Halifax constable and former police media relations officer, Paul MacDonald, discusses how the media often fails to do a good job in reporting on crime and the workings of the criminal justice system and how this can lead to problems in policing. This speaks to the organizational structure of newsmaking and how reliant the media is on knowledge owned by the police. The issue of exaggeration is developed by looking at fear of crime and how crime reporting creates an emotional ontology, wedding audience to police in the fight against crime. Coverage of the 2005 Toronto Boxing Day shooting is examined.

Similarly, in Chapter 8, Tony Thomson, a sociology professor, looks at the historical relationship between the media and the police, discussing and criticizing how public relations has come to be an important part of policing. Using the example of Crime Stoppers, the analysis looks at how soliciting the help of the public through the media extends the influence of the police further into the community than would have been possible otherwise and is itself an exercise in public relations. Unfortunately, however, soliciting the public's help through invoking the idea of community can alienate the very audience ads try to enlist. An analysis of how this works through video Crime Stoppers ads is presented in the sample study.

In Chapter 9, Darrel Pink, lawyer, discusses sensationalism in the news and how difficult it is to work with reporters when they often do not have an adequate understanding of the criminal justice system and how it works. The concept of sensationalism is developed through the example of the Homolka–Bernardo case in Ontario, where the law was used to prohibit the media from reporting certain information, while tabloid speculation in the United States and Britain was rampant. The theme of sites of social anxiety is taken up and discussed in light of recent sensational cases in Canada, and the analysis tracks the development of the term "serial killer" in the 1980s, mapping its ambivalent use in news and entertainment.

In Chapter 10, Deborah Woolway, radio producer, discusses the theme of pack journalism in the context of the inquiry into why Donald Marshall, a Nova Scotia Mi'kmaq, spent eleven years in prison for a murder he didn't commit. This theme is taken up in a look at the media coverage of the Westray mine disaster and the subsequent criminal and legal issues that surrounded its inquiry. The consequent uniformity in news reporting caters to an emotional sense of personal tragedy instead of illuminating the underlying causes of such a disaster.

A recommended reading list is provided but no references or endnotes. This pedagogical style is chosen to invite readers to consider the persuasiveness of the analysis.

Changes for the Second Edition

A second edition of a text usually signals that the book has been successful. *Constructing Danger: The Mis/representation of Crime in the News* has been in use since it came out as an undergraduate crossover text for courses in sociology, journalism, media studies, criminology and women's studies. It has been reviewed several times in criminal justice and other publications, has been adopted across the country, has never been out of print, students like using it, and I am still contacted by instructors who use it in their courses.

This book was important because of its pedagogy: it led the reader through an analysis, from an opening expert's statement on relevant issues, to reading the news through actual samples, to its analysis. Keeping its essence, I return to *Constructing Danger* and rework it for several reasons.

First, the analysis is complemented by *newer examples*. The section on serial murder discusses the case of Paul Bernardo. A more relevant case would now be Robert Pickton. Another section discusses AIDS and how contagious diseases are re/presented in the media. A more relevant case to accompany that analysis would now be SARS or swine flu. Another section discusses fear of crime in a day when school violence was just beginning to be defined as a social problem.

Second, the sample is *more national*. Where there was an analysis of a race riot in Halifax, today we might use one from Montreal or Vancouver. The difficulty in identifying a national news story is in finding a balance of Canadian stories versus stories that Canadians consume. Living in a globalized news environment, locality ceases to matter. And that itself is an issue worth exploring.

Third, the analysis focuses *more on emotion*. The original emphasis on "mis/representation" draws attention to ideological distortions in the media. This presumes the media could do a better job, a different job, a job that media analysis could outline. It assumes that the media should do the work of criminology and make media coverage better reflect the knowledge that criminologists produce. Instead, while dissecting distortions, or "necessary illusions," continues to be an important part of media analysis, I focus on the emotional impact of how crime is portrayed in the news and how an emotional reading of themes such as anger, fear and disgust is basic to human life. Where the dominant paradigm in media analysis is on rational-logical problems, as if all we have to prove is that the media exaggerates or distorts issues, what counts at heart is how those stories are read/heard/viewed by readers/listeners/viewers who use emotion as a skill in their participation in reading as a process.

Thus, the revisited project keeps the structure and analysis from the 1995 edition, embeds it in a revised research template to bring it more up to date and develops the emotional angle through topical examples. These exemplars guide the reader through a critical analysis of crime in the media. Aside from scholarship that addresses fear as an unwarrantable and unwanted consequence of crime news, there is little research on an analysis of emotions in crime news, creating a unique focus for a crime and media book.

The re-working substantially augments the material of the 1995 edition with reviews of new academic literature, the inclusion of new examples and their analysis and an enriched focus on the emotional angle. In line with the pedagogical orientation of the original edition, content analyses of crime stories lead the reader to and through an emotional reading of the news, teaching the reader how to re-read the news through the vehicle of examples of emotional coverage. These examples are ordinary news stories, but ones that exemplify emotion: the Toronto boxing day shooting (2006), the Greyhound bus attack (2008), abductions by pedophile Peter Whitmore (2007), the Toronto SARS scare (2003), the Grand Manan arson case (2006), the 9/11 terrorist attacks in New York, Robert Pickton goes to jail, Conrad Black goes to jail and so on.

It is not unusual for media analyses to focus on how fear is increased because of media reports, with the emphasis is on how fear is exaggerated or unnecessary. *Instead, the analysis in this book privileges emotions as warrantable resources for media consumption rather than unintended byproducts of bad reporting.*

In presenting mini-analyses of exemplary news stories, the point is not to develop journal-article length analyses of these topics but rather to use them as heuristic vehicles to develop a *sensibility* for how to explore media analysis. This preserves the accessibility of the 1995 text while updating it with current examples.

This book brings together key issues along with recommendations for how to read the news. This book is not about magic solutions for better reporting, but rather is designed to enhance a reader's literacy in how the media constructs and (sometimes) mis/represents the world. This is a text that can be read along with the news, not a textbook reporting research facts or a how-to manual that breaks down research into easy exercises. The book is not abstract, and examples are used throughout to ground the analysis. In each chapter the specific techniques used to analyze the news are explained, and the topics and themes explored in the various chapters all fit together with references supplied for further reading. The important task is to learn all over again how to read the news for ourselves, not just to echo the conclusions other people have come to. If we stand on hills, we can see farther.

1

A String of Stranger Sexual Assaults
The Construction of an Orthodox Account of Rape

Distortion can mean many things: an issue may be exaggerated, down-played or slanted. The complaint is that the truth is not being accurately portrayed. The assumption is that there is a truth at heart, somewhere, if only we can strip away the confusion. Although it is difficult to know the full truth about the extent of sexual assault in our society, some distortions are obvious.

This chapter begins with a brief talk by Sharon Fraser, a journalist and broadcaster, who points out how issues are usually presented from a male-centred point of view in the media. As a result, women's issues are often absent or distorted. Since sexual assault affects women pervasively, it is important to look at the way in which it is presented. And while the media might believe its own myth that the news is objective and doesn't reflect any one point of view, Fraser believes the news implicitly reflects a male perspective.

The next section, Reading the News, uses the issue of a gendered perspec-tive to examine how sexual assault is reported in newspapers. Several news accounts reveal how the media communicates explicit and implicit messages about sexual assault. From a series of news reports from the summer of 1993 in Halifax to the Sample Study of a full year of coverage in the *National Post* in 2007, we look at articles that warn women of the danger of sexual assault by strangers. We examine various patterns in how sexual assault is presented in the news.

The third part of the chapter, Analyzing the News, examines distor-tions in crime news using an "orthodox version of events" model. While maintaining relative silence about sexual assault in general, this orthodox or standard account makes it appear that the real danger is from strangers in public places, thereby reinforcing rape myths. Furthermore, by making the police the authority on crime, women's experience is underrepresented. We suggest that through an "emotional" reading of the news, perhaps this experience can be recovered. Studies I have found useful for thinking about sexual assault in the news are Walby, Hill and Soothill (1983), Soothill (1991) and Benedict (1992).

Sharon Fraser's Talk

I was going to say stop me if you've heard this before, but I don't think I'll ask you to do that because I was accused rather harshly in *Frank* magazine of being repetitive and I said well of course I'm repetitive. These issues won't go away, so someone has to keep harping on them and I guess it's me. I'm going to talk just in general about women's coverage in the media, being a woman, working in the media and also how the stories are covered.

I once asked a radio producer friend to put me on his radio show once a week and I'd do a five minute newscast on how that week's news would be interpreted by a feminist woman. He was aghast that I would even ask that. "I couldn't do that," he said. "If we had you on we'd have to have all the other groups on too." "But who in the world are these other groups," I said, "the Kinsmen, the Rotary Club?" I don't think of women as a group. I also don't think of all the people outside the straight, white, male, able-bodied power structure as being special interest groups. Indeed, the people who use the expression "special interest" tend to be the ones who have a very special interest indeed. And it's very well massaged by our mainstream media.

Not very long ago, I was interviewed on this subject by an interviewer who said, "How can you say this, I feel that we're constantly doing women's stories, native issues stories, stories about the disabled." "But," I asked, "who is defining the issues?" I used the example of a newspaper called *Atlantic Fisherman*, where I used to be the editor. I made a decision when I was there that I was going to cover the fishing industry from the point of view of the people who catch the fish and the people who work in the plants. I went to them and asked them what was important. Then I would go back to my office and phone the cabinet ministers, the bureaucrats and the company presidents. They weren't used to this and they didn't like it. And my interviewer didn't like my suggestion that a group of white males were sitting around in a newsroom tossing ideas back and forth, and then going out and asking a list of already formulated questions.

Years ago when I was a student, I used to tell the teacher I was frustrated because I wanted to know about the people, how they lived, what their houses were like, what toys the children played with, what food they ate, who cooked it, and what did they wear. I would have been fascinated if I could have found this information, and many years later I realized what was missing was the history of women and children. And now when I read or listen to those outlets that are responsible for recording our day-to-day history, I see the same thing happening all over again. In general, what makes the news and how it's reported has very little to do with the reality of most women's lives.

In a story meeting I was in while working as a writer-broadcaster in the current affairs department of CBC Radio, the three people in the meeting who spoke before me brought up story ideas about a new potash mine, rising mortgage rates and changes in the downtown traffic patterns. They had big plans to talk to the minister of natural resources, the president of a financial institution and the mayor. When it was my turn, I reported that the tellers in my bank had all been told when they came in that morning that they were being cut from full time to half time. Their wages were being halved accordingly, and they were losing all their benefits. They were given no notice, and they were not even afforded the courtesy of an explanation. Before I was even part way through this short presentation, I was aware of six eyes glazing over with indifference and I could sense the barely stifled yawns. When I finished the producers said, "So, what's the story?"

I thought I had given enough for a story proposal, but I went a little further and said I think it happened this way because the tellers are women and whoever is responsible for such decisions would simply assume the women were working for supplementary family income, and that's when the yawns became audible. "Oh no, not that women's stuff again," and somebody else said, "We've already done women's stuff this week." Finally the producer said, "If you can prove it, if you can get the manager of that bank to tell you by three o'clock this afternoon that the tellers' hours were cut because they're women, you've got a story, otherwise forget it."

We still live in a society where what is seen to be important and significant is determined by a male agenda. Our institutions, the education system, the governments and certainly the media have never acknowledged the realities of women's lives and therefore have covered women's issues as afterthoughts and fillers at best, with tongue in cheek and journalistic contempt at worst. Just as women and children are the first to fall through the safety net of our economic system, stories that deal with women's issues are the first to be cut when editors and producers lack space and time.

The notion that there are no women's issues, but only people's issues, is one that keeps being raised with the implication that with the cooperation of all the sensitive and helpful men we know everything's been taken care of. We've now reached an equitable society, and now, could things get back to normal? But there are women's issues; they're women's because they've been there forever and men haven't done anything about them. If women don't keep them in the forefront, those issues will become invisible again. Some of those issues are child care, reproductive rights, pay equity, women's health, sexual harassment, sexual assault, domestic violence and incest, pornography, stereotyping in the media, all those issues that are responsible for so many glazed eyes and stifled yawns in so many newsrooms.

There are people's issues but even they are not covered in a way that's meaningful to a majority of women. The coverage is geared toward straight, white, middle-to-upper class, able-bodied males, men with jobs, mortgages, car payments, stocks and bonds, credit cards, insurance policies, all those trappings which our media assumes to be common to everyone.

Women who are in the news business, women who work in the media, are something like women who play roles in male politics. I would like to see as many women as possible get into both, but the truth is, unless the male agenda is changed in some very fundamental ways and unless the women in question have a strong sense of women's politics, it often doesn't matter too much whether the person filling the seat is a man or a woman. Women too have been socialized to believe our concerns are not very important and we shouldn't whine so much about wife battering and rape when there are more important things to cover, like wars and strikes and uprisings.

I've had this conversation many times about covering stories from a different perspective and with a rewritten agenda. Every time I've been greeted with a shocked response that news is news, and you can't cover it with a point of view. The last time it happened it was with a radio producer. I said to him, "Well, whose point of view do you cover the news from now?" He said, "No one's, the news is objective."

Wanting better media coverage of issues is important because the media is a conduit to government; it influences public opinion. People outside the power structure require, in fact demand, that their voices also be heard.

Reading the News

Sharon's talk raises the criticism that the media reports issues from a male-centred point of view. This bias places women into particular roles, such as victim, and yet at the same time ignores issues important to them. In the reporting of sexual assault, for example, if distortions result in mis/representing sexual assault from the perspective of women, this can re/create false understandings of sexual assault as a crime, which affects what women know about the world and their risk of assault.

Sexual assault provides a good example of gendered news because it is predominantly a gendered crime: most sexual assaults are committed against women, and it is widespread. In what was news at the time, a 1993 survey found that one-half of all Canadian women had experienced at least one incident of violence since the age of sixteen, and one-quarter had experienced violence at the hands of a current or past marital partner. A 1994 study estimated that although an alarming 39 percent of all Canadian women had experienced at least one incident of sexual assault since the age of sixteen, only 6 percent of these incidents had been reported to the police.

Imagine the surprise in the 1990s to find that official statistics captured only 6 percent of sexual assaults. And then imagine how many of those might be reported in the media? Not much has changed since then, but the question remains: Given that sexual violence is so widespread, does the media cover it in a way that works in the best interests of women?

News articles come in many different forms, from small "'briefs" to larger stories. Article 1.1 is an example of the former, extracted from a much larger article recounting crimes of the week. It is small and descriptive and does not have the female victim's perspective of events.

Article 1.1 "Police Blotter"

Sexual Assault. A woman was sexually assaulted by a man as she walked through a laneway near Bloor Street West and Lansdowne Avenue. (*National Post*, May 28, 2007)

This account is typical of news briefs or capsules, which provide a synopses of various local items and are used to cover a wide variety of issues, not just crimes. They are usually short and convey the impression that sexual assault is isolated, and while the facts are true, they are constructed in such a way as to lead readers to not understand the context, extent and severity of the crime.

The point of view is that of the police, the assault happened in public and appears to have been committed by a stranger. This format leaves little room for detail or to create a context that would help the readers to understand why the assault occurred as anything other than a public predator crime. In addition, while such crimes happen, what is the consequence of focusing on such crimes to the exclusion of others, such as date rape, for example? The result is a so-called rape myth, that is, that sexual assault is mainly committed in public by strangers. Other myths that can occur in sex crime reporting are that rape is sex and that women precipitate the crime. Such myths might justify and excuse rape from a certain male point of view, but certainly not from a woman's.

The first edition of *Constructing Danger* looked at a period in July and August of 1993, when the Halifax news media reported what they called a string of sexual assaults committed by strangers. The fifty-eight news articles published over six weeks were often lengthy and located near the front of the newspapers. Thirty-five were accounts of the crimes, and twenty-three were secondary articles, such as columns and opinion pieces.

Article 1.1 illustrates the typical brevity of many news accounts of sexual assault, especially those involving strangers, but the reporting of the string of sexual assaults also brought out other issues. Since none were committed by acquaintances, it reinforced the rape myth that sexual assault is predominantly committed by strangers.

The topicalization of stranger-related sexual assaults brackets out assaults committed by acquaintances, creating a news frame for interpreting the world. Assaults committed against women by men they know in friendships, relationships and families, at work or at school are not seen as part of the pattern. Since sexual assault is generally given low priority in the news and acquaintance-related assaults continue to receive very little attention, the dominant theme is stranger-danger. Against the backdrop of relative silence concerning sexual assault in general, the spotlight is turned on strangers.

The first of what became the string articles were innocuous and occupied little space in the newspapers. If these assaults had not become part of a string of news items (which can only be constructed in hindsight), it is doubtful they would have received much attention at all. The articles were relatively short and appeared in the news briefs. Even with scant detail, or perhaps because of it, they constructed a typical idea of what sexual assault looks like: a woman was attacked by a male stranger, who then escapes, and the police become involved. This is a mis/representation or false stereotype because most women victims are sexually assaulted by men they know. With the account organized from an official point of view, the only person who comments on the incident is a police officer, which promotes the seeming objectivity of the report and further isolates it from women's experience.

The version of events found in the media during this period was homogeneous: these assaults against women were perpetrated by strangers, they were unrelated (but related as a string) and the police were urging all women to be cautious. In describing the crime in this way, the reporting creates a typical sexual assault article, in which women are attacked in public places by men they do not know, and women are warned to take steps to prevent the violence, putting the responsibility for safety on them rather than on men.

Later articles in the 1993 string were longer but also contained the typical elements of sex crime reporting: a crime occurred, a woman was the victim of an unknown male attacker, the police are involved and there is a warning for women to be careful. Various textual elements or themes were found to construct the story.

The image readers get of women in this type of report is that they are victims of sexual assault, their attackers are strangers, they are not safe in their own homes, they have to be careful to avoid being victimized, and the police are the experts on how women experience such crimes. These longer articles convey a more serious tone but do not necessarily examine the issue in a better way than the briefer reports.

What is not seen in such accounts is any analysis of men as perpetrators of sexual assault, of sexual assault as a crime in general, why women are blamed for not keeping themselves safe or criticism of how the criminal justice system deals with this kind of crime. These concerns did become briefly topicalized during this series of sexual assaults, but only as public forums on safety were organized and the police were criticized for not adequately responding to community concerns. Let's turn now to a more extended analysis of sex crime news.

Sample Study

The study of the media usually involves constructing some sort of a sample of what readers read and then speculating on the consequences. Readers read, watch and hear local news, and they also watch, read and listen to the national news. Consuming national news creates a national reader, in the sense that readers are getting the same messages across the country.

In this chapter, the *National Post* was selected to see what a national reader would read on sexual assault in the course of a year. An auto-ethnographic strategy is used to read that news sample for analysis.

Articles were searched in *Canadian Newspapers Fulltext FP Infomart* using the search term "sexual assault," limiting the search to the *National Post*, for the period January 1 to December 31, 2007. The articles retrieved were further selected on the basis of whether the headline and abstract contained, or would lead one to believe, that the article was about sexual assault. Only news items were selected, not columns, editorials or letters to the editor.

Of the 187 articles that came up in the search, 132 were selected for analysis. Data that were initially recorded were title, date and page number, word count, location of offence, relation between victim and perpetrator, stage of event in the criminal justice system and speakers whose voices were in the article. Later, emotion words and quotations were abstracted as well. The objective is to see what might characterize the orthodox account. What follows are the main patterns of what is called the "orthodox account" of rape.

1. *Relation.* In cases where the relation was known, 42 percent involved strangers and 58 percent involved acquaintances. This is not quite half and half, but certainly buoys the impression that cases are almost evenly divided between those committed by strangers and those committed by acquaintances. This is the first part of the orthodox account.

In about a third of the cases that involved acquaintances, a person who was outside the circle of family or friends was named as the assailant, including teachers, coaches, drivers and a judge. In general these people were named as having exploited their position of authority or trust. The remaining two-thirds of the cases involved family or friends.

Nineteen articles were about an accused exposing others to the HIV virus. This, of course, usually involved spouses or ex-lovers and is usually called aggravated sexual assault.

2. *Location.* In cases where the location was stated or could be inferred, 46 percent involved public places and 54 percent occurred in private. The former included parks, woods, school grounds, stairwells and public transit.

The latter included residences, a private party, a doctor's examining room and a private office. Again, while not quite half and half, it sustains the impression that the cases are almost evenly divided between those committed in public and those committed in private. This is the second characteristic of the orthodox account.

3. *Stage*. The third major categorization was what stage of the criminal justice system the reported case involved. Fifteen cases (13 percent) were reported as having occurred and were sometimes framed as warnings to the public by the police. In forty-eight cases (41 percent), an assailant had been arrested or was facing charges.

Given the time frame examined in the study, the person named as charged might have been the alleged perpetrator in a previous article. About a dozen cases were reported serially, at various times and stages. Some cases were reported, with perpetrators charged, in the course of the year, while other cases came to trial and were concluded in the time frame. No case was reported, resulted in charges, came to trial and was concluded in the year.

Thirty-nine cases (35 percent) were reported as being at trial, and 11 cases (10 percent) were reports of sentencing decisions. These two sub-categories were selected out because they presented occasions for comments by judge, lawyers and members of the victim's family. Four cases involved defendants who were acquitted or against whom charges were dropped. One involved a team of lacrosse players accused of assault at a private party, while another involved a man who had pled guilty to an assault Paul Bernardo later admitted committing. The third and fourth cases involved police officers who had been charged and acquitted of sexual assault.

Thus, the third feature of the orthodox account is that attacks are known to the police and result in charges, go to court and usually result in convictions.

4. *Speaker*. The fourth categorization of articles concerned the main speaker in the news reports. Officials of the criminal justice system tend to be the prominent speakers. The police were the main source of information in fifty-two (39 percent) articles; judges, lawyers and other officials such as doctors, psychiatrists and institutional spokespersons, in forty-three (33 percent) articles. By that count, police, prosecutors, judges and lawyers account for the main source of information in at least three-quarters of all articles. Victims were able to be identified as speaking in only twelve (9 percent) of the articles, and in nine (7 percent) cases their mother, father or sister spoke.

Direct quotes were available in about three-quarters of the stories, with police (27 percent), officials (11 percent), judges (9 percent), defence attorneys (10 percent) and prosecutors (7 percent) accounting for almost two-thirds of quoted statements. Adding in witnesses, medical professionals, academics and organizational advocates (9 percent) meant that three-quarters of direct quotes were from an institutional perspective. Quotations directly attributable to family (8 percent), defendants (7 percent), victims (4 percent), and friends (2 percent) accounted for the rest.

Most articles had only one speaker, and in that case, it was usually the police. Some articles could have a judge, lawyer and victim all speaking in the same article. However, victims and their families were usually mute, speaking in about one-sixth of all articles. When they did speak, it was usually at the conviction or sentencing stage, and it was often quite emotionally. Since victims are usually absent, emotion is the way we reconnect to them.

This is the fourth characteristic of the orthodox account: victims are seldom heard from and are seldom used for evidence of what happened or for their feelings about the crime. Victims are invisible to the public and silent as interlocutors of the event. They rarely speak, but when they do, it is often with emotion. After realizing this during the auto-ethnography, it was decided to look for emotion words in the articles in general and specifically in the quotations.

5. *Emotion.* Certain words were used commonly in the articles. The word "aggravated" was used in about one-sixth of the articles, usually to refer to aggravated sexual assault or metaphorically to indicate the level of violence. Prosecutors spoke of victims being "terrorized," and police referred to "strings" and "series" of sexual assaults. Judges called defendants "repulsive," "loathsome" and "losers" with "no remorse." Prosecutors called defendants "lying, evasive and unbelievable" and criticized the release of offenders who were "walking time bombs" or "waiting to reoffend."

Victims also described being on an "emotional roller coaster," how their "future had been destroyed" and that they had "waited years to report" the crime. One woman who had been infected with a disease by her partner, who was then charged with aggravated sexual assault, said that she had tried to kill him with her car. A daughter who had testified against her father in an incest case said he "was dead" for her and she hoped that he would "suffer in hell."

These words were poignant and would usually be seen as extraneous to an objective account of a crime. Yet when the instances of emotion words were counted up, an interesting pattern emerged. A majority of the quotations exhibited controlled emotion (42 percent); with anger (19 percent), contempt (13 percent), sadness (13 percent), surprise (10 percent), happiness (2 percent) and fear (2 percent) making up the rest.

This is the fifth characteristic of the standard account: direct quotes were used in 74 percent of cases, but, overwhelmingly, the emotion is flat, controlled and neutral. Given that an institutional view dominates in the use of speakers, the absence of human emotion is not surprising. How then should we react to news of events we will never see, told in a neutral voice by people we will never meet, of crimes that happen to people from who we don't hear?

Only in two of the 120 articles considered in the sample were contextual details provided on the nature of the sexual assaults. With this missing, the context became what the articles reported: isolated events, committed in public by strangers, in private by acquaintances, recounted by authorities in a neutral voice.

In summary, for the "national reader," the typical account of sexual assault has incidents almost evenly divided between stranger/acquaintance and public/private. In most cases an assailant has been arrested, and there has been a concluded trial. Officials dominated in the discourse, while victims were largely silent. Furthermore, there is a notable lack of emotion in the talk quoted in the articles. This is what I call the orthodox account, the standard account that readers read. Its features become the main way that sexual assault is portrayed, and thus, to be thought of.

Analyzing the News

The question posed at the beginning of this chapter was whether media issues are presented from a gendered point of view, that is, a male point of view. We take the most difficult case, a gendered crime, sexual assault, and see that women often appear as silent victims, that there is a tendency to reproduce rape myths based on location of the offence and relation to the offender and that an institutional view becomes the authoritative voice on the crime.

One method for the analysis of crime news is the "social panics" model, which is based on the idea that crime is exaggerated in the news, creating an unreasonable and distorted fear among the public. An analysis of social panics is important when looking at how news accounts are constructed and how certain stereotypes are reinforced. For example, a social panic could be based on exaggerating the level of stranger-related crime in relation to sexual assaults committed by acquaintances. Given the amount of media coverage and the associated public concern, it could be argued that the string of sexual assaults reported in Halifax during the summer of 1993 created a social panic.

However, there are several problems with using a social panic model: the focus on exaggeration while forgetting that a crime in fact has been committed, the possibility that some crimes are underrepresented, and neglecting to analyze how crime news might be distorted. In focusing on news as true or false, we can lose sight of how subtle distortion can be, distracting us from other issues. The crime and its possibility fade into the background as we focus our interest on the transparency of accounts.

The cynical temptation is to say, "well, it just shows that you can't trust everything you read." However, in general, we aren't cynical or doubtful and we do trust the media to give us the correct information about events. Distortion of sexual assault draws attention away from the very real nature of the crime and from the responsibility of the media to report stories in an unbiased way.

Let's examine some ways sexual assault news might be distorted.

1. *Rape myths.* Biased accounts of sexual assault are ideological, part of the problem and part of the crime. The distorted cultural messages our society receives about sexual assault are part of the reason the crime can occur. Myths such as it only happens to bad women, only strangers commit the crime, rape is sex, the offender is perverted, women provoke or somehow deserve rape, and women fabricate rape stories or cry rape for revenge, are all perpetuated in news accounts of sex crimes.

These myths are not simply wrong; they exist for a reason: to displace men's responsibility onto women. The discourse about sexual assault is anchored in cultural myths and consists of rhetorical tropes that carry meaning and come to mediate practical social relations. Our attention is drawn away from the experiences of women as victims of sexual assault. Saying that women are not cautious, were walking in the wrong place or put their trust in the wrong man shifts the blame onto the victim as if they are somehow responsible for the attack they suffered at the hands of another.

This journalistic pattern of victim-blaming is part of the normal cultural construction of sexual assault. To find this idea reproduced in the news is not surprising, nor is it acceptable, but it did not seem very common in this sample. More subtle a distortion was the silence around sexual assault, which can be examined by using a model of "ways of knowing" about crime.

2. *Venn circles.* Comparing the representation of crime in the news to another source of information is called a critical comparative approach. A typical comparison is to contrast the representation of crime in the news to police statistics. In seeing how widespread sexual assault is, for example, we are better able to appreciate if there is a silence on sexual assault in the news. In a venn diagram, there are three circles, each representing a body of knowledge: for example, crimes known to the police, crimes reported to victimization surveys and crimes reported in the news.

From the first edition, we know that 34,352 cases of sexual assault were reported to the police in Canada in 1992. After screening out what the police believed to be unfounded cases, the official incidence was 29,543 sexual assaults. Only 59 percent of sexual assaults were cleared by charge, 34 percent of cases went to court, and 12 percent of perpetrators were found guilty.

The difference between the incidence of sexual assault reported by Statistics Canada and those recorded in the *Canadian News Index* demonstrates the relative invisibility of sexual assault in the news. In 1990, for example, about 28,000 sexual assaults were officially reported to the police in Canada, but the seven major dailies polled by the Index carried only slightly more than two hundred stories, which is one news story for about every 140 reported cases, or less than 1 percent of the total reported sexual assault cases.

We also know from victimization surveys that the vast majority of incidents (94 percent) were not reported to the police. If only 6 percent of total cases were reported to the police, the real number of sexual assaults in Canadian society in 1992 was more like 500,000. On other words, there was only one news article per 2,333 assaults, which means that only about 0.04 percent of assaults were reported in newspaper articles. This underreporting makes sexual assault seem far less common than it really is.

The official numbers form the objective baseline from which to measure how well the media reports sexual assault. However, when we consider how many sexual assault stories are reported in major newspapers every year, we do not find numbers to reflect either the official incidence or the estimated one. In terms of our venn diagram of ways of knowing about sexual assault crime, victims knew of 500,000 cases, the police knew of 28,000, and the public knew of about 200 cases.

Against this background of relative silence about sex crimes, any coverage would seem extraordinary, especially if it is flagged as unusual. Sexual assaults do not appear in the news in numbers that reflect their true incidence, and those that do appear are often not reflective of reality, as in the case of sexual crimes committed by stranger-predators. This distorted image in the news becomes part of how victims and non-victims think about the world.

In a circular way, this dominant image of what sexual assault looks like then becomes part of the crime. If the typical sexual assault article dramatizes stranger-related assault, then jurors, lawyers, judges and the police formulate sexual assault in a similar way. Perhaps the police, for example, are likely to discount a report if it does not "add up." This, in turn, is a recursive relationship: court decisions can affect public perception of sexual assault, as in the case where a judge credited a man for having spared his daughter's virginity despite having molested her for more than two years.

In 2007, Statistics Canada says that there were 21,449 cases of sexual assault reported to the police and classed as founded. Of these, 20,933 (98 percent) were level one (low or no other injuries to the victim), 375 cases were level two (with a weapon or causing harm, less than 2 percent), and 141 cases were level three (aggravated assault, wounding or maiming, less than one half of 1 percent). The rate per 100,000 was 85.

For this edition and using the *National Post* as an indicator of publicity, 132 articles represent 21,449 cases reported to police. Another way of saying it is that roughly one out of every 162 cases makes it to the news. In about one out of six articles, the charge was aggravated assault, compared to less than half of 1 percent of official cases.

The ratio of offences committed by strangers versus acquaintances (using police data) in 2007 is 18 percent compared to 82 percent. However, the news sample makes it seem as if the ratio is almost even, exaggerating the proportion of stranger-related offences and downplaying those that are acquaintance-related. This is an important criticism of the news because it makes women feel that assaults committed by familiars don't fit the crime.

However, in calculating the true level of representation, we again have to turn from official police statistics as inadequate as a way of representing the problem. What we find in doing victimization surveys is that about 91 percent of sexual assaults are not reported to the police. Why don't victims report?

Victims don't report if they feel the incident is minor. Incidents of sexual touching are less likely to be reported to police (94 percent unreported) than incidents of sexual attack (78 percent unreported). Is this because victims compare their experiences to the crime they read in the news? Victims of sexual assault also stated that they did not report the incident to the police because they felt it was not important enough (58 percent), because it was dealt with in another way (54 percent), they felt it was a personal matter (47 percent) and they did not want to get involved with the police (41 percent).

So what is the real number of sexual assaults in society? According to self-reported victim data from the 2004 *General Social Survey on Victimization*, about 512,200 Canadians aged fifteen and older were the victims of a sexual assault in the previous year. The rate was 1,977 incidents of sexual assault per 100,000 population, many times higher than the official rate of 85.

Again, using the *National Post* as an indicator of publicity, 132 articles stand in for half a million cases reported to researchers. Another way of saying it is that roughly one out of every 3880 cases makes it to the news. This is only one paper, but it is a national newspaper.

In terms of our venn diagram of ways of knowing about sexual assault crime, victims knew of about 512,000 cases, the police knew of 21,000 and the public knew of about 132 cases. The characteristics of the last, filtered through the double reporting of police and media do not match the characteristics of the first.

3. *Incidence data.* Further comparisons are telling. In 41 percent of the cases read in the sample, a suspect was arrested and facing charges. In reality, sexual offences are less likely to be cleared by police than other types of violent offences, with charges laid in a third of sexual offences compared to half in other types of violent crime. In the news sample, 68 percent of cases resulted in a conviction. In reality, sexual offences result in a finding of guilt 49 percent of the time, less likely than for other violent crimes.

Of crimes that are reported to the police, four-fifths are committed by an acquaintance. When we look at the victimization survey, the proportion committed by an acquaintance drops to slightly more than half. To be fair, the relation between victim and offender reported in the news represents that reported in the victimization survey better than that reported to police.

Victims of sexual assault report that their most common emotional reaction is anger (24 percent), followed by confusion and frustration (20 percent), shock and disbelief (16 percent), annoyance (16 percent), and fear (15 percent). While many victims of sexual assault did not report their victimization to police, many did turn to informal sources of support, such as friends (72 percent), family (41 percent), co-workers (33 percent) or doctors or nurses (13 percent). Victims of sexual assault felt less safe than those who had not been the victim of a crime, with 27 percent of sexual assault victims saying they felt unsafe when walking alone at night. One in six (17 percent) victims of sexual assault indicated that they routinely stay home at night because they are too afraid to go out alone. A high proportion of sexual assault victims (63 percent) indicated that over the previous twelve months they had changed their routine.

4. *Emotion.* As we see here, the problem is not a panic but a silence. This in itself upsets our traditional way of analyzing crime in the news. In terms of a public knowledge or discussion of sexual assault, we have some distorted stories of overly violent incidents committed in public by strangers, which often get solved and go to trial and result in convictions. But overwhelmingly we have no stories at all.

Sexual assault is not overplayed in the media but is made virtually invisible in comparison to its official and actual incidence. Using police statistics and victimization survey results as a methodological tool for the examination of news accounts demonstrates the invisibility of sex crimes. In understanding this general background of under-reporting, the articles on sexual assault that do get printed in the newspapers can be analyzed: Do they present crimes committed by strangers; are they high profile assaults; are they cases where the accused is acquitted; what does the language look like; do we hear from the victims?

The things victims say are strong: "You may still not believe that you have done anything wrong, but I know otherwise"; [I have been through] "an emotional roller coaster full of sadness, fear and pain"; and "We were supposedly in a place of protection... well, it wasn't a place of protection, it was a place of hell."

Mothers also spoke: "No one was there on that night to protect her preciousness. My heart bleeds because of that. You took her precious soul from me, my shining star, my beautiful angel"; and "She was a happy, successful girl, loved by her family and friends."

Contempt and anger are evident: "I was trying to kill him... I was going to run him over, put the car into reverse and run over him again to make sure he was dead. Then I was going to kill his family and then I was going to kill myself"; and "It would be easier to accept that he died… than to learn that he is this cruel and hurtful person… The lives of my family were ripped apart and turned upsidedown in seventeen minutes."

While such quotations are rare, counting can only get us so far. It is not just that these quotations are few in number but that they are so far between. In explanation, the largest distortion in the news about sexual assault is that it is predominantly stranger-related and that it is much more likely to occur in public places than private. Other distortions are an over-representation of arrest and conviction than actually occurs. More subtle, perhaps, is that the dominant voice is institutional, with judges, lawyers and police providing most of the accounts of what happened.

During the 1980s, the number of sexual assaults reported to the police steadily increased, but coverage in the news decreased. The increase in reporting to police, while low, reflects a general change in society's attitudes about sexual assault and perhaps its better treatment of victims in the criminal justice system. The decrease in media coverage, however, is more difficult to explain.

While recent statistics show that the ratio of police cases to news stories remained about the same between 1992 and 2007, the ratio of news stories to victim's stories changed dramatically. The former ratio went from 1 to 140 in 1992 to 1 to 160, while the latter went from 1 in 2,333 to 1 in 3,880. There is still the same proportion of police cases making it to the news, but we hear from fewer victims.

Public knowledge about the crime of sexual assault has several layers. For example, although, obviously, all sexual assaults are known to the people they happen to, only 6 percent are known to the police and less than 1 percent is communicated to the public through the news. This process of attrition introduces distortions, some subtle, others not. The media cannot represent the complete picture, in part because of a lack of information but also because of the priorities and agenda set by the media itself. Victims of crime are more likely to report those incidents committed by strangers, which are more likely to be believed by the police and in turn are more likely to be picked up by the media.

At the end of this chain of attrition, the public sees only a select few of the stories culled from the huge number of assaults committed, and these stories are slanted towards sensational crimes committed by strangers. The public receives information that implies that interpersonal violent crime committed by strangers is rampant and that the world is becoming an increasingly dangerous place to live. Thus is fear constructed, which has consequences for how people live their lives.

The media, then, is part of the system that makes sex crimes invisible. If a crime is seldom reported, then silence becomes the norm; if a crime is often distorted, then this is distorted message is presented to readers. In contrast to a social panic model, this is the "orthodox version of events" model.

In looking at how accounts are constructed, we can see how our attention is directed to a preferred reading of events. This directing, or deixis, occurs in the creation of the typical account. When an account directs our attention to one interpretation, it elides, or misses, other possible versions. An orthodox version of events is constructed in the course of the reporting on sexual assaults when attention is consistently drawn to certain features.

News accounts are also doubly constructed as they are truncated versions of police definitions of crimes and they fit social stereotypes of what the crime should look like. In these constructions, aspects of the initial event that are features of a crime must be intended, that is, collected together by the news account. Through the inclusion of selected features and the exclusion of others, accounts retroactively accomplish, or transform, the event into a crime. For all intents and purposes, and for most people, what is in the account is the crime. We have no perspective to see any other reality.

Various features of the account (the assault, a victim, an attacker, the police) become prescriptive aspects of the crime. These textual features are intended to be read as a reworked description of a sexual assault; thus, the event becomes the textual reconstruction of the event. The account conveys information to extra-local readers who are far from the event (as observers, not participants) in a number of ways: by transmitting official information from the police (who are the authorities); by creating in readers (the public) a sense of passivity, perhaps in response to the one-way flow of information; and by substituting categories such as attacker and victim for people in the actual event. An event first experienced by the victim is reworked, translated and shown through a series of filters to become a crime experienced by the reader.

Coupled with the relative absence of reporting on sexual assault, a slanted construction of crime is reported in the news. Newspapers typically rely on the police or on trials for information, reflecting both a law-and-order perspective and an institutional perspective, rather than those of victims, social organizations and other professionals. The overwhelmingly institutional focus means that the definition of crime is often constructed by the police, and the police emerge as authorities in the news accounts.

In the string of sexual assault news accounts examined in the first edition, the police point of view dominates. The police were named in the headlines, and their opinions tended to be cited first and given the most space. In the secondary news articles, however, this dominance shifts. Experts, organizational representatives, citizens and journalists are also cited. An important difference, of course, between primary and secondary news accounts is that the former report the so-called facts of the case, while the latter are more speculative. It is only in the secondary news articles (columns, opinion pieces) that an alternate point of view, not dominated by the police interpretation of events, emerges. In this process, news organizations create a privileged interpretation of sexual assault by excluding the woman's point of view and replacing it with a more authoritative perspective. This might not be a problem if not for the fact that the dominant perspective tends to recreate mystification around sexual assault.

Police provide the descriptive information from an organizational point of view: a report that an assault occurred, a description of what happened and an opinion on whether they thought it was connected to other assaults. This is the general structure of the "discourse of events," and it defines the character of the crime and the role of the victim and the offenders. The textual ordering of the event constructs the social reality of the crime. The very words used by the police and reported in the media construct the character of what happened: "alleged assault," "assault," "attack" or "false report."

The police can also offer various explanations of the crimes, which become another part of the orthodox version of events: victims were said to have left windows open, offenders follow victims into stairwells, media reports might bring people out of the woodwork to copycat or it's blamed on the warm weather. Official explanations can be sympathetic to victims or excuse offenders, and thus can be evaluated to what extent they buy into rape myths.

Police often urge women to be cautious, not to let people they don't know into their homes, to use common sense and not take shortcuts, to resist, to scream and not to use pepper spray. The problem with this is that it puts all the responsibility for safety on women.

The dominant discourse or orthodox version of events focuses on stranger-related sexual assaults, while disingenuously admitting their relative rarity, and depends on the authority of the police. This orthodoxy emphasizes how not to become a victim and stresses the danger of public places. Thus, news accounts focus on the details of the crimes, the stranger trope and the police version of events. A final aspect of the construction of orthodoxy is the suppression of alternate voices and emotional accounts. Only in secondary news accounts are conflicting points of view on such topics as the ineffectiveness of the police even barely developed. Most importantly, the crime, and the fear of crime in particular, as experienced by women is absent from this orthodox version. For this reason emotional discourse is an occasion to resist orthodoxy. It is in the emotion of victims and the dispassionate voice of authorities that we can begin to trace the lines of power.

In conclusion, despite the importance of the social panics model, because it focuses more on distortion than on distraction it fails to analyze deeper ideological constructions in the media and how these constructions reflect gender distortions, which work to the detriment of women and society as a whole.

Gendered violence in society needs to be re-analyzed, and the ways in which the media reports sexual assault need to be reformed. Tackling commonly held rape myths is a good place to start. It is easy to reproduce the status quo. It is much harder to challenge it.

Summary

This chapter began with the idea that women's issues are not represented in the news. I have used the issue of sexual assault to show that news accounts are constructed in an orthodox way to create a particular version of events. My argument is that a series of silences and distortions work to misrepresent crime in the news.

However, it is not enough to show that the media gives us distorted knowledge; this knowledge exists for a reason and as a reality. Ideological knowledge is normal knowledge. The focus on stranger rape and away from acquaintance-related sexual assault, for example, is how newspaper accounts structure knowledge of the world in ways that work to the detriment of women and the advantage of men. It is not that stranger rapes are more important but that they are seen as having more import for the public as knowledge of crime.

The emphasis in the first edition was on a sensationalized "string" of sexual assaults in Halifax. In this edition we focus on a whole year of reporting in a national newspaper. What we find is that this "news as usual" discourse reveals little information that is useful to women as they live in this world. This is illustrated by a comparison of the patterns of crime in the news to the patterns of crime known to police and to victims. Reporting of sexual assault that contains greater detail might not necessarily be better, and it can exacerbate public fear.

However, I think the most important new element in this analysis that can work against the invisibility of sex crime in the news is emotional discourse. Testimony from victims and their families connects us as readers to real people and aids in persuading us to the impact of crime.

Overall, the textual construction of crime is circular: as the news constructs a panic about gender and danger, it draws upon the warrantability of that claim as a condition of its production. The media can play up fear of strangers because that is a pre-existing cultural idea. Because news is constructed extra-locally, discourse that reflects dominant ideas reproduces the unequal relations of the genders in a way that is beyond our control. Reporting of sexual assault that relies on normal notions of gender and danger to give its text reasonability reaffirms those ideas. However, in those few spaces where we read emotional discourse we become reconnected to others and the crimes become more visible.

2

Women Who Work as Prostitutes
The Sex Trade and Trading in Labels

Women who work as prostitutes are often negatively and stereotypically labelled by the media. This is not surprising given that prostitutes have been seen as fallen women, seducers and vectors for contagious disease. In sociology, the idea of labelling refers to how groups become stigmatized in society in such a way that they are thought of poorly. The labels come to represent the group, dehumanize the individuals and provide others with too easy a way to categorize and discredit people. They become a master status.

Anne Derrick focuses her talk on how women who work as prostitutes are narrowly stereotyped in the media. In her work as a lawyer she has had occasion to legally represent women in the sex trade and has observed the type of labelling they receive. For women who work in the sex trade, "prostitute" or "hooker" becomes their main identity through the media, an identity that categorizes everything else about them.

In the next section, Reading the News, some examples are provided of how the media labels women who work as prostitutes. Often, the media's representation of them is shallow and reinforces the negative image of the profession. For example, media coverage often uses the word hooker, failing to address the wider aspects of violence and exploitation. In addition, little concern is shown about the organization of the trade, how poverty might be a motivation to work as a prostitute or how prostitution can be dangerous work.

In the Sample Study, news accounts from the *Vancouver Sun* published between 1989 and 1992 are used to look at how murdered women were portrayed and how the definition of who these women were was central to what was done about them. It is argued that this sets the stage that allows the work of a serial killer to continue for so long. The findings are then taken up in Analyzing the News, which carries the ideas forward to look briefly at coverage of missing women in 1998 and 1999, and in particular how the characterization of prostitution in the media is part of the crime itself. It is easy to blame women for prostitution when that is the predominant image in the media. It is argued that the dominant emotional context is characterized in what John Lowman (2006) has referred to as a "discourse of disposal." Studies I have found useful for thinking about prostitution in the news are Jiwani and Young (2006), Stillman (2000), Pitman (2002) and Hallgrimsdottir, Phillips and Benoit (2006).

Furthermore, the definition of prostitution found in the *Criminal Code* of Canada is not represented in the news accounts, enabling further misrepresentation of the crime. By stereotyping women who work in the sex trade as hookers and by misrepresenting the character of the crime, the media fails to provide an understanding of prostitution that addresses the violence and exploitation in these women's lives and is part of its reproduction.

Anne Derrick's Talk

I am going to discuss some opinions I have developed after some exposure to representing clients who are themselves subjects of controversy. I have had some clients who welcome that controversy or at least welcome their role in it, and then I have had clients who have not welcomed their role at all.

One of the obvious examples of clients who do not welcome the controversy that they attract is the case of women who work as prostitutes. I try to use that term deliberately — "women who work as prostitutes" — because part of what I am going to say relates to the fact that I think one of the great weaknesses in our media is the tendency to label.

My experience made me acutely aware of this carelessness with language when I became involved with representing women who work as prostitutes. This was in relation to an action that the government took against a group of women who were plying their trade in the downtown area of Halifax. The government tried to get an injunction against them in 1984, and I became involved as one of the legal counsel to them.

I made connections with prostitute rights activists in other parts of the world and other parts of Canada. So when I was in Toronto I got together with a woman named Amber Cook, who worked for a very long time as a stripper and also did work as an activist for prostitutes' rights. I met with her, and while I was talking to her about her work all of a sudden she bursts out, "Why do you keep calling them prostitutes? They are women who work as prostitutes." She was a very big, striking, tall woman and she completely intimidated me. I felt like a stupid, white, middle-class, rude person who had been very careless and insensitive with my language. I hear Amber's voice in my head whenever I speak about prostitution.

I was exposed to a number of things in the media when I represented the women back in 1984–85, and I will present them in no particular order. First of all, I thought that the media was generally sympathetic to the reality of these women's lives, sympathetic to learning more about what the women were experiencing or certainly how being under siege by a very unsympathetic and hostile government and ruling class was affecting them.

Along with that sympathetic disposition, however, I also found the media to be very lazy: lazy about their analysis and lazy about how they would access information. The easiest thing to do was to ring me. I became a sort of spokesperson on the issue of women on the street. They called me up and they would ask me my views and want to do an interview with me and it was easy to do that. They had my phone number and they knew where to find me, and it saved all the trouble of maybe having to do some reading or speak to some other people, or think harder about the issues, or try to present them in a more challenging or provocative way.

One of the other things that they did in addition to the easy route of contacting me was say: "Could you put us in touch with a prostitute?" "Would you be able to find us a prostitute?" I do not completely castigate that. I think it's very important to recognize that what women as prostitutes experience must be learned and understood from their perspective. It must be obtained through their eyes and through their voices, and middle-class lawyers are not to be relied upon to talk authoritatively about the issues.

Unfortunately, it also puts the burden on the women to talk about the issue of prostitution. For a vulnerable and largely invisible population who don't invite controversy or media attention, I think that is a very difficult burden to bear. If the media is lazy about these issues, then they do not properly occupy their role as critiquing the viewpoints of others. They need to challenge these viewpoints such that the onus is removed from the women and placed more squarely where it belongs, on the shoulders of the media and of other members of society.

In the media, you have the viewpoint of one group and so you want to get the viewpoint of the opposing group. When you are dealing with the issue of prostitution, the gentrified middle class talk about "what a terrible problem prostitution is and how inconvenient it is in our neighbourhoods and how we must get rid of it and our children are going to see used condoms." That is all reported and then you go to find the token prostitute and you ask her what she thinks, or you speak to the token prostitute's lawyer and you ask her. I have a mixed view of my own role in speaking out in the issue of prostitution, but I chose to do so certainly at the time because there wasn't anyone else to say anything.

There is a legitimation that goes along with being heard in the media. All of that legitimation is placed in the hands of the middle classes, who were protesting against women working the streets and therefore causing the government to act in this draconian fashion. And yet, no one to speak on the other side of the whole issue to say, "Why is it that prostitution is the problem? Why is it not that poverty is the problem. Why is it not that the way our society is structured is the problem?"

Without this more critical analysis on the part of the media, the issue is very much presented, you know, "What do we do about this problem of prostitution?" The middle class or the ruling class then say, "Well, we stamp it out, we get an injunction, we quarantine the women if they happen to be HIV carriers."

There are some real difficulties around the vulnerability of unpopular, unattractive populations being victims of easy reporting where there is not enough critique, there is not enough analysis and there is not enough willingness to go beyond simply presenting the two sides of the story.

The other important thing I learned is that the media is very important in terms not only of influencing public opinion, but also that if you are heard, if you are speaking out, if you are being reported, then you must have something that is worth saying or worth listening to. I think that this is a tool that can be very useful in the hands of populations like women who work as prostitutes in being able to speak about what they know best — better than anybody else — and being able to be heard speaking about that and therefore acquire some credibility.

Unfortunately, that hasn't happened with as great effect in Nova Scotia as it has in other jurisdictions where there have been prostitute unions developed and where women have grabbed media attention. For example, I think about the occupation of churches in England and France in the 1970s, where that was a very effective, strategic move for capturing public attention and focusing the public mind on what is really going on for women on the street and what responsibility society has in relation to that.

The issue of how the media deals with women who work as prostitutes is very much an issue of dealing with people who are acceptable and people who are not acceptable. The result is this terrible labelling that occurs, and I am made most aware of this whenever a woman who works as a prostitute is murdered. It is always "the prostitute is found murdered," or a "woman who is a prostitute is found in a dumpster behind an apartment building." I feel confident if someone murders me it is not going to be a "lawyer was found murdered." Maybe that will be somewhere in the story, but I will have a name, some other identity, but these women, this is their identification, they are a prostitute, that is it. It is not that it is their livelihood or that is their occupation, that is their identity, that is who they are. That is hard for me to fathom other than it is part of this "Are you an acceptable person or not?"

If you are an acceptable person you have a more developed identity than if you are not an acceptable person; then you have your label and you wear that like a yellow star or a pink triangle. I think women who work as prostitutes share this experience with people who are HIV positive.

It is the same with people who are accused people or criminals. The other day the newspaper reported that the Dartmouth courthouse is going to be renovated and that judges will no longer have to share common elevators or staircases with criminals in leg irons. It is quite true that some people who are convicted as criminals are placed in leg irons, but some people who are on remand and are innocent until proven guilty are also placed in leg irons.

There is very much this sense of carving up who you are in society and applying the label and leaving it at that without any further analysis. I think the media has been guilty of this, but they are also conscious of it being done by others, which is an important realization. I hope these divisions between acceptable and unacceptable people are critiqued more effectively by the media themselves.

For example, I think of the Sutcliffe, Yorkshire Ripper case in England, where the judge made comments about how women were being found murdered and the outrage when "decent women were found dead."

I think that the media is guilty of buying into those kinds of divisions, which reinforces the acceptance that there are some people who are disposable in society and there are some people who are not. That has a dramatic and definite impact on people's lives in the struggle against AIDS and certainly in the struggle that women in the street experience in terms of being very vulnerable to violence, being murdered and having those murders effectively investigated, because of the way they get reported on and they get labelled and the way public opinion is informed about them.

There is the example on the west coast of the Green River murders, where well over one hundred women have been murdered over the last number of years. There have been ongoing concerns about the way those murders are being investigated and concerns about how the press has been dealing with that phenomenon, which makes one very confident that if these were white, middle-class college coeds, there is no way that it would have gone to the extent of over one hundred women who happened to be prostitutes being murdered and there seeming not to be an effective investigation accompanying that.

I think there is a lot that can be done to improve what I perceive to be the basic sympathy at least in the media, trying to better understand the experience of women in the phenomenon of prostitution in our society. However I think many of the habits, which are easy habits and which result in the media not being sufficiently critical and not being sufficiently self-critical, continue.

Reading the News

Let us look at how women who work as prostitutes are stereotyped in the media. These stereotypes involve derogatory language and typifications about the profession. For women who work in the sex trade, being a "prostitute" or "hooker" becomes their primary identity, a stigmatized reputation provided to them by others, an emotional label. Ironically, this stigmatized reputation is seen by some as a deviant variation on women's ordinary sexual work. Stereotypes about women who work as prostitutes are significant because the way prostitution is presented in popular culture inevitably becomes part of how the crime is treated in the criminal justice system.

In 1993 the *Halifax Herald* ran a story headlined, "Slain woman local hooker," which illustrates how labelling and stereotyping can become the theme of a newspaper report. This news account of the violent death of a woman who worked as a prostitute appeared on the front page with a banner headline. The slain woman was described primarily in terms of her purported occupation.

Article 2.1 "Slain woman local hooker"

A young woman found shot to death Tuesday in North Preston has been identified as a Halifax prostitute who was expected to testify against a man accused of beating her with a stick. Cole Harbour RCMP officers, who have set up a special tip line to aid their investigation into the slaying of 17-year-old Kelly Lynn Wilneff, would not comment on any link between the two cases. They also said they don't have any "specific" suspects. (*Halifax Herald*, February 19, 1993: A1)

The account is deceptively simple in its descriptive detail. A woman was found murdered and was only identified after an anonymous tip. She had worked as a prostitute, as evidenced by the fact that she had been charged twice with communicating for the purposes of selling sexual services. She had been the complainant in an assault case against a man but didn't appear at his trial. There was a warrant for her arrest, and also for the plaintiff, Kevin Whynder, who had not shown up at the previous hearing. The police did not indicate there was any connection or that they have any specific suspect in mind. However, the police indicate they are in charge of the investigation, the task force on prostitution is hoping the death will send a message to other young women, and they are still looking for information. So, we have a crime of murder, a victim who was a prostitute, the police are involved and there is a warning to other young women.

The article accomplishes its matter-of-factness through the descriptive character of the writing, even though there is an interpretation that some women live deviant lives and there are dangers associated with that lifestyle.

The facticity of the article then is not simply anchored in the writing style but also in that it trades upon an easy version of reality. The report does not challenge a stereotypical version of prostitution but confirms it, in the process confirming sexist assumptions. This is a dominant version.

Interestingly enough, on the following February 26, the newspaper's ombudsperson wrote an article commenting on the number of calls made to the paper objecting to the use of the word "hooker." In fact, that article on this case was the only one to use "hooker" in the headline. In other articles the victim was described as "a Halifax prostitute," a "17-year-old prostitute" and "a part-time Halifax prostitute who worked the streets to support a crack cocaine habit." The ombudsperson does not state what is insensitive about the use of the word "hooker" or if it was a mistake in this one particular case. However, at the time this word was commonly used by the media in their portrayals of women who work as prostitutes, as a sampling of headlines from Halifax at the time shows.

Exhibit 2.1 Newspaper Headlines

"Female hookers caught, while johns often walk, court told," *Halifax Herald*, January 16, 1992: A5

"Dartmouth police target hookers," *HH*, August 15, 1992: A6

"Hookers must charge pimps — youth worker," *HH*, September 19, 1992: A4

"Hooker outreach program in jeopardy even after boost," *HH*, March 27, 1993: A7

"Parents rescue teenage hooker," *HH*, November 4, 1993: D13

"Judge doesn't buy $5 hooker story," *HH*, November 20, 1993: A5

"Hooker cried wolf once too often, say police," *HH*, December 2, 1993: C19

"Assault defendant denies hooker link, admits sex with girl," *Daily News*, December 8, 1993: 9

"Man found guilty of crimes against hooker," *HH*, December 9, 1993: A4

"Hooker won't testify in upcoming trial," *HH*, March 5, 1994: A5

"Hooker's memory failure foils Crown's case, Alleged pimp acquitted of five counts," *HH*, May 14, 1994: A4

"Woman distraught as brother jailed for beating hooker," *HH*, June 4, 1994: A4

"Dartmouth dogged over hooker issue," *HH*, June 8, 1994: A9

So if the word "hooker" appears quite often in news articles on prostitution, is it used in a negative and derogatory sense? Does the use of the term in the news reflect sexism in society? There are 220 words in English for a sexually promiscuous woman (and only 22 for such a man), and these words are predominantly negative. Even the word "john" is problematic, because it does not carry the derogatory connotation that "hooker" does. "John" is just faceless, anyman, while "hooker" is the deviant other.

In 1994 another woman who worked as a prostitute was found dead. The headlines used the words "slain prostitute," "prostitute's body found" and "hooker." The accounts were much like the one above, simple in their description: a woman was found murdered, was identified as a prostitute, has a history of drug abuse, is reported to have had men looking for her, the police are in charge of the investigation and won't say there is any specific suspect in mind and so on. Most of the news articles on this particular femicide were limited to the aspects of this case alone.

However, two articles in the first few days of coverage put the violence into the larger context of violence against women who work as prostitutes, moving away from the sensationalized and isolated treatment found in the other news stories. Such coverage is both unusual and important, for most media accounts of crime report incidents as if they are isolated, failing to show how they are part of a larger pattern of criminal activity.

Article 2.2 "Halifax streets growing meaner for dozens of prostitute victims"

Halifax streets have been particularly violent for prostitutes recently, with dozens of violent incidents ranging from beatings to murder. This week's death of Kimber Lucas, 25, adds another name to the growing list of prostitutes victimized. Lucas, 25, was a prostitute and drug abuser. She was also seven months pregnant. (*Daily News*, November 26, 1994: 5)

The article states that dozens of violent incidents have occurred recently, including five femicides, two incidents of aggravated assault and one case of attempted murder. The other murders are Kelly Wilneff, described as a seventeen-year-old prostitute and crack addict; Anna Marie Mason, twenty-three, said to be a part-time hooker and mother of three; Kelly Lynn Whynot, a seventeen-year-old prostitute, and Jean Hilda Myra, thirty-one, mother of three and, again, said to be a part-time prostitute. There is no mention of the other incidents of violence referred to or of evidence the streets really are growing meaner. However, the account creates a context for prostitution-related violence in a way that few articles do. It documents a pattern of violence rather than focusing on the seamier side of the sex trade, avoiding the voyeurism of most news accounts on prostitution.

Besides labelling, crime news re/creates a second distortion by focusing on prostitution as deviant women's work. The use of the words "hooker" and "prostitute" are unidimensional and ignore the role men play in the sex trade industry. There are far more men involved in the buying and selling of sex than there are women. Men pay for sex with women and men, men organize the trade as pimps, men create the laws and by-laws, and predominantly it is men who police it. However, men are seldom the subject of enforcement.

Prostitution as a crime is identified as a problem related to the presence of prostitutes providing the service, rather than to johns, pimps or the social conditions that give rise to prostitution in the first place. The enforcement of prostitution law in Canada has historically been isolated and sporadic, influenced by moral entrepreneurs, and often simply results in the police moving the business from one area to another.

Newspaper reports represent a normalized point of view, authorizing and reproducing a version of reality that locates the problem solely with the prostitutes. This point of view has typically been the approach in the policing of prostitution as well: to focus on the women who work the street not on the other aspects of the organization that maintain it. In this way, the topicalization of prostitution in the media mirrors the criminalization of prostitution by society.

However, there are occasionally important fractures in the ideology around prostitution. Not everyone agrees with the dominant perspective that prostitutes alone are the problem. While there are attempts to control prostitution, sponsored by business and property-owner associations, which arise out of frustration and the perceived inability of the police to do anything about the problem, there are also advocacy groups that seek to address the conditions under which prostitutes work. Usually in the news the hookers are identified as the obvious problem, but the role of the customers is sometimes referred to as well.

Against this general background of selectively topicalizing the work of prostitutes, it's remarkable that in 1993 articles started to appear on a police crackdown against pimps in Halifax. It was announced that a prostitution task force would receive money from the Department of the Solicitor General. A flurry of articles were published about pimps being arrested, charged and tried, and about prostitution rings, abductions and women fleeing the street. Even though this slant focused more on the exploitative side of the business rather than the moral, it still left the role of the johns virtually invisible. The policing of prostitution and the reporting on prostitution parallel one another; both focus disproportionately on the women who work in the sex trade rather than on those who use and maintain it.

In summary, deviance is not simply behaviour that violates the dominant rules of a society; deviance is also the result of the labelling of behaviour that is felt to violate cultural norms by those who are in a position to do that labelling. A labeller is as necessary as a behaviour to label. We have explored here the idea that prostitution is a label based on a negative stereotype that focuses on the sex trade as deviant women's work. In this process of topicalizing women as offenders and victims in the business of prostitution, attention is directed away from the activity of men.

Let's turn now to a more extended analysis of the news, in order to focus on the link between media stereotyping and policing of prostitution.

Sample Study

Dominant narratives always reproduce the status quo, using explanations of crime and justifications for crime control that reinforce positions of power. Because those without power have little voice, deviance is usually portrayed as a problem of the underclass, a problem that can be solved by a law-and-order approach. For many it is easy to buy into such an approach because it doesn't involve questioning current arrangements or relations of power.

This study uses news articles from the *Vancouver Sun*, for the period of January 1, 1989, to December 31, 1992, retrieved from *FP Infomart*. Because the previous section dealt with some cases involved murdered women who were called "hookers," the search term "murder" is used. This creates 519 results, of which 55 appear to deal with prostitutes.

In these articles the point of view of the police and criminal justice system predominate. The police are the source of information 54 percent of the time, with lawyers, Crown prosecutor and judges commenting an additional 8 percent. Advocates (11 percent), women who work as prostitutes (3 percent), and family or friends (8 percent) are minor sources of information in the articles. When others (academic, defendant, victim, landlord, minister), who speak 16 percent of the time, are factored out, the criminal justice side is the source of information 74 percent of the time, while it is the woman's side 26 percent of the time. The dominant point of view reflects the relations of power regulating (deviant) women's sexuality.

Headlines using the word "hooker" appear often, as Exhibit 2.2 illustrates:

Exhibit 2.2 Newspaper Headlines, *Vancouver Sun*

"Slayings of 14 hookers unsolved: 'Overkill' links some slayings," February 4, 1989: A1

"$10,000 reward offered in hooker's death," February 16, 1989: A3

"Police probing links in slayings of hookers," March 18, 1989: A14

"Slain hooker remembered as a sweetheart by others," June 7, 1989: A12

"Police probe Mount Pleasant in hooker deaths," June 8, 1989: B7

"Hooker toll rising," September 1, 1990: A2

"Man held in hooker slaying suspect in other deaths," September 1, 1990: A1

"Suspect sought in hooker killing," December 31, 1990: B3

"Hooker made near-fatal mistake," May 2 1991: A1

"Hooker's killer gets life term," May 6, 1991: A1

"Man charged in death of hooker: Police concentrating on case at hand before probing links," January 23, 1992: A9

1. *Dominant explanation.* Looking at the actual texts allows us to see what explanations are offered to the public. The dominant explanation is that offered by the police: the transient lifestyle of the women is why they have

disappeared and also why it is so difficult to investigate the crimes, as in the case of Tracey Leigh Chartrand.

Article 2.3 "Possible links seen in slayings"

"She was never really reported missing by anyone," said [police]. "Several months ago we caught wind of the fact that she had not been seen by friends or associates, and as a precautionary measure police initiated an in-house investigation to determine whether she had in fact disappeared." (*Vancouver Sun*, April 17, 1989: A3)

This is the version against which other versions contend: Tracey is missed but not reported missing The police resist the idea of a serial killer operating in the area who is targeting prostitutes, even though they consult with U.S. federal police about the Green River killer and a possible suspect's forays to Vancouver. One of the longest articles in the sample details explicitly the actions of a violent individual who pleads guilty to killing Nancy Jane Bob.

Article 2.4 "Profile of a sadist"

"He got his satisfaction from the violence," said [police]. "The more women resisted, the more violent he became. With one of his victims he choked her till she was bleeding from the nose, ears and mouth and he had an orgasm."

"I thought I was going to die," [said the victim]. "He held me down and strangled me. I went unconscious. I remember kicking the door and when I came to I was on the ground... He dragged me into the bush and left me there. He's a real horror show."

"They were the low life of the low life. They don't know any better. They're stuck in a rut and can't get out," [the defendant] said. "I hated it. I wanted to be with Linda. I wanted to take care of her. I think they're [prostitutes] so dependent on their habit they lose their senses." (*Vancouver Sun*, May 2, 1991: B1)

An article from the same day, titled "Hooker made near-fatal mistake," repeats the dominant explanation that these women lead dangerous lives and that their deaths are either misadventures or the result of psychotic individuals who target them because they are hookers. They are not targeted by psychotic individuals as women (which would make them members of a major group) but rather as prostitutes (which makes them members of a minority deviant group).

2. *Resistant explanation.* Some resistance to the dominant explanation is embedded in the allegation made by friends of the missing women that police had not looked for the disappeared because they were sex workers.

Article 2.5 "Police probing links in slayings of hookers"

"The public has to wonder if it's because of the profile of these people that more isn't being done to solve these mysteries," said [lawyer]… "Basically all of the women killed have been poor and have turned to this life in desperation. They're on the low end of the political totem pole," he said. "It's not an easy case for the police, but just because it's not easy and there's no hue and cry to catch the perpetrator doesn't mean it's impossible." (*Vancouver Sun*, April 18, 1989: A14)

This second explanation, that the sheer number of missing women means there is a serial killer at work, has been subterranean but becomes increasingly popular and exists alongside and in opposition to the official police version that there is nothing unusual in the pattern of murders. It is a competing explanation for what has happened to them. The police say they are looking at hooker-related murders and they visit the Green River task force, but they also say their theory does not involve a serial-type killer. In 1990, when fifteen prostitutes have been killed in the lower mainland since 1982, the police still say they do not have a serial killer on the loose.

This (lack of an) explanation for the murders dovetails with the "women as hookers" explanation. It is a shallow discourse that does not admit of the women's humanity. It is an emotional disinterest. The following news article comes in the wake of the killing of Katherine Mary Lou Daignault, a "Mount Pleasant prostitute."

Article 2.6 "Prostitute deaths probed for link"

[The mayor] said it's a "significant" number of homicides, but he doesn't believe there is a pattern developing that would require extra police effort, such as establishing a task force….

"The scary thing is it doesn't seem to slow things down. An incident like this doesn't have any effect. Now they [other prostitutes] hear another one got it and they go right back to work. They seem complacent about it," [police] said. (*Vancouver Sun*, June 6, 1989: A10)

The resistance to the (disinterested) explanation offered by the police and mayor is published in a letter to the editor a month later, when a reader says the idea that women are complacent about their own safety is outrageous. She points out that these women work to put food on the table and a roof over their heads "despite the fear that they could be the next raped, strangled, naked body discovered." She says that it is too easy to blame the victim and suggest that the women's deaths are their own fault. This resistance is offered in a few personal notes about the murdered women. Parents, sisters and friends say things like the following:

Exhibit 2.3 Personal Comments

"The least popular the person, the more Linda would like them, the more she wanted to help them so they would be more or less accepted. She'd give them self-confidence," [friend] said. (*Vancouver Sun*, February 4, 1989: A10)

"She loved to show off her daughter's picture and cook curried chicken for other residents. She… would regularly help a blind woman manoeuvre the halls to the communal bathroom and took the time to chat with the elderly who never seemed to have any guests." (*Vancouver Sun*, November 9, 1989: B6)

"Being on the street terrified her," [friend] said. "She was always scared going out — but she had no choice. What she didn't get from welfare she had to make up on the street. It was all for her children." (*Vancouver Sun*, January 23, 1992: A1)

While the resistance to the dominant explanations is sparse it is also strong. It is an emotional discourse, which opposes the disinterested authoritarian one. It is also one that opposes the cognitive simplicity of "it's just hookers" to offer a more complex version of events.

Overall, to develop a critical perspective on crime in the news, we need to see the accounts that are offered there as possible versions of why things happen and what should be done about them. These accounts are authored with a voice, a perspective, although sometimes the voice is so seemingly objective that it just seems to be stating the facts. In those occasions when opportunities open for contrasting versions, we can better see both the artificiality and the constructed character of factual accounts. It is to be open to a different way of talking.

Analyzing the News

In media coverage between 1989 and 1992 there are a couple of explanations offered for the murders of the women: that the deaths are a result of the prostitutes' lifestyles and that there might be a serial killer at work. These are not equal discourses: the first blames the victims and (perversely) allows the second.

Developing a second sample for study, we see that in 1998 and 1999 similar issues arise when women start to go missing from downtown Vancouver's sex trade. The number of disappeared goes from ten in 1998 to thirty-one in 1999 as friends and family tell their stories to reporters. However, unlike the murdered women there are no bodies and no one to care unless someone notices their absence.

1. *Explanation one.* The dominant explanation is that offered by the police.

Article 2.7 "Missing women cases probed: Vancouver police will review 40 unsolved cases dating from 1971, but they doubt a serial killer was involved in any disappearances."
"They could have wanted to change their names for any number of reasons," [police] said. "They could have gone to another town with a new identity. They could have gone to the States. They could have married and they don't want anyone to know what's going on." (*Vancouver Sun*, September 18, 1998: B1)

This explanation is as empty as the places where these women once walked.

2. *Explanation two.* A disturbing voice enters into the public discourse when the media begins to carry emotional accounts of missing women. The debate about the missing sex workers spins around the police version and the families' version, constantly sparring with the spectre of a serial killer. The discussion becomes political as a result.

Article 2.8 "Missing on the mean streets"
"If these women were not street involved, there would be an outpouring of concern and immediate action to find their killer," [prostitutes' advocate] said this week...

"What are the police waiting for? We've got a population group that is being chronically murdered and maimed," [another advocate] said. "We know they are. We know they will be in the future, and somehow we've made a choice that their safety is not a priority. And the really scary thing is that some place we're comfortable with it. That's what's scary." (*Vancouver Sun*, March 3, 1999: A13)

3. *Explanation three.* There is also a third, more subtle, explanation for the missing sex workers, which centres around the idea of a "discourse of disposal," which governs the city's regulation of street prostitution. The discourse of disposal has two parts. On the one hand, under federal law, communication for the purposes of the procuring sex in public space is illegal. Because police and city officials have increasingly cracked down on the sex trade, street-level sex workers are forced to work in extremely dangerous places. At this level the discourse of disposal means that there is a physical geography of exclusion where policy and practice work to segregate sex workers in dangerous areas. As a result, police and municipal government are directly implicated in the disappearances of the thirty-one women. They are responsible.

Moreover, there is also a rhetorical discourse of disposal evidenced in the way in which prostitution is marginalized in public debate. In this way the discussion of what to do about the missing women cases becomes increasingly politicized. These competing accounts are more than cognitive choices because the sympathy that springs up for the families and friends of the lost women creates a discourse of sympathy, which works in direct opposition to the disposal discourse.

The discourse of disposal is evident in several ways: the explaining away of the disappearances; the dangerous character of sex work itself, which needs controlling; and the negating of the real lives of the women. This last is constantly reaffirmed in what relatives say about the missing. Let's look first at how law and policing works to make prostitution disposable, and then we will turn to the actual discourse.

1. *The law.* In 1978 the prostitution law (Section 195.1) was based on the new notion that every person who solicits any person in a public place was guilty of prostitution. Prior to 1972 the law only criminalized women and did not apply to males.

This idea was successfully challenged in the same year by an appeals court on the grounds that soliciting meant being pressing or persistent. In the early-1980s, there was a lot of concern about street prostitution and the need to do something about it. In response, various municipalities in Canada enacted by-laws to curtail street prostitution in the early 1980s. Both Montreal (1980) and Calgary (1981) enacted by-laws to prevent the use of the streets by prostitutes or their clients.

In 1983 the Supreme Court of Canada struck down the Calgary by-law as an attempt to enact criminal sanctions, which was exclusively under federal jurisdiction. Montreal's by-law was also struck down in 1984, effectively stymying similar by-laws in Vancouver, Niagara Falls, Regina and Halifax. Given that soliciting was difficult to prove, and that municipalities could not act on their own to control prostitution, the law was very difficult to enforce.

In 1984, the B.C. attorney general sought an injunction to restrain prostitution-related activity as a public nuisance in a specific residential area of Vancouver. The N.S. attorney general applied for a similar injunction to restrain the public nuisance of prostitutes in Halifax. The N.S. application was refused on the basis that the province was trying to control a matter that fell within federal jurisdiction.

In an attempt to control prostitution, occasional efforts were made to publicize and criminalize the activity of male johns, pimps and sex workers. In the early 1980s, Toronto, Halifax and other cities publicized the names of customers in the news, but soon discontinued it simply because of a lack of interest on the part of the newspapers.

The idea of publishing johns' names is an interesting one, for it shifts the media from crime reporting to crime control. This action moves the media from a reactive position to a proactive one, accepting without question, it would seem, that prostitution is deviant, the law is above question and the media can act to control crime.

On the basis that the law was unenforceable and in order to control the so-called public nuisance factor, in 1985 the soliciting provision was replaced by a section broadly prohibiting communication for the purposes of prostitution. Initially, this new law was overturned by the Nova Scotia Court of Appeals as contrary to the *Charter of Rights and Freedoms* in 1987. The Halifax police then changed their method of policing to a more passive one, reflecting a widespread uncertainty about the enforceability of the new law.

In 1990, however, the Supreme Court of Canada ruled that communications between a prostitute and a customer were not protected under the *Charter*, even though it constituted a warrantable infringement of a person's *Charter* rights.

In 1992, a Halifax woman charged with prostitution argued that the enforcement of section 213 of the Canadian *Criminal Code* (communication for the purposes of prostitution) was discriminatory because more women are charged under that statute than men, even though "it takes two to tangle." The lawyers showed that between June 1, 1990, and November 30, 1991, 84 percent of those charged under this statute were women, and argued that this was discriminatory under the *Charter of Rights and Freedoms* because the law was being unfairly applied. A provincial court judge ruled that the difference in charge rates was not sexist and did not violate the *Charter*, a decision upheld at the Court of Appeal. The issue was made to seem one of police resources, that it was easier to catch women than men. Halifax had the highest ratio of charges against women in the country.

A traditional rationale for gender asymmetry in prostitution-related charging has been that there are not enough female police officers to go undercover to arrest johns, an answer which begs the question of why police personnel is gendered and points to an implicit gender bias in the law and its enforcement that mirrors the social stereotyping of prostitution as women's work.

The statute under which the Halifax woman was charged is one of several that define the offence of prostitution: keeping a common bawdy-house where prostitution regularly occurs (section 210), procuring or pimping (section 212) and offence in relation to prostitution (section 213). The last is the one most often applied and is usually called communicating for the purposes of prostitution. The law states: "Every person who in a public place or in any place open to public view communicates with any person for the purpose of engaging in prostitution or of obtaining the sexual services of a prostitute is guilty of an offence punishable on summary conviction." More importantly, section 213 criminalizes the behaviour of both parties in the transaction if they ask for or offer sex for money. However, the media finds it difficult to focus on the customers (men), just as do the police and members of the public. Men are virtually never portrayed in the media as the beneficiaries or organizers of prostitution, despite the fact that there are more men involved in the buying and selling of sex than there are women.

Despite the preponderance of men in the trade, women are more likely to be arrested on prostitution-related offences. Official statistics make it appear as if men and women are equally charged, yet there are many more men who engage the services of prostitutes than women who work in the sex trade. Moreover, the Canadian average disguises provincial differences in charge rates.

The media can sometimes find itself criminalized for its involvement in the sex trade. For example, in 1990, Toronto Metropolitan police charged *Now* magazine and four of its directors with communicating for the purposes of prostitution for placing classified personal sex ads in the paper. However, three weeks later all charges were dropped, as the Crown and attorney general found there was no basis for the charges.

The preceding is a brief summary of how prostitution is physically segregated by law. Now we turn to how it is discussed in the media.

2. *Discourse of disposal.* There has been considerable variation in the amount of newspaper coverage on prostitution over time. The quantity of coverage, as well as its content, is important for what it says about prostitution as a public issue, and for how society deals with it as a problem.

The chronology of prostitution law parallels the change in media coverage. In the late 1970s, the law was changed to make it more gender-inclusive and to redefine the terms of the offence. The enforcement of the solicitation clause soon proved unworkable in the early 1980s, and media coverage started to rise. In the first edition, I documented the sharp rise of prostitution-related coverage in the mid-1980s. At the peak of news stories in the mid-1980s, the law was changed again. Interest started to decline but still remained relatively high through the late 1980s as the law was clarified through the court system. There was substantial discussion on whether the law was working to deter prostitution and the public nuisance that accompanied it.

For example, a search for "nuisance" in the *Vancouver Sun* for 1985–1990 finds a series of articles on prostitution. Interestingly, of the fourteen items, two are columns, six are editorials, and only six are articles. There is also more of a critical point of view, as the police are criticized for arresting more female prostitutes than their customers and the mayor is criticized for suggesting that the law is not punitive enough.

Article 2.9 "Hooker law flawed"
Increasing the criminal sanctions might put more people in jail and more names in police files, but that would only increase the hypocrisy. (*Vancouver Sun*, December 1, 1989: A16)

By 1991 the crisis in law enforcement was over, and media coverage returned to normal.

In this way the media reflects social issues of the day, although often without the critical perspective or historical point of view that we might wish. But the media does not simply take up social issues and report them like a mirror, for it is in a position to create and distort them as well. We have already looked at stereotyping and labelling of prostitution in the media. News coverage of prostitution in the 1990s after the communicating law was clarified participated in the public debate as well. The question is, how did that coverage characterize the problem of prostitution? With this recursive interchange between prostitution law and the media, the newspapers take up pre-existing issues in society and focus them as in a prism, perhaps distorting them, sometimes criticizing them but always transforming them in the process of reporting.

Prostitution does not receive a lot of attention in the news, and as we have seen it is often distorted, failing to make the connection to larger issues of violence against women, portraying prostitution in a way that is derogatory to women and making men invisible. This distorted and incomplete picture plays a role in the social mis/construction of prostitution in our society. The predominant image of prostitution we get is one of women standing on the street in fishnet stockings and a miniskirt, but in actuality there are more men than women engaged in the buying and selling of sex. There are the pimps who organize the trade and exploit the women; there are the johns who demand the trade and exploit the women; and there are, of course, men who work as prostitutes themselves.

Interestingly, an examination of the local media coverage of Vancouver's missing women in the late 1990s finds competing explanations for what happened. The dominant explanation is that offered by the police a decade earlier: the transient lifestyle of the women is why they have disappeared, and why they would turn up again, and it is their dangerous occupation that puts them at risk of violence. Other versions contend against this dominant version, which is based in both a physical segregation of sex trade workers and a rhetorical discourse of disposal.

However, some members of the public refused to accept the police's explanation that nothing out of the ordinary has happened to the missing women. This resistance to the dominant explanation began at least in the late 1980s, exacerbated by allegations made by friends and family of the missing women that police had not looked for the disappeared because they were sex workers. This contrary opinion is of course resisted by the police. There is also the suggestion that there must be a serial killer working Vancouver, an idea that is also resisted by the police.

In 1999, when the mayor offered a financial reward for information leading to the arrest of those responsible for crimes occurring in Vancouver at the time, a series of garage robberies and a series of violent home invasions against the elderly, he was criticized for not taking the disappearances seriously. Facing a crisis of legitimacy, he suddenly announced a $100,000 reward for information leading to finding the missing women.

The second explanation, that the sheer number of missing women means there is a serial killer at work, had been subterranean but became increasingly popular and existed alongside the official police version that nothing untoward has happened. This contrast of explanations shows how interpretations enter into the reading of events. A special episode of *America's Most Wanted* traded on the explanation that serial killers were preying on inner-city prostitutes. The episode used a bad-neighbourhoods stereotype, which made the idea that this was happening in the Downtown Eastside easily picked up and reproduced by the local media.

Overall, the coverage of prostitution in the 1990s was an inextricable part of how violence against women who work in the sex trade can happen. The dominant discourse is disinterested, that these women are society's disposables; yet increasingly it is confounded by an emotional discourse that someone cares. The difficulty is getting those caring voices represented in the mainstream media.

Summary

It would seem that the media is part of the crime of prostitution in many ways. First, the media labels and stereotypes women who work as prostitutes, presenting them as "hookers" who are engaged in deviant women's work. The media not only ignores the role of men, but it also glosses over the violence and exploitation of the trade, focusing on deviance as the critical issue. Furthermore, the media influences crime prevention strategies by highlighting prostitution as a problem and can become part of a strategy itself when it chooses to do such things as publicize the names of johns. By not questioning the deeper causes of prostitution, the media upholds the legitimacy of the law, how it is policed and why a moralistic law remains on the books.

Finally, the press can be used against prostitution but can also become criminalized itself, as when it publishes personals ads that seem to solicit prostitution. To use the media to publish opinions contrary to the dominant discourse is difficult but not impossible.

There are historical trends in how prostitution has been characterized as a problem in Canadian society, and understanding the relationship of the media and the crime means understanding their intertwined nature. It is not a linear relationship but a reciprocal one, based in a normalized and continually maintained system of sexism, a sexism made possible (on the basis of) and evident through a discourse of disposal.

3

Domestic Terrorism
The News as an Incomplete Record
of Violence against Women

Violence against women, and the ability of the media to represent it in the news, is the focus of this chapter. In her talk, Debi Forsyth-Smith places violence against women in the context of how the media covers women's issues in general. Included in her discussion are some recent trends and the need for further change.

In Reading the News, a sample of articles dealing with violence against women in relationships is used to find out how well the newspapers deal with the issue. Various measures are used, such as the size of the article, whether it portrays the violence as unusual and whether it locates a specific crime in the context of violence against women in general. This is a typical approach for a conventional analysis of crime in the media.

In the Sample Study section, two sets of articles are considered in terms of how the victim and perpetrator are portrayed, how blame is placed for the crime (directly and indirectly), who makes those claims and the putative effect on the media audience. First, a pilot sample was selected from the *Calgary Herald* for six months between December 2008 and June 2009 using the term "murder suicide." This newspaper was chosen because Alberta has the highest rate of spousal homicide-suicide in Canada. After some conclusions are drawn, the sample is compared to a second news-set, this time a six-year period, from January 1985 to December 1990.

The issue of violence against women is addressed more broadly in the Analyzing the News section. Other sources of information pertinent to the analysis of violence against women are considered, and statistics on femicide and wife battery in Canada are examined. This chapter highlights how the media has only recently taken up this issue and still provides an imperfect record of violence against women. Coverage tends to be isolated and sensationalistic and consequently further mystifies the problem by contributing to its invisibility and pervasiveness. The emotion is confusion and dismay, and the theme is "interpretations." Studies I have found useful for thinking about domestic violence in the media are Bullock and Cubert (2002), Lamb and Keon (1995), Messner and Solomon (1993), Ryan, Anastario and DaCunha (2006) and Taylor (2009).

Debi Forsyth-Smith's Talk

One of the things I want to get across is that the whole issue of how the media has focused attention on women's issues has been given a tremendous amount of attention over the last twenty years, beginning with certainly the task force on the images of women back in 1978, which first really identified sexual stereotyping and the fact that there were a significant lack of women working within the context of the broadcast media in particular.

As a result of that task force, research was done to identify specifically what areas were really lacking in terms of the representation of women. There was the research done in 1984 which identified news coverage, programming coverage and advertising as well. I think the biggest news of all in that respect is that the exact same research was repeated in 1988, and there has been no significant change statistically speaking since 1984 despite legislation and despite increasing numbers of women working in the broadcast media.

There's also some research being done right now in the national media archive in Vancouver, which I think is quite significant in terms of what it says about the coverage of women's issues. How they define women's issues is significant in itself. Certainly the whole identification of women's issues has been put in a framework of a confrontational approach. For example, when you talk to the National Action Committee you always have to have an opposing group, when you talk about the abortion issue you always have to have the opposing viewpoint in the context of media coverage. In terms of the National Action Committee and the coverage that's been afforded to their work and their views on issues, there is usually an accompanying response from a group such as REAL Women.

We saw the same thing happen in Halifax in just the last six months when a new organization was formed, sort of a moral majority group or a right-wing group. The issue was over their name, when another women's group by the name of Voice of Women opposed the name, the United Voice of Women. The whole coverage of that episode was about the name issue and not getting to the root of what really were their issues and their positions. I think that a very important context of the coverage of women's issues is that there's so much attention paid to opposing sides of the issue that the substance of the issue is rarely covered.

With specific respect to the issue of violence against women, an identifying point where that began to get greater volumes of coverage would be the Montreal massacre in 1989. Certainly from a national perspective, the coverage on the Montreal massacre comprised the majority of the coverage in broadcast media and television news in particular. It composed the largest percentage of their coverage on women's issues for the entire year at about 15 percent, and both national broadcast outlets gave it about the same amount of attention.

What was interesting about that experience is the framework. For example, the CBC *Journal* did a broadcast on the massacre, and it was introduced as a discussion of the increased level of violence against women and the fact that this was not an isolated incident any more, and that it was happening more frequently, in women's lives in particular. However, what ensued was really a discussion about the psychological makeup of mass serial killers. There was really very little discussion of violence in women's lives. But since then the coverage by all various mediums has seen, quantitatively speaking, a significant increase.

The difficulty is that once again we're focusing on the most sensational end of the spectrum. I had a call from a television reporter a couple of weeks ago who horrified me by asking if we kept any pictures of battered women in our resource centre so that they could be used as part of his story.

The whole range of violence has not really been given substantive coverage in terms of the degree and type of violence that women experience in their lives, and I think that's really what's missing. There's certainly lots of action if you want to talk about broken bones, and broken ribs, and black eyes and so on, and you can draw a parallel between our cultural understanding of the whole issue of violence against women and the way that it is presented to us for consumption by the media.

And that, I think, presents a lot of difficulties when it comes to putting the issue of violence against women in context. Again, the research has indicated that when we're talking about sexual violence against women and children, it really is the most extreme and sensational cases that get coverage in terms of what kind of cases are reported and how they're reported, and often the victimization of the woman becomes secondary to the context of the story. For example, the remarks of judges and the remarks of lawyers becomes the story, rather than the story of the victimization of the woman.

It is interesting that in this process of identifying what are women's issues, what gets us bogged down is what we see in the media. Identify what are issues that are of concern to women and you have the usual list: pay equity, poverty, violence, you have all of those things, but I think there's a wider issue here which is that these issues are people issues, and what's missing from the media coverage is the feminization of those issues with the perspective of women and speaking from a women-centred viewpoint.

So I think that there are several things that should be noted. We do have federal legislation with respect to employment equity in our media and our broadcasting industry. We do have sexual stereotyping guidelines which are presently a condition of licence under the CRTC but are in danger of being removed because the broadcasters have made a significant case to the CRTC that in fact everything's OK now, which every bit of research that has been done has indicated is simply not the case.

The broadcasters, however, have gotten together in a very significant way and developed some red herrings to distract us from what's really needed, which is some significant enforcement of those guidelines. The CRTC is delighted to accept the broadcasters' pitch for self-regulation because they don't have the resources or the people power to enforce guidelines any more. The latest move by the CRTC was to call for submissions on the whole issue of sexual stereotyping, for which they supplied three weeks' notice. Through the efforts of the organization MediaWatch, that's been extended. It's doubtful, though, that even significant public representation on that issue will change the approach that CRTC has to this issue, which is to put the responsibility on the broadcasters and subsequently on the viewing public.

I think we have to redefine what we're referring to as women's issues. One of the very serious concerns that women themselves have is their dealings with the mainstream media, particularly women who are working on equality issues, and providing them with some support to deal with that. They obviously want their issues mainstreamed but at the same time they feel abandoned by the kind of coverage they receive from the mainstream media.

I think the other issue that's worth mentioning is the fact that even though the research numbers show very little difference between 1984 and 1988 in terms of the portrayals of women and the images of women, there has been even less of an increase in the numbers of women who are involved in the positions of power within the media. And that really hasn't changed at all. It is still male city desk editors and male news directors who are calling all the shots. And I think we've heard what that's like for a woman who is working inside the media in terms of selling stories.

I think, though, that the fundamental concern that women I have talked to with the media is the one-dimensional approach to women's issues. In other words, getting back to the REAL Women versus feminists for example, getting down to the abortion versus the anti-abortion forces, that is the only dimension that is applied to many of these issues, is getting those two sides of the story but not allowing in any sort of multifaceted dimension on the coverage.

The final thing that I want to mention is the critical need that we have when we're talking about an issue like violence against women, to pressure the media not to increase its quantity of reporting but to widen the dimensions of the kind of coverage that we have, and to lead the story of violence against women into the impact that it has on society as a whole and other levels of our society, such as the costs that are associated with it. And I don't mean in a very shallow way, I mean in a far more dimensional way, you know, the health care costs, the costs to generations of families who are victimized by violence in their lives. Tremendous more work needs to be done on the psychological and emotional violence that's being done to women not only in the context of their domestic relationships but in the context of women's lives in general in our society, and I think that's something that's really been missing from identifying what we call violence. And perhaps it's redefining violence against women altogether.

Reading the News

To summarize some of the main features of the talk, it seems that the media does not do a good job of presenting information about violence against women. It is not women-centred and is not broad enough, tending to reduce issues to a contest of opinions. The reality of media reporting is changing, but there still is a ways to go.

The news does not tell readers much about the reality of women who are battered in the home. The terms used in the media for women in violent relationships misinterpret the experience and thus become part of the problem. For example, the term "spousal abuse" misnames the problem, by making it seem as if either spouse is equally at risk or fault. "Wife-beating" is also problematic because it does not identify women who are assaulted in common-law relationships or battered by a boyfriend. "Domestic violence" has come to identify family violence in general but fails to specify the gendered and intimate character of the problem.

"Violence against women" is specifically related to women's relationships with men. The Canadian Panel on Violence Against Women released a report called *The War Against Women* in 1993 that documented widespread abuse and recommended zero tolerance of violence against women. The results of a survey by Statistics Canada, excerpted in an editorial in the *Toronto Star*, indicated that 51 percent of women had experienced physical or sexual violence at least once. More than 78,000 women are admitted to shelters for battered women in Canada each year.

Violence against women in relationships was widespread. A report published in 1994 indicated that three in ten women currently or previously married to men in Canada had experienced at least one incident of physical or sexual violence at the hands of their partners. Risk was highest for young women and for those in partnerships that had begun less than two years previously. However, the criminal justice system was accused of not taking the crime seriously enough.

Violence against women in relationships is an underreported crime. And in spite of the pervasiveness of domestic violence that does come to light, it is underreported in the media as well. Only a few articles on the topic appear in the media; those that do comprise a small sample of the cases that occur in society, just the tip of the iceberg. The same filters in reporting that we saw in the analysis of sexual assault are at work here. The result is that domestic violence is portrayed as an isolated event and the systemic reality of violence against women in this society is denied.

In the first edition of *Constructing Danger*, a news brief was used, "Calgary man sentenced for assault in intersection" (*Globe and Mail* April 9, 1990: 11), to illustrate some of the inadequacies in the media's treatment of violence against women. The article described a man who assaulted his former wife in a busy intersection after kidnapping her. The reader got the end of the story: he had been convicted of kidnapping, sexual assault causing bodily harm, break and enter, he was a manic depressive and had been sentenced to a mental institution. Furthermore, the way the incident was written up made it appear unusual and bizarre. The report provided no explanation of how the crime originated, the underlying nature of the man's emotional instability, how the assault may have been connected to former abuse in their relationship, the frequency of the abuse or the private terror that many other women experience before they finally leave or seek help. The account was isolated and decontextualized, and as such it served as a good example of media coverage.

The main reason for publishing the story was probably that bystanders had cheered the man as the near-naked woman tried to escape. The fact that the man was reported to need psychiatric help and that the assault happened in public further emphasized the unusualness of the event, unconnected except for its violence to the ordinary reality of many women's lives. Thus the dominant interpretation it created was how unusual it was.

A similar article used in the first edition, "Man goes on rampage in Virginia" (*Halifax Herald*, April 28, 1993: D16), began virtually the same way. A man beat up his former girlfriend and then acted in what seemed a totally bizarre way by going on a rampage. The attacks resulted in charges for various criminal offences and were described in a concise, matter-of-fact way. Again, no background information is given to help readers put the crime in context. The report appeared in the news capsule section of the paper, which indicated the relative unimportance of the story from the newspaper's perspective. If it hadn't been for the rampage, it is doubtful the item would have been carried on the newswire and reprinted thousands of miles away.

These examples were used to show how violence against women tends to be portrayed as unusual and episodic. There is little or no analysis, the coverage focuses mainly on the individuals in the case and no context is provided to help the reader understand these incidents are anything other than unusual. The reader becomes a voyeur by chance, catching a glimpse of tragedy in someone else's life, unable to do anything about it and finding it difficult to even treat as serious. The reader also becomes an interpretive enabler, assisting in the marginalization of violence against women.

This individualism of bizarre events can easily lead to blaming the victim, asking how she got herself into such a situation and why she hadn't left, as if being a victim of violence can discredit a woman's reputation. Such articles portray the violence without context or interpretation, easily supporting the claim that this is what can happen to bad girls. This decontextualization and legitimation of violence against women can be found not only in the text of articles but also in headlines.

In order for the reader to be able to deconstruct the layers of the story and interpret its meaning, articles need to focus more on the background of the cases and to critically analyze the legal system and its response. The reason background and contextual details are often missing is perhaps because more work is required to get them (a good organizational reason for bad behaviour), which might be an explanation but is not an excuse. Article 3.1 is typical of the period. The police are the main source, and there is no (apparent) motive.

Article 3.1 "Deaths probed"

RCMP describe the shooting deaths of a... couple as a murder suicide. The bodies of [the man] 72, and [the woman] 57, were found [with a] rifle... nearby the bodies. RCMP have no concrete motive. (*Calgary Herald*, August 30, 1990: B2, by staff)

On the other hand, Article 3.2 from the same period attempts to get at a larger background for a murder-suicide, trying to explain it as an epidemic, as copy-cat and as a macho need for control, but as we can see, it falls short of the mark.

Article 3.2 "'Powderkegs' walk streets"

The man who shot down a city mother and then killed himself might have been one of the "hundreds of walking powderkegs"... says a leading Calgary psychiatrist... an expert in suicide at the University of Calgary... as he warned that the city may be in the midst of a suicide epidemic follow-ing recent highly-publicized cases... [He] said a number of issues including alcohol or a family history of being abused can trigger a murder-suicide... [but] highly-publicized suicides also lower barriers." We don't put the idea in their heads but there may be someone else in the same situation who is already thinking about it. Maybe the barrier is lowered just enough that the person goes ahead with it. This is so unusual. We've had enough incidents that a year from now people who are looking at examples of epidemics will be picking this one." (*Calgary Herald*, March 7, 1990: A1, by Mario Toneguzzi, Joanne Ramondt)

The murder-suicide described in the article was one of three incidents at the time; the others included a mother charged with first-degree murder of her infant; a man who went to his estranged wife's house, shot her in the leg and then later shot and killed himself; and a young man who was allegedly suicidal when he crashed his car into another car killing himself and three other people during an RCMP high-speed chase.

The expert went on to temporarily abandon the epidemic theory to advance the idea that in some cases men commit murder-suicide because they have lost control of their lives, and he called for education and discussion to treat the violence. However, an expert in domestic violence was also quoted as saying that he was leaving the field in frustration at the lack of funding for his program to treat wife batterers, even though it had an 85 percent success rate. That's an important part of the context of interpretation which is often missing.

Article 3.1 portrays the murder-suicide as a mystery, and 3.2 tries to create a larger context of interpretation, albeit based on the epidemic idea. Article 3.3, also from around the same period, creates a context that normalizes murder-suicide within the gender relations of marriage.

Article 3.3 "Men who can't cope"

Two words — domestic dispute — disguise a grim, often gruesome reality... male violence against women, of husbands murdering their wives. Often it is sparked by the wrenching process of divorce and escalates into a violent showdown — a domestic dispute — ending in a murder-suicide. It's a familiar pattern, repeated all too frequently in towns and cities across Canada... [On Sunday] 42-year-old Edward Evans shot and killed his estranged wife and then committed suicide... As usual it was the man, unable to cope with drastic, depressing emotional stress who picked up a gun and killed. It is understandable in such circumstances to simply blame the individual for personal failure. But this obscures a deep-rooted pattern of violence. Much of the blame goes to a society which fails to teach boys and men how to cope with emotional stress without resorting to blind rage and insane violence... men commit nine out of 10 murders... not news to people [running] shelters for battered women [or]... to men who have undergone anger-management courses in an attempt to stop abusing their wives. (*Calgary Herald*, July 21, 1992: A4, Editorial)

This article begins to get at different reasons for domestic violence: masculinity, violence, culture and socialization. It creates a larger context of interpretation but still stops short of questioning whether the legal system is sensitive to women's needs. In Article 3.4 information is provided on the need for the legal system to respond more effectively to the issue of domestic violence and protect women who are its victims.

Article 3.4 "Peace bond information to be given to police"

Nova Scotia women will no longer have to carry copies of peace bonds in order to prove to police that the orders exist. By Jan. 31, police dispatchers will have their own copies of peace bonds, provided by court officials soon after they are issued… on a police computer network, [and the] computerized Canadian Police Information Centre… Earlier this year, [the attorney general] promised to look into the speed at which peace bonds are issued after critics charged it can take up to three weeks after making an application to obtain the order… that police do not respond quickly enough to complaints about peace-bond violations and women are forced to persuade judges to renew an order by citing new instances of violence. A peace bond is a court order for one person to stay away from another. (*Halifax Herald*, December 23, 1992: A3, by Janice Tibbets)

The article mentions the problem women have had in getting the police to acknowledge and enforce peace bonds against their husbands. The article makes it seem like a simple technical issue of getting the right information out and does not go into how criminal justice system officials often have misconceptions about wife abuse that get in the way of their doing anything about it. The article reports a legal step forward but also does not go into the difficulty of implementing change around gendered issues such as wife abuse.

And then there came a case that would change the world.

Article 3.5 "Battered wife couldn't take it anymore"

Ottawa — At least eight times, Angelique Lyn Lavallee dragged herself to Winnipeg hospital emergency rooms… Sometimes she had a split lip or broken nose… black eyes, broken ribs and multiple cuts and bruises. Lavallee, now 24, told skeptical doctors she had a history of falling off horses. More often than not, they didn't believe her.

Then on Aug. 31, 1986, Lavallee cracked — and the truth of her life with David Kevin Rust… came pouring out. During a noisy and boisterous drinking party, Lavallee, cowering in a bedroom closet, took the loaded .303 calibre rifle Rust handed her in a dare and blew the 24-year-old man's head off as he walked out the room. "He said if I don't kill him first, he would kill me… when everyone left. I was scared. All I thought about was all the other times he used to beat me." Lavallee never went to jail. An 11-man, one-woman jury believed her story of regular threats and beatings [and]… acquitted [her] of second-degree murder. It was the first time in Canada that a woman was acquitted of murder using the defence of battered wife syndrome, a medically recognized phenomenon where a woman is unable to leave a relationship despite physical, sexual or emotional abuse. This week, the tragic story — and the legal issues surrounding the defence — made it to Canada's highest court... The Supreme Court reserved judgment. (*Calgary Herald*, November 3, 1989: A1, by Stephen Bindman)

This case changed the world because it showed the legitimacy of women fighting back against domestic violence. It created a challenge against an easy assumption that victims can sometimes be perpetrators, and vice versa; but more deeply the challenge was what to do about violence in relationships.

The story shows that the case was challenged by the Crown and appealed all the way to the Supreme Court. An interesting feature of this news item is that it goes on to portray a confusion over interpretations between the two lawyers who paint vastly different pictures of Lavallee and her actions. The government lawyer, George Dangerfield, said there was no evidence that Lavallee was an abused woman who killed to prevent further abuse and he also ridiculed the term "battered wife syndrome." He said it added a patina of scientific respectability to both an action and a phrase which does not deserve it.

Lavallee's defence lawyer, Greg Brodsky, said there was plenty of evidence at the trial chronicling a regular pattern of violence. He cited a history of verbal jousting and threats, such as "if you keep it up you're going to get it" and, finally, physical violence which was witnessed by others. The defence attorney said that in such cases the jury has to be told why, when you are taken to the hospital because of those beatings, you tell them you fell off a horse or that you walked into a door. The defence offered the interpretation that in such cases the victim dare not say how the violence happened, and for that reason this is a special syndrome. However, the Crown offered this opinion: "This was a combative woman, a woman who was antagonistic, who for her size was quite strong, who fought back on every occasion when antagonistic arguments grew between them."

In the end. Lavallee's appeal was accepted, her defence was accepted, and Canada was the first country in the world to recognize battered woman's syndrome. However, such a conclusion came at the end of a fight over inter-pretations, a fight that was carried to the public through the media.

In summary, the news can tell different stories. It can convey a mystery as to why a murder-suicide happened. It can begin to show how the structure of the family allows abuse to happen and prevents a woman from doing anything about it. The news can also begin to get at issues of gender and maybe even what the justice system can do about it.

If good news is informative, it can offer an overview of the situation of women who are battered and point to how the social organization of women's lives can contribute to the violence. The news must also get at the role of the criminal justice system in controlling the violence, a feature that tends to be absent in crime reporting.

Sample Study

1. *The "slain and slandered."* The study of victims of homicide in the news is not new, and neither is the study of female victims of domestic homicide. The usual items included in the analysis are how the victim and perpetrator are portrayed, how blame is placed for the crime (directly and indirectly), who the claimsmakers are who make those claims, and what the putative effect on the media audience would be.

Some research into how femicide victims are portrayed looks at issues of newsworthiness, whether a context is revealed and the patterns of victim blame. Some research suggests victims are blamed both directly and indirectly for their own murder. Direct tactics might include using negative language to describe the victim, criticizing her actions such as her not reporting past incidences or mentioning "consorting" with other men as contributing to her murder. Indirect tactics of victim-blaming might include using sympathetic language to describe the perpetrator, emphasizing mental, physical, emotional and financial problems that might have caused the perpetrator to act as he did or highlighting mental or physical problems in the victim.

2. *Pilot study.* To see how this idea works out, a pilot sample was selected from the *Calgary Herald* for six months, from December 3, 2008 to June 3, 2009. This newspaper was chosen because Alberta has the highest rate of spousal homicide-suicide in Canada. The objective was to study local and regional primary and secondary pieces on domestic violence that involved the murder of a woman and the suicide of the male partner.

Using the search term "murder suicide," twenty-one full-text articles were retrieved from *FP Infomart*. Three articles were excluded as irrelevant because they used the term erroneously, two cases happened in Los Angeles, another two were for a case in Quebec, and another was for the conviction of a doctor who prescribed drugs to a wrestler who killed his family.

In terms of articles that covered local cases, twelve articles were selected for analysis, in order to determine whether "framing" issues were relevant for analysis. "Framing" is a media analysis term that focuses on the "context for interpretation" created or offered in the article. Two articles were news briefs, five were secondary articles after the fact, leaving five primary articles. A tertiary piece on domestic violence was included for discussion here, although it will not be included in the sample for analysis because it did not deal with specific cases. Exhibit 3.1 summarizes the cases and the coverage.

Exhibit 3.1 Domestic Homicide Cases and Coverage

"Lall murder-suicide"; 5.27.09: B10, brief; 5.27.09: B3: "those left behind are still searching for answers; Calgary's worst murder-suicide has been blamed on mental illness"; "widely described as a loving family man, suffered hallucinations... young father who doted on his wife and young daughters... heard voices in his head and believed he was possessed by the devil."

Unknown; 5.7.09: A3; "friends... say they were a close-knit family."

"Buzo-Kawaja case"; 5.7.09: B1; 4.6.09: A1; 4.6.09: B1; 2.21.09: A15: "[the woman] previously had restraining orders... [her] partner jumped to his death... and did not leave a note... the couple had an extremely troubled relationship the woman had tried to break off several times... it is not as simple as walking away from the violent partner... the period after the woman leaves the relationship is usually the most dangerous; a good, caring, loving woman who had never given an indication of problems at home; [the brother] worried... but had no inkling things would end this way... [the partner] lost jobs, drank frequently and developed a habit of fighting... making threats and eventually resorting to physical violence... we didn't expect this to happen; it appears to be a domestic dispute that went terribly wrong."

Dupuis-Rogerson; 12.13.08: A13: "she's very social, a very nice lady."

What patterns can be discerned from this pilot study? First, the event is often described as inexplicable: the man was loving, the couple seemed happy, and the woman did not deserve what happened to her. Second, sometimes there were warning signs: the man had difficulties, or the couple had a history of conflict. Third, there is an attempt to find a reason: mental disorders, alcoholism and unemployment. Fourth, what is said about the tragedy is affected by who is saying it: police, friends and family, and advocates.

Two cases, the Lall murder-suicide and the Buzo-Kawaja case dominated the news coverage. The general explanation in the first, despite the searching for explanations a year later, is mental illness. This is a residual explanation, in that nothing else makes sense, and he was never diagnosed or treated. The explanation in the second appears less equivocal, as there is a history of misbehaviour on the part of the man and conflict in the relationship. In the first case there are cautions about the need to seek help for mental illness despite the social stigma. In the second, there are cautions about the difficulty of leaving a relationship.

An interesting difference between the Buzo-Kawaja and Lall cases is that the former is more unequivocally framed as domestic violence, while the latter has more the air of mental illness being the only explanation that makes sense. Perhaps there was more of a tendency to blame the victim in (stereo)typical domestic violence cases in the past, whereas how could the victim be blamed in a case where the perpetrator had a mental illness. Do these explanations misdirect or dismiss the violence? Is there a blaming of the victim, directly or indirectly?

As mentioned, direct tactics for blaming victims could include negative language to describe the victim, not reporting previous violence or reporting issues such as substance abuse. Indirect tactics could include using sympathetic language to describe the perpetrator or citing circumstances like unemployment to try to excuse his actions. However, in the pilot study there does not seem to be obvious direct or indirect victim blaming. What does seem clear is that people are trying to understand what happened. They are struggling to interpret the events, a struggle over interpretation that surfaces in and is topicalized by the media accounts. Something more subtle also comes into play: cognitive biases.

Cognitive biases are used in the interpretation of events. For example, there is a tendency to criticize the victim for not calling the police. This is a "just-world" bias, that good people do the right thing and bad things happen to bad (incompetent) people. "Hindsight bias," on the other hand, might focus on the (now) obviousness of warning signs, as in getting a restraining order. We do not want to be context-dependent and just focus on the violence, but we also do not want to be context-independent and just focus on the politics. Cognitive biases might be useful models to aid in the analysis of interpretations.

3. *A second pilot study*. This time we used an earlier six-year period, from January 1985 to December 1990. Nineteen articles were available, of which seven were screened out because they were U.S. cases, involved a different crime or were commentaries. The twelve articles left included various cases of murder-suicide: male on male, female on male, an attempt and a case of infanticide. These were screened out, leaving seven articles on five cases over a six-year period of coverage. In actuality the five cases were from 1989–90.

The articles are short, either briefs or on average 200 words. Police are the usual source, with acquaintances, neighbours and sometimes family included. Explanations include "domestic problems," "depressed state," "no concrete motive" and "nobody knows." These are crimes where the victims are silent, and the absence of help is noted.

Compared to the first sample, the lack of coverage, the paucity of detail, the reliance on official sources and the absence of a context are striking. This was normal news coverage of domestic violence in the 1980s, a virtual silence compared to coverage twenty years later. What is also interesting is that the incidence of domestic violence has decreased over time in society, as measured by police, at the same time as the number of newspaper articles about intimate partner violence has increased. The incidence of domestic violence and its portrayal by the media are inversely correlated, which shows the public is receiving more information about fewer cases. Also, in comparing the two samples, there was a marked use of advocates as sources and a larger discussion of context in the later sample.

In terms of putting our criminological analysis to work, some research has found that it is possible to work with journalists to develop a "best practices" handbook on news coverage of domestic violence murders. For example, the Rhode Island Coalition against Domestic Violence worked with reporters and then compared print coverage of domestic violence murders prior to developing a handbook to after, and found significant changes were made. These included an increased tendency to label the murder of intimates as domestic violence and double the use of advocates as sources. As a result, the domestic violence murders, which had previously been framed as unpredictable private tragedies, were more likely to be framed as social problems requiring public intervention.

This example of action research, or "participatory communication," shows the importance of naming interpretations and the possibility of changing them. The next section takes up the idea that violence against women in relationships is largely invisible. The news is a record of events, but it is an imperfect one that often misses or disguises the systematic character of violence against women. The news tends to represent violence against women as episodic, isolated and individualistic, and confusions exist as to how to interpret events. But maybe this is open to change.

Analyzing the News

Some of the problems with newspaper articles on violence against women in relationships are silence, sensationalism and individualism. The limited number of articles on domestic violence that do appear tend to highlight outrageous crimes and ignore the scope and enormity of the problem. This is similar to the problem in *researching* the news, getting enough information to see these kinds of patterns.

Reading and researching the news are connected, in that researching means going back over and re-reading the news to see what the patterns are and to see how well the media records violence against women, for example. In this section I discuss the use of a news index to research the news. Though most people are not likely to engage in this type of research, it can indicate how important specific issues are to the news media. Then I look at some statistics on patterns of violence against women in relationships that will put both reading and research in context.

1. *The Canadian News Index.* The first edition of this book used the *Canadian News Index* (or *CNI*, now called the *Canadian Index*), which is a topical index

of articles published in seven major Canadian daily newspapers. The *Index* began in January 1977 and is published monthly with a cumulative year-end index. Its scope and history provide an important tool for an analysis of Canadian newspapers. If you pick a topic such as homicide, for example, the *Index* lists the titles and page numbers of articles published on that topic among the papers it surveys. The articles can be retrieved from microfilm or through interlibrary loan, so it is a good source of information from which to construct patterns of topical news reporting.

However, this method has several limitations. For example, not all news articles are indexed. Items of significant reference value, synopses and feature articles are indexed, but routine news reports are not included and duplicate wire service articles are screened for content. With respect to crime stories, daily update reports are rejected in favour of summary articles. Most stories are indexed under the type of crime they report ("securities — fraud" for example) but some are found under more topical titles, such as the "BCCI scandal" (the collapse of the Bank of Credit and Commerce International in 1991). In general, then, it is difficult to know how much variation there may be in the rules of inclusion and exclusion. Sometimes it is difficult to determine the type of crime the indexers feel a story represents, but the *Index* provides a good guide, short of actually doing a newspaper survey.

However, it is not always easy to find certain articles or topics: for example, infanticide is grouped under "homicide," and Mount Cashel can be listed under "Hughes Commission" or the "sexual abuse of children." Even though there are many substantive differences between manslaughter, first-degree and second-degree homicide, and infanticide, the categories do not always correspond to those used in the *Criminal Code*. If one wishes to use the *Index*, one needs to get used to its limitations as a socially constructed record.

So, overall, several problems emerge when using the *Index*. First, because not all articles are represented, it cannot be regarded as a uniform database upon which to do research. However, it does contain a considerable number of citations spanning several years. The second, deeper problem is that articles are organized by topic or subject, which provides a secondary filter. The *Index* creates topics as they become socially relevant and thus reflects the topics the media is interested in reporting.

The very lack of information can be an important aspect of the topic. For example, "family violence" did not appear as a category until 1980, "battered women" appeared in 1985 and "violence against women" and "men who batter" became categories only in 1990. There were eleven citations under "family violence" in 1980, and this number had risen more than 450 percent to fifty a decade later. "Battered women" had ninety-seven citations in 1985, and this figure dropped 42 percent to fifty-six by 1990. "Men who batter" had a mere six citations in 1990 and eleven a year later. The number of citations in each of these categories is hardly reflective of the pervasiveness of the crime, to say the least.

Charting the chronological development of the topic of "family violence" shows that it has a relatively long history as an issue but very few citations. The more specific topic of "battered women" is newer and has had more citations but still a low absolute number. "Violence against women" is the newest category and starts to place violence against individual women in a larger context. Naming the source of the problem — "men who batter," however, does not seem to have a high priority.

Domestic violence existed long before it began to appear in the *Index* or in the news. However, the topicalization of the problem in the media occurs in a reflexive relationship to the construction and definition of the problem in society. The categories provided in the media reinforce and limit how we see the topic in society; at the same time, the media reflects changing social sensibilities. Topics can remain invisible or hidden in the world and in the media simultaneously. For example, gay-bashing is subsumed under "assaults" and is largely hidden in society, while "date rape" has only recently surfaced from the "sexual assault" category just as it has recently been recognized as a prevalent social problem. It is also extremely difficult to sort out femicides or homicides committed against women, because there is no category that labels it as such.

So, while imperfect, the *Index* is still an important record of articles published in the news. There are limitations to the way the items are organized and, in order to do a proper analysis, a reader has to be aware of them. It is difficult to know how the recording is done, yet the *Index* enters into the social construction of "matters of fact" by appearing to exist as a true record, a claim the media in general also makes.

2. *The Google News Archive.* Using a more modern, popularly accessible index, Google News creates a similar pattern. Using the term "wife abuse," Google News indexes the abuse of wives back to the early 1900s and articles with headlines such as "wife kills husband to end years of abuse." Article 3.6 provides an excerpt from an early case.

Article 3.6 "Tale of beatings by Jelke is told in court by wife"

Mrs. Eugenia Woodward Jelke, testifying in support of her cross-petition for divorce, charged her husband today with a series of physical assaults, throughout their nine months of married life. Her husband, F. Frazier Jelke, also heaped continual abuse upon her, Mrs. Jelke said in Newport country superior court. The room was crowded…. The continued controversies and assaults made her desperate, she said, because she had tried to please him. She said the manner of life exhausted her and she was frightened of him… She testified she said to him: "If you love me so much, why do you beat me up?"

He replied, she said, "Every man has the right to beat his wife." (*Pittsburgh Post-Gazette*, May 24, 1933)

The case is important enough that *Time* magazine sees fit to present it as a milestone in 1933. The divorce petition between Jelke, fifty-two, a Manhattan broker, and Eugenia, twenty-seven, an Alabama socialite, was denied after a "sensationally disgusting trial" on the grounds that both were guilty of extreme cruelty. The judge found that she had been cruel to her husband when she cursed him, bit his ear and tore his shirt and that he had been cruel to her when he blackened her eye and abused her in the presence of others. The judge ended in blamed her in saying that for her it was a marriage of convenience and an opportunity to indulge in luxury.

Article 3.6 details incidents from a prominent case, which is probably the reason why it is reported at all. The article also suggests a novel method for re-collecting articles from the past to construct a history of publicity around wife abuse. The Google News Archive search shows articles through the decades, increasing dramatically in the 1970s. While the cases are individualistic and not connected together as a pattern or theme, they do reveal the context of interpretation at the time.

The Google News Archive is useful because what can be collected together from such cases is the way the media presented the information at the time. The Jelke case reporting is remarkably open in its presentation of the facts and its (and the judge's) interpretation that the abuse is mutual.

In a similar way, the Sugar Ray Leonard case, in the early 1990s, mystifies wife abuse in its reporting of the fighter's use of cocaine, as shown in Article 3.7. This mystification is part of the context of mis/interpretation at the time. Apparently a celebrity story of drug use is more important than a celebrity and wife abuse story.

Article 3.7 "Leonard tells of drug use"

Leonard admitted to substance abuse after *The Los Angeles Times* today published excerpts from his divorce proceedings that quoted his former wife, Juanita, as saying that Leonard used cocaine on occasion and physically abused her while under the influence of alcohol... "He at one point would harass me physically and mentally in front of the children," his former wife was quoted as saying. Leonard said "I'd be lying," to deny he and his wife had never fought, but said the incidents mentioned in the court proceedings were "taken out of context, exaggerated." (*New York Times*, March 31, 1991)

3. *The interest in making lists.* Looking at another type of record, the first edition of this book had a list of women killed in Nova Scotia between 1989 and 1993, compiled from information supplied by the Nova Scotia

Advisory Council on the Status of Women and from local newspapers. A picture emerged of women who were killed by men they knew. In fact, of all solved cases in the list, not one woman was killed by a stranger! There were twenty-two solved femicides, eight unsolved and two cases of missing women, for a total of thirty-two over this four-year period. The unsolved cases constitute 25 percent of the total, falling close to the national average of 23 percent for cases "not cleared" by a charge.

That record of gendered violence places the information in a pattern that is hard to retrieve from the media. The media tends to focus on individual cases, which isolates crimes, making it harder to see them as part of a larger pattern. The Advisory Council list, on the other hand, is based on an interest in interpretation.

This pattern of violence against women in relationships is important to topicalize, identify and name. In case after case in the Advisory list, the relationship of the perpetrator to the victim is named: husband, boyfriend, estranged partner, old boyfriend. The great majority of women murdered knew their killer. Unsolved femicides are a minority of the cases but could involve acquaintances as well. Acquaintance-related homicides are easier to solve than stranger-related ones, but in some cases the police know who the perpetrator is but do not have enough evidence to lay charges.

4. *The context of violence.* In some cases it may be years before charges are laid. In 1991, of 753 homicides in Canada, 582 were cleared. Eighty-seven percent of these involved family members or acquaintances and, of female victims, 92 percent were killed by family members or acquaintances. The percentage killed by a stranger was 13 percent in general: for women, it dropped to eight percent. A woman was four times more likely to be killed by a current or estranged intimate than was a man (120 cases compared to 31). A woman is far more at risk at the hands of someone she knows than a stranger. In 44 percent of all cases of immediate familiar-related homicides, there was a previous history of domestic violence.

Changes in the law that have made stalking an offence highlight the growing sensitivity of lawmakers to the problem of violence against women in society. These changes have been fuelled in part perhaps by highly publicized cases involving battered women, some of whom had to kill their abusive partners in order to save their own lives.

"Battered woman syndrome" (BWS) has been recognized in Canada, but it is not an easily won defence, in part because it requires revision of the concept of what constitutes a reasonable defence in the face of "imminent danger" (section 34, 1995 Canadian *Criminal Code*). In early 1990, the Supreme Court of Canada reinstated the acquittal of a woman tried in Manitoba on a charge of second-degree murder after she had shot her abusive boyfriend. In their ruling, the justices wrote that "it is not enough to consider what a 'reasonable man' might do in certain circumstances, because 'the factor of gender can be germane to the assessment of what is reasonable.'"

That case, discussed above, involved Lynn Lavallee, and what the Court did was change the context of interpretation so as to reduce the confusion over how to interpret such cases, and the dismay that such cases could happen in the first place. As a result, prominent cases of women who killed their abusive male partners have been reviewed, and the media is increasingly focusing on the topic.

5. *A special case.* Adele Gruenke was not as fortunate as Lynn Lavallee. In 1986, she was convicted of killing an older man who she alleged had demanded sex from her. She had accepted money from him in the past, was under a lot of psychological stress about her own health, and when she declined his advances he said he would kill her mother. She court disbelieved her defence and convicted her of first-degree murder. Crucial at trial was a confession given to clergy, which was the basis for an appeal to the Supreme Court in 1991.

What was interesting is that the same psychiatrist whose evidence was so pivotal in Lavallee's case also testified for Gruenke. The psychiatrist did not use the term "battered woman syndrome" but testified she was apparently suffering psychological distress over her illness and his actions. The doctor also offered evidence at appeal but it was not enough to sway the court.

After Lavallee won her appeal, the Self Defence Review Group was formed under Judge Ratushny to review cases where women had been convicted for murdering men to see if the BWS defence might apply. Gruenke's case was sufficiently interesting that Judge Ratushny accepted it as one of ninety-eight cases that might merit review after Lavallee.

The judge interviewed only fourteen women out of the ninety-eight applications, and Gruenke's file was one of only seven referred to the Manitoba Appeal Court. The Appeal Court was asked to consider psychological evidence as to Gruenke's mental state at the time of the crime. However, the court determined it did not constitute new evidence and dismissed the appeal in 1998. Gruenke was released on parole in 2004, although news items were more interested in her husband, in jail for killing a police officer.

Much has changed. Most jurisdictions now have guidelines to reinforce the need for police to lay assault charges under section 266 of the *Criminal Code* when there are reasonable grounds to believe an offence has been committed, regardless of the wishes of the victim/complainant. This change in policing comes after years of criticism of the police for being part of the problem, for not charging men who batter and putting the responsibility on the woman to leave the abusive situation. And, as mentioned above, in the 1990s the federal government passed legislation on stalking that would make it illegal to harass someone by repeatedly following, watching or phoning them (part of a larger set of *Criminal Code* amendments). The law defines the offence of criminal harassment (section 264) and sets a maximum penalty of five years' imprisonment. This law follows legal measures already available in many U.S. states and adds more weight to pre-existing statutes related to intimidation and uttering threats.

Perhaps such laws signal a new commitment on the part of the criminal justice system to take violence against women seriously. But these changes have also occurred alongside a shift in society's understanding and interpretation of violence against women, and an effort to sort through the attendant emotional confusion.

Summary

The news is both a resource and a topic, a source of information and a reflection of social awareness. Regarding the topic of violence against women is represented in the news, women's issues have been getting more attention, but improvements are needed. The treatment of violence against women in relationships is incomplete and presented in a way that removes it from the context of the very structures of male power and violence that allow it to happen in the first place. This means that the news is an imperfect record of the extent and character of violence against women. Furthermore, there is both cognitive confusion and emotional dismay as to how to interpret what has happened, sometimes blaming the woman, sometimes recognizing the power structures at play. This can be traced through a study of news items over time.

What we see is that as a true reflection of what goes on, the news is often flawed, consistently overlooking some issues and playing up others. Silence on violence against women becomes part of the social structure that perpetuates violence and thus has to be part of the story. Ignorance becomes an ideological tool; if we misunderstand the world, we are systemically unable to do anything about it. We need to record violence in a way that will help us to understand and change the world for the better.

4

The Mount Cashel Orphanage Inquiry
The Inscription of Child Abuse

Inscription is a term that describes how the media takes up socially deviant categories and reproduces them. For example, an assumption already exists in society that homosexuality and child sexual abuse are linked. In a process of inscription, the media takes up this idea, exaggerates, strengthens and reifies it and makes it seem an established fact. By placing the idea in print, a stereotype becomes a fact. This process of inscription or objectification is usually taken up in a method called frame analysis.

Gary Kinsman talks about the Hughes Royal Commission of Inquiry into Mount Cashel, which was the investigation into the so-called sex scandal at the Christian Brothers orphanage in St. John's, Newfoundland. Kinsman describes how the work of the commission recreated the link between homosexuality and child sexual abuse, especially because it focused on allegations of sexual violence against male children. The media took up this imputed link, with consequences reaching far into the community.

In Reading the News, examples are given of how inscription worked in the media treatment of Mount Cashel and how violence against children was represented as homosexual acts rather than as abuse or pedophilia. In the Sample Study, a news sample was selected for frame analysis based on the search for a pedophile ring in Cornwall, Ontario. Using the search category "project truth," 110 articles were found in the *Ottawa Citizen* between 1997 and 2007. Most articles were simply statements from police briefings or officials, and coverage usually came from only one source and uncritically repeated statements by claimsmakers. In Analyzing the News, some of the larger patterns of child sexual abuse reporting are developed, showing how skewed coverage actually disguises the reality of sexual violence against children. In this chapter, inscription is the theme, the frame analysis of discourse in newspaper coverage is the method, and anger and outrage are the emotions. Studies I have found useful for thinking about child abuse in the news are Best (1990), Cheit (2003), Doyle (2000), Jenkins (1992), Lippert (1990) and Macmillan (2002).

Gary Kinsman's Talk

The Hughes Royal Commission of Inquiry in St. John's, Newfoundland, looked at the cover-up of sexual and physical assault on residents of the Mount Cashel Orphanage in the mid-1970s. My research is a critical analysis of the workings of that commission and its relationship to media coverage.

When I first went to St. John's, I had some knowledge of the different controversies around sex-related matters involving priests and adolescent boys, what had gone on at the orphanage and about the commission. I arrived in this context as a gay man who had done work on sexuality and the policing of sexuality in a number of different locations across the country.

One thing that became clear to me was that the media was picking up and amplifying how the work process of the commission was associating homosexuality with child sexual abuse. Given my own experience, I've been trying to understand the relationship between this royal commission and the mass media coverage, and how it was organizing a mythological association between homosexuality and child sexual abuse.

The media was using the framework that there was a relationship between homosexuals and child sexual abuse. I'll just read you an account of one of the outcomes of this media coverage and the whole climate that has been organized against homosexuals in Newfoundland since some of the royal commission charges have been laid. I'm not saying that the violence against gays is in any way caused by media coverage or by such things as the Hughes Royal Commission, but I think they shape the context in which violence has taken place.

This comes from a letter that was published on June 4, 1989, in a St. John's newspaper: "Being a homosexual in Newfoundland is a difficult lifestyle due to the ignorance of the majority regarding homosexuality. The social difficulties associated with my lifestyle I have learned to accept and have learned to cope with until a recent incident of gay-bashing. The incidents seem to be on the increase since the media coverage regarding the church-related sexual assaults on young boys. I was a victim of gay-bashing as I was walking home from a gay club downtown — surrounded by three adult males who verbally and physically abused me because they saw me leave the gay club. They informed me they were doing society a justice by getting rid of 'another faggot child abuser.' The cuts, the bruises, the broken ribs will heal, but the anger, frustration and fear will be a part of me for a long time. The fear not only stems from being beaten because of my sexual preference but also because of the sarcastic attitude of the Royal Newfoundland Constabulary officer when I reported the incident, requesting surveillance in the area so as to help others avoid the horrible beating I had received."

Now this is not just an experience that this one man had, or that I've had; this is a generalized experience that lesbians and gay men have in

Newfoundland. It has certainly set back the struggle for lesbian and gay rights, as the provincial government is saying that sexual orientation protection in human rights legislation for the province is a "no go," at least for the present. This also had an impact in Nova Scotia, where the government used what was going on in Mount Cashel, the evidence that was being produced in the Hughes Commission and the media coverage, as a justification for why sexual orientation protection should not be enacted there as well.

How was it that this royal commission and the media coverage were once again associating homosexuality with child sexual abuse? Some accounts have been put forward in the lesbian and gay community suggesting homophobia, that individual journalists or the commission counsel were prejudiced. However, I didn't think the individual attitudes and prejudices of some of the commission counsel or some of the journalists involved in covering the royal commission actually could account for what was going on. It was a much more systemic social process. The reassociation of homosexuality with child sexual abuse was also being put together in an extralocal way, outside of our everyday lives, in the work process of this royal commission and in the work that journalists were doing in selecting out the major stories for that day.

The social process of associating homosexuality with child sexual abuse involves the gender inversion of the problem of sexual assault and harassment towards young people in our society. The perception that has been created and disseminated through the Hughes Commission and the media is that young boys are the major targets of sexual assault and harassment in our society, and that is not accurate. Feminists' concerns over violence against women, and sexual violence and harassment towards young girls in particular, have been obscured through the way in which the Hughes Commission Inquiry process has been taken up in the media coverage.

This is a quote from the Working Group on Child Sexual Abuse's submission to the Hughes Commission Inquiry. They say, "The commission, however, has presented a somewhat skewed vision of abuse because it is primarily a judicial inquiry into the events of one institution... the general public is starting to believe that abuse is a religious affliction, that young boys are the primary targets, that sexual abuse is primarily a homosexual issue, that abuse happens primarily in institutions or other state-sponsored systems."

The lesbian and gay studies group at Memorial University organized a forum to dispute the association of homosexuality with child sexual abuse. We managed to gather the media's attention to another way of looking at the stories; for about a week they gave us a fair amount of coverage. The media went to the commission counsel and asked them questions almost as if we had instructed them, and we learned from the responses how it was that homosexuality was being created as the problem.

Royal commissions do important work for state institutions and agencies. They are used when a government faces a legitimation crisis, when the criminal justice system seems no longer to have worked properly. A royal commission is a way in which the government can set up an independent body that is going to investigate these questions. There's a number of common features to these types of commissions of inquiry, such as terms of reference which are given to them by the government and the funding they're allocated by various state agencies.

Key to analyzing the Hughes Royal Commission are the terms of reference, which structure its work and limit what it addresses. Analyzing those terms of reference begins to account for how the homosexualization of the problem could take place and also how, by focusing only on a male institution, questions of what was going on with girls and women have been completely obscured in the commission process.

Royal commissions are supposed to be independent and autonomous from the everyday workings of the state and various institutions, but that is not actually the case. One of the ways in which the state comes into play is through police evidence and through different legal documents that have been produced in various state agencies. However, the appearance of independence and impartiality has to be constantly constructed. Judge Hughes never wanted to deal with media coverage but would take time at the beginning of the day to challenge the way in which the media was reporting on what was going on at the royal commission.

On the other hand, the commission would get taken up by the mass media as an authoritative source of news. In the *Evening Telegram*, the only daily newspaper in St. John's, it was consistently a front-page story for the first couple of months, and it also became a major news story across the country.

So there's a relationship between the way in which the commission took up what went on at Mount Cashel, the different accounts put forward to explain it, and how the media would then pick that up. As well, the commission takes up forms of knowledge that have already been defined by the dominant power relations in our society. One aspect of this inscription is how the term "child sexual abuse" itself is mobilized by the commission and used in the terms of reference. The people who originally raised the question of violence against young people in our society in the early 1970s were feminists doing grassroots work, raising these questions in the political context of a critique of family relations, the power of adults in our society and the power of men over younger people. There is a gendered character to this violence.

But as this term has entered into the official bureaucratic procedures of social work, government agencies and institutions, particularly through the work of the Badgley Commission in the early 1980s, all of those earlier political concerns have dropped away. We now have an administrative category of child sexual abuse, which no longer raises the same types of political connotations or criticisms of patriarchal relations in society and the way in which masculinity is constructed and associated with violence and aggression. That's one question that the commission is not exploring, the roots of where violence toward young people comes from.

The term "child sexual abuse" was not available in 1975 in the official agencies who knew of abuse at Mount Cashel and prevented it from becoming a public and visible issue: the criminal justice system, the social work system and the Catholic Church itself. But now, many of those same institutions are trying to make this a crucial issue that must be addressed. Child sexual abuse has entered into the Newfoundland context as an official, administrative category.

The second process of inscription that the commission and media depends on is the homosexualization of the issue. In the 1950s and into the 1960s, there was a consistent construction of sexual violence and harassment as not private but public and in particular associated with sexual deviancy and homosexuality. The mythology that homosexuals or gay men are child molesters doesn't have any accuracy, but it's still an interpretive framework used to account for and explain the problem. That discourse has been remobilized and has entered into some of the initial media coverage of Mount Cashel. When Shane Earl went to the *Sunday Express*, the way in which those initial stories were framed was that homosexuality at Mount Cashel was the problem. And in the book *Unholy Orders*, this is provided as an interpretive framework for reading what went on.

Police work also defines homosexuality as a problem for the commission. The original Detective Hillier report in 1975 investigating the problems at Mount Cashel was entitled *Homosexual Acts and Child Abuse at Mount Cashel Orphanage*. That report has now been used as a central piece of evidence in the commission, recreating in the 1990s this association of child sexual abuse with homosexuality.

So the Hughes Commission is producing homosexuality as a problem, making that available for the mass media, which has taken it up as a framework of interpretation, not because of the individual prejudices of the commission counsel or of some of the journalists, but as an intrinsic part of the work process of the inquiry itself. The documents, and the knowledge upon which they depend, label homosexuality as the problem. The commission takes up that knowledge, and does not challenge it but rather takes it for granted. The commission takes up the standpoint of seeing homosexuality as part of the problem, and the media coverage takes up that way of framing the issue.

Reading the News

Gary Kinsman criticizes how the media uncritically adopts the idea that homosexuals are responsible for male child sexual abuse. There is far more sexual abuse of female children than of male, most abuse is committed by heterosexual men, and pedophilia is the sexual disorder responsible. Furthermore, child sexual abuse is more a matter of power and the desire to control than of sexual orientation. However, the organizational process of making connections between homosexuality and child sexual abuse and of writing up the crime in this way inscribes and constructs stereotypes as if they are "matters of fact." This is a different problem than misrepresentation because it is not that that a mistake is made, but simply that the problem is characterized in a certain way which is mistaken.

1. *The Mount Cashel Inquiry.* The inquiry into abuse at Mount Cashel dominated the news for some time. For 1989, the *Canadian News Index* lists 238 citations on the Hughes Commission. However, early articles on Mount Cashel appear relatively innocuous, as the news brief in Article 4.1 shows. It does not mention homosexuality or details of the abuse; if anything, it is quite technical in form.

Article 4.1 "Sexual abuse inquiry considered"

St. John's (CP) — Government officials are considering calls for a public inquiry into sexual abuse in Newfoundland… There have been several calls for an inquiry in the wake of a series of charges against Newfoundland priests accused of sexually assaulting young boys. (*Globe and Mail*, March 1, 1989, Brief)

In the article, the problem is defined as one of studying existing data and going through information in order to make a decision whether an inquiry should be called. The matter is an official one and does not include criminal charges against priests who allegedly committed sexual assaults against young boys. Various politicians, organizations and bureaucratic officials are involved in deciding whether there will be an inquiry. The character of this article is further influenced by the fact that it appeared in the national press and was consequently compressed to include just the facts. Articles that appeared in the Newfoundland press at about the same time are lurid in comparison, detailing personal shame and tragedy. In Article 4.1, there is no sense of personal shame or ordeal, simply talk about a bureaucratic process.

Article 4.2, published one year later in a St. John's newspaper, cites testimony from the Hughes Commission Inquiry on whether there was homosexuality and sexual abuse at Mount Cashel. The article is interesting precisely because it does not offer unequivocal testimony of abuse by brothers at the orphanage. In fact, the witness does not recall any abuse at Mount

Cashel, although he does remember some homosexual behaviour among some of the boys.

Article 4.2 "Former Mount Cashel resident knew of homosexual activity"
For the first time in weeks, a former resident of the Mount Cashel Orphanage took the stand at the Hughes inquiry Thursday. But unlike other young men who have told the commission devastating tales of abuse, Craig English did not talk about being molested or beaten by Christian Brothers... Mr. English testified that he knew of sexual activity among a small group of eight-to-10-year-olds at one of the Mount Cashel dormitories in 1975. Now 23, Mr. English is a nephew of Br. Edward English, one of several Christian Brothers charged with sexual abuse after police re-opened their aborted 1975 investigation of the orphanage. The witness didn't discuss his experiences at Mount Cashel with police until last week, when he was reached at his home in Toronto. He made no complaints to investigators at the time... Mr. English couldn't remember being interviewed by anyone at Mount Cashel 15 years ago concerning his care and education.

The inquiry also heard from Tom Mills, senior Crown attorney for eastern Newfoundland. Involved in the prosecution of young offenders in 1985, he recalled one case in which a youth had pleaded guilty to several criminal offences... While the young offender had alleged sometime before 1985 that he had been sexually assaulted by another boy [in the Whitbourne Boys Home], the lawyer said he felt no obligation to report the allegation because authorities were aware of the charge. "The allegation that (the boy) had been sexually assaulted by another boy was already information in the hands of social workers representing the director of child welfare," Mr. Mills said. "The indication that I received was that an investigation had in fact gone on..." Mr. Mills acknowledged the boy's parents had expressed concern that their son might be sent to the Whitbourne home... concerns were raised in the House of Assembly and in the media during the period... In April 1985, the report of a judicial inquiry cited negligence in the death of Alonzo Corcoran, 16, who froze to death in late January, 1984, after he and another youth escaped from the Whitbourne facility. (*Evening Telegram*, March 23, 1990: 1, by Cathy Finn)

In Article 4.2, the witness does not talk of being molested or beaten, unlike other young men who had told devastating tales of abuse. He did not know of any sexual activity, except among young boys. While the headline states there was homosexuality at Mount Cashel, in the article it was only among young boys — and sexual experimentation among children is not the same as sexual orientation. This witness is unlike other witnesses who did allege sexual abuse and furthermore is a nephew of one of the charged

Christian brothers. So, the article constructs homosexuality as having occurred while undermining the credibility of the witness.

More interestingly, and unlike the putative promise of the headline, the bulk of the article is taken up with the testimony from a lawyer about a young boy who alleged sexual assault by another resident at a different institution, a secure custody youth facility, an event that was never reported. What this does reveal is that the problem of abuse at provincial institutions was a problem known about by the authorities. The inquiry subsequently heard that abuse was reported at Cashel years before to police and to social workers but that nothing was done. This admits to gross negligence within the system.

Several months later at a Supreme Court trial, testimony was heard about sexual behaviour on the part of priests, which served to more strongly anchor the connection between the sexual abuse and exploitation of young boys and homosexuality. Article 4.3 is unequivocal about the nature of the acts and who they were done with. There is testimony that a priest gave a homeless boy a place to stay in return for unnamed sexual favours, that they had sex, and that there were sexual acts with other men. It is unclear from the account whether the sex was coerced or abusive, but the article anchors the point that these are men who have sex with males and that they are priests who were later charged with sex-related crimes.

Article 4.3 "Priest sheltered boy for sex, trial told"

St. John's, Nfld (CP) — A Roman Catholic priest picked up a homeless 16-year-old boy one night in 1976 and for six weeks gave him a place to stay in return for sexual favours, the Newfoundland Supreme Court heard Thursday. The boy, now 30, was testifying against Father Gordon Walsh, 41, who is on trial on two sexual abuse charges... At another all-male Christmas party he said he was fondled by Father James Hickey — who is currently serving a five-year sentence after pleading guilty to more than 20 sex-related charges. The complainant said he'd been in and out of foster homes and orphanages his whole life — including the infamous Mount Cashel orphanage. (*Halifax Herald*, May 11, 1990)

Various other media articles can be found that cumulatively fed into the perception that homosexuals were the problem. During a 1990 Newfoundland Supreme Court trial on indecent assault and gross indecency, the actions in question were defined as homosexual acts. And in 1991, during another Newfoundland Supreme Court trial, the prosecution defined the defendant as a "homosexual," as if that proves his guilt. In another article on the same case, the accused was said to be "an admitted homosexual."

The consequence of these characterizations is that they link homosexuality to sexual abuse against children. The specific criminal charges arose out of the Hughes Inquiry, which itself constructed the same linkages. As Kinsman points out, the inquiry picks up a way of framing the problem that already exists in society, and through its discourse reproduces that frame, which in turn is picked up by the media. This process of inscription happens organizationally, through the examination of witnesses, the submission of documents, the press briefings and so on. The unasked question, however, is why homosexuality is being linked to abuse and pedophilia in a way that heterosexuality never is? Articles that point out that homosexuality is not the same as pedophilia are rare, although they do exist.

Cashel was the test case, perhaps, for sensitivity to institutional abuse. During the 1990s, news arose about abuse in boys and girls homes, reformatories and training centres across the country. However, this did not necessarily mean that old mistakes weren't repeated with new revelations. In 1994, a Halifax newspaper ran the cover headline "Pedophilia & Homosexuality — A connection?" The columnist was writing about the inquiry into abuse at the Kingsclear Youth Training Centre, and how the New Brunswick Coalition on Human Rights Reform disagreed with the imputed link between homosexuality and pedophilia at the inquiry. Citing questionable statistics, the article said "only 1.1 percent of men are exclusively homosexual," but that "homosexuals are, at minimum, five and a half times more likely to molest children than are heterosexuals." The fact that the human rights group had requested a clarification of the difference between homosexuality and pedophilia was described by the columnist as merely political correctness.

On the following day, the provincial paper reported that the Gay and Lesbian Association of Nova Scotia planned to launch a human rights complaint against it. A clinical psychologist was quoted as disputing the initial column, saying that most pedophiles are heterosexual, particularly in cases of incest. From there the issue quickly faded from vitriol to accusations of censorship.

Let's now look at another case where a link was made between homosexuality and child abuse, the case of the London porn ring.

2. *The London porn ring.* On November 11, 1993, police in London, Ontario, announced the seizure of 230 videotapes of children engaged in sex acts. The front-page news story, based on a news conference at police headquarters, reported "shocking details" of child porn ring activities involving a dozen male children aged ten to fourteen. London police chief Julian Fantino sat at a desk with 180 pornographic video tapes and a camcorder on display. The chief was quoted as saying, "We're dealing with people who have no morals, whose whole enterprise is to corrupt children. These people are predators and children are vulnerable."

Two weeks later it was announced that girls as young as eight had been filmed being invited for sexual touching. Months later officials announced that a young inmate at a correctional facility who had been linked to the pornography ring/trade in London may have exposed other inmates to HIV.

In May 1994, the police chief called for a province-wide police task force to be set up immediately to combat the "burgeoning child pornography trade" in Ontario. The solicitor general of Ontario announced that there would be a coordinated effort to crack down on kiddie porn. The Liberal critic was quoted as saying, "This is a cancer that goes to the core of this society, and it must be rooted out... we are facing a very real evil here with predatory adults preying on defenceless children." Subsequently, Project Guardian was announced, a coordinated effort between the London police, the Ontario police and the Toronto police forces.

The police eventually laid 371 charges against forty-five men: forty-six charges involving boys under fourteen, one charge of making child pornography, twenty of possessing child pornography, and the other half of obtaining the sexual services of a person under eighteen years.

However, there were several problems with the so-called London kiddie-porn ring. Gerald Hannon, writing in the *Globe and Mail*, estimates that about 85 percent of the sixty or so young men interviewed by the police were fourteen or older, legally able to have sex. There was no organized ring, and although pictures were taken and shared, that does not make them pornographic. And the famous press conference with the hundreds of pornographic videos taken from the schoolteacher's home? They ranged from *Abbot and Costello* to *Zorro*.

Most of the boys knew each other, and participated in a (im)moral economy where they had sex with each other, and with, or were observed by, the older men. In exchange they got money, food and shelter. They were hustlers who were coerced by the police to reveal the men's names, who were caught up in a change in the law which made it an offence to possess sexual images of anyone under eighteen years.

The London kiddie-porn ring probably never existed. In the Sample Study we look more in depth at how the Inquiry into a so-called pedophile ring investigated the alleged link between pedophilia and child abuse in Cornwall.

Sample Study

In 2006, a public inquiry opened in Cornwall, Ontario, to investigate allegations that a pedophile ring had operated in the community since the late 1950s. Stories had circulated in the community that the ring passed its victims among its members, which were said to include members of the Roman Catholic clergy, police and probation officers and other professionals. In 1992, a specific allegation by an altar boy that he had been abused by a priest and a probation officer was followed by the archdiocese paying him $32,000 to drop charges laid with police. However, in 1993, a police officer recorded interviews with a suspect who alleged the existence of an organized ring of pedophiles. The Cornwall police were unable to substantiate any such claims.

However, the allegations continued to circulate and were serious enough that in 1997 the Ontario Provincial Police launched an operation called Project Truth, which resulted in about 115 charges against fifteen men. However, when the cases went to court, few of the charges were upheld and there was only one conviction. The case was in tatters, and in 2002, the OPP said there was no proof of an organized ring. Because of ongoing concern, however, the public inquiry was announced in 2004.

One of the key witnesses, Ron Leroux, was supposed to tell the story of a pedophile ring of prominent Cornwall citizens. However, under questioning he said that the pedophile clan story was made up because a police officer, Constable Dunlop, had been pressuring him. He told the inquiry that he never read anything put down in his statement and that the story he told of robed cult members inserting candles into rectums was taken from a book about a U.S. pedophile clan. When he was asked by inquiry counsel for his definition of a pedophile, he said "a queer." Dunlop himself was dismissed from the police force.

Interestingly, there was a report prepared for the inquiry on the media coverage of allegations of historical abuse of young persons in the Cornwall area from 1986 to 2004. It looked specifically at whether the frames journalists selected, or the facts they reported as causing the problem, changed over time. It also looked at who the agenda setters were, what the ideology of the paper was and the geographic diffusion pattern. Using frame analysis means looking at how journalists selected certain aspects of an event and made them salient by defining the social problem as having certain causes and remedies.

The final database for the report included 1329 discrete print media articles, 224 of which were letters to the editor. A subset of 555 articles was selected to create a representative two-week sample. Among the findings were that over 70 percent of coverage came from local publications, peaking in 1994 and then again in 2001. The bulk of the coverage was simple news stories, with only 5 percent being more in-depth articles.

Opinion content, editorials and columns compromised about 20 percent of all coverage, quality was lower than expected for the complexity of the issue, and there was a general failure to follow journalistic best practices. For example, rather than quote multiple sources, over 50 percent referenced no sources. Rather than use contrasting sources, items might use two sources from within the same organization. And instead of balancing in-depth pieces with commentary, community gossip and hyperbole dominated. One-third of the coverage used government officials in the frame, slightly less were victims, and police comprised almost 20 percent of the sources used.

The frame analysis showed that certain topics were used to highlight conflict and create sensationalism: pedophile ring, criticisms of the police and judicial system, and an alleged cover-up conspiracy. The most prominent frame was that the police and other levels of the criminal justice system were culpable for the social problem through their ineffectiveness or incompetence. The second prominent frame was the crusading hero of Constable Dunlop, and the third was a lack of in-depth investigative type journalism.

Using those ideas about framing, a news sample was selected for analysis. Using the search category "project truth," 110 articles were found in the *Ottawa Citizen* between 1997 and 2007. Consistent with inquiry research, most articles were simply statements from police briefings or officials. Coverage usually came from only one source, did not analyze how the alleged abuse could have happened and uncritically repeated statements from local MPP Gary Guzzo and from Dunlop that there was a need to get to the bottom of the scandal. There were also unsubstantiated allegations that justice officials were covering up the abuse.

Coverage was sparse in the years leading up to the trials (1997, three articles; 1998, three articles; 1999, three articles; and then five articles in 2000). In 2001, defendants died, were found unfit to stand trial, were acquitted or had charges dropped. This was the height of coverage, with thirty articles published in 2001. Coverage dropped to twelve articles in 2002 with another trial stayed and the police announcing there was no ring, and then to three articles in 2003. In 2004, another trial was stayed and the government announced there would be an inquiry.

While expert evidence offered at the inquiry was based on a larger and less local sample, the frames offered there were also found in this analysis. Interestingly, another sample, selected from the *Globe and Mail* between 2000 and 2005, returned fourteen articles, also mostly news items but less dominated by the hyperbole of crusaders. Instead, there was a series of columns on the "witchhunts," paralled interestingly enough by Article 4.4, an excerpt from an alternative gay-oriented publication called *Xtra*, which presents a very different point of view than was in the rumours, allegations that nonetheless became the mainstream.

Article 4.4 "Gays face fallout after Cornwall pedophile witchhunt"
Opinion / Lives ruined and gay community vilified
Cornwall — Hollywood scriptwriters would have been hard-pressed to come up with a more intriguing plot: a pedophile ring with a membership list of prominent citizens holding wild sex orgies in a secluded cottage a few miles east of this quiet community of 46,000. The ring was said to include a Roman

Catholic bishop, priests, the Cornwall police chief, other high-ranking police officers, a probation officer, a Crown attorney and some of the community's leading businessmen. Vulnerable boys, some as young as 10 years old, were, so the story went, lured to the den of iniquity with gifts and money. The clan used them as personal sex toys with rituals that included men clad in white sheets lusting after their naked, young prey who had candles inserted into their rectums... A four-year OPP investigation... to investigate the way institutions such as the Roman Catholic Church, law enforcement agencies and the Children's Aid Society, handled complaints of sexual abuse... included hundreds of interviews by a four-man team, found no evidence of the ring. But that only added fuel to rumours of a high-level cover-up... [A] controversial website, Projecttruth.com... fed the pedophile-ring frenzy that gripped the community. Within weeks of the site being set up, it had 30,000 hits. Copies of Leroux's statement were downloaded hundreds of times and distributed in factories and coffee shops. Soon, everybody was talking about the "pedophile ring" as a fact and names were tossed around like frisbees. The witchhunt was in full gear... The gay and lesbian community became particularly vulnerable as the line between homosexuality and pedophilia became blurred. I can still remember a call from a member of the citizens coalition, a group headed by Dunlop's brother-in-law Carson Chisholm, calling me to complain about the alleged cover-up and how my newspaper (the *Cornwall Standard-Freeholder*) wasn't doing enough to expose "these homos." When it was pointed out to the caller that he was lumping homosexuals and pedophiles together, his remark spoke volumes. "They're all queers. Instead of burying them they should just chisel their heads and pound them into the ground." Don Johnson, a former Crown attorney and now the city's top criminal defence lawyer... never bought into the pedophile ring story. "I knew it was bogus right from the start. It was a piece of fiction taken from a book," he said. Unfortunately, a large chunk of the city's population suspended disbelief and accepted the story as gospel. But then came the inquiry that was going to expose all the lies and deceit by the people in power and have clan members running for the proverbial hills. (*Xtra.ca*, October 19, 2007, by Claude McIntosh)

On the eve of the inquiry, a dominant news frame is typified by the following quotation in an editorial:

Article 4.5 "Cornwall cases need inquiry"

How is it possible that Cornwall police and Ontario Provincial Police initially concluded there was no basis for charges in the sex-abuse allegation, then there was a completely different conclusion, and more than 100 charges were laid against 15 accused, under another police investigation? When charges were finally laid, why were there major errors, such as the Crown's failure to disclose information on the case to the defence, resulting in a scrapped trial? Were these errors and delays that should have been avoided? And if sexual assault cases dating back decades were short on evidence or weak in some other way, why were they pursued when the chance of conviction was slim? What lessons do we learn here? (*The Ottawa Citizen*, Wednesday, October 20, 2004: B4, editorial)

The Glaude Inquiry finished in early 2009 after hearing 180 witnesses over a period of four years. It released its report in December, at a cost of $53 million. It concluded, in part, that while there was no evidence of a pedophile ring, there was a failure by institutions to protect children from abuses committed by their own members.

The three different cases, Cashel, London and Cornwall, share some similarities. They involve young people as (purported) victims, adults are (belatedly) accused of predating them, and there is a strong whiff of homophobia involved. These examples show how the link between homosexuality and pedophilia is very much alive for some people and that the topic continually receives play in the news.

The latter two cases, London and Cornwall, can perhaps too easily be seen as moral panics, where the fear that children are victimized by homosexual adults is all too transparently contrived. The claimsmakers, especially the police, are able to use their positions of power in the community and their voice in the media to inflame moral concerns that are relatively baseless.

However, the point is not to unmask moral panics and show them as baseless. Youths probably were exploited in London, and the Cornwall case did begin from a single case of abuse alleged by an altar boy against a priest. However, in the latter case, and certainly in the Cashel case, it is important to observe that the story shifted and morphed from one of the institutional abuse of power to individual cases of perversion, flamed by the emotional fire of outrage.

Some questions that need to be asked include: Why was the media so willing to take up the imputed link between homosexuality and abuse and reproduce that discredited stereotype? Why does it not show as much interest in labelling heterosexual child abusers, and why is child abuse in the family hardly discussed in the media at all? And finally, whose interests does it serve to construct the link between abuse and homosexuality and detach abuse from the context of its actual occurrence? In the case of Mount Cashel, is our attention distracted from larger issues?

Analyzing the News

The particular way child sexual abuse was inscribed during the Hughes Commission Inquiry detached it from its most common location, in the family, and homosexualized it in the process. Moreover, in focusing on the abuse of boys by brothers in this inquiry and on priests in others, the fact that the abuse was made possible by an institutional structure of traditional, male authority was overlooked.

In topicalizing the violence this way, the usual pattern of the sexual abuse of children was disguised, and the abuse in this particular instance was mystified. This kind of obfuscation can be found repeatedly in news coverage in general. But this is not simply a mistake, because it reveals the power of discourse to create interpretations.

It is obvious, of course, that the Hughes Commission on Mount Cashel served as a lightning rod for issues of abuse and was probably a catalyst for reports of institutional abuse in general. Certainly, in the intervening years, there have been inquiries in many other provinces. In 1990, the *Toronto Star* published details from a 1960 confidential report into male sexual abuse in Ontario at St. Joseph's Training School in Alfred and St. John's in Uxbridge. The consequent inquiry resulted in two hundred charges against twenty-nine men at these Roman Catholic reform schools. The investigation eventually widened to include five provincial reform schools.

There were also charges of widespread sexual abuse against adolescent girls at the Grandview School for Girls detention centre in Cambridge, Ontario, before it closed in 1976. In 1992, the police investigated sexual abuse that occurred in the 1960s at the Kingsclear Youth Training Centre in New Brunswick, and at the East Saint John Boys' Industrial Home, the New Brunswick Protestant Orphans' Home and the Dr. William F. Roberts Hospital School. The subsequent inquiry was also accused of blurring the very important distinction between homosexuality and pedophilia.

In 1994, the Nova Scotia attorney general announced an inquiry into violent sex abuse at the former Shelburne School for Boys, an inquiry that was subsequently widened to include the Nova Scotia School for Girls in Truro.

1. *Media patterns.* The first edition of this book showed that there were important differences in the amount and duration of news coverage of issues related to the abuse of children between 1978 and 1992. The topic "child abuse" had the longest running history in the *Index*, beginning earlier than incest, for example. Child sexual abuse doesn't begin to be a subject topic until much later. The sexual abuse of children became a category in 1989 and, at 469 stories, had the highest number of citations in 1992. There would appear to be a blossoming of child sexual abuse cases or, more likely, the media has suddenly discovered an interest in them.

The Hughes Commission Inquiry received brief but heavy coverage nationwide, with 238 citations in 1989, dropping to forty-five citations in 1990. However, as the *Index* only covers major Canadian papers, this number does not even begin to get at the local Newfoundland newspapers such as the *Evening Telegram*, where coverage was probably at saturation level.

Many of the citations listed under "child sexual abuse," in fact, were for trials of people named at the Hughes Inquiry. The total number of cases under this category, then, is inflated by articles that would have been listed under the Hughes Inquiry two years earlier. The interest in the sexual abuse of children is conceivably an interest in other well-publicized cases, as well, which again would inflate the citations and not reflect abuse within families.

In 1991, the Hughes report was published and the Mount Cashel trials started; in 1992, there were the Martensville trials in Saskatchewan, the investigation at the Grandview Reform School in Ontario, the case of the Duplessis orphans in Quebec, the ban on the film *The Boys of Saint Vincent* and the scandal at the Christian Brothers schools in Ontario. There was thus a lot of interest and publicity about the sexual abuse of children, especially males.

The topic of "child abuse" has the longest continuous coverage. It climbed in the 1980s, with the highest number of citations in 1987, and then steadily fell thereafter. As the number of child abuse stories in general dropped (from 248 in 1987 to 115 in 1988, 110 in 1989, and 87 in 1990, an overall decrease of 65 percent), stories on the sexual abuse of children rose (from 256 in 1990 to 469 in 1992, an overall increase of 83 percent). The coverage of "child abuse," which includes cases of physical abuse, does not seem to have been affected by the sensational cases mentioned above. The topic of "incest" had the lowest number of citations overall, averaging slightly more than a dozen per year over the ten-year period from 1983 to 1992; most of these would have been against female children by males in their family.

One way these figures and trends can be interpreted is to conclude that sexual abuse of boys by adult males in institutions is far more newsworthy than child abuse in general or incest against female children in families. Nor surprisingly perhaps, the coverage is more extensive and more sensationalistic in cases where it is the least likely to occur.

The exaggerated interest in extra-familial abuse of males becomes a problem if most abuse of children occurs in the home against females, for it means that sexual violence against female children has become invisible through lack of coverage. Furthermore, it means that while newspapers cover homosexual pedophiles, they are actually missing the far greater pervasiveness of violence against children in the home by heterosexual male family members.

The interest in this edition is not in updating these statistics on media coverage but rather to look a different matter — the discourses that inscribe a problem. What is apparent is that when it comes to children, media coverage is highest of abuse by non-family members.

2. *Crime patterns.* The statistics on child sexual abuse indicate that the

magnitude of the problem is quite large. According to a subset of 122 police services representing 61 percent of the national volume of crime, in 2003, children and youth under eighteen years of age were the victims of 22 percent of violations against the person.

Gender is also an important factor. In a 1991 report of a survey of police departments in Canada that analyzed almost 300,000 criminal incidents, 2,000 of which involved a violent crime against a child less than twelve years old, 56 percent of the victims were female. Among child sexual assault victims, over two-thirds were girls.

Intimacy is also a factor: in sexual assault cases, 41 percent of the accused were family members, and the percentage was higher for girls (48 percent) than for boys (33 percent). Sexual assaults against children are more likely to happen in a home setting (girls 75 percent, males 63 percent) than in a public area. Similarly, in 2003, six out of ten physical assault victims and half of sexual assault victims under the age of six were assaulted by a family member.

The type of assault was an issue too, with sexual assaults comprising 50 percent of the total and physical assaults 28 percent. Boys tend to be more at risk of (non-sexual) physical assault and were more than 70 percent of its victims. For other sexual offences, such as invitation to sexual touching, two-thirds of the victims were girls.

The picture of reality we receive from the cases considered above is one with a preponderance of sexual abuse, especially against boys. These cases seem to get the most media attention, as evidenced by the heavy coverage of Mount Cashel and the high number of child sexual abuse citations. In contrast, criminal statistics bear out the fact that child sexual abuse occurs more frequently than physical abuse and is largely against female children. However, the sexual abuse articles in the media are inflated by stories from inquiries into institutional abuse against boys. Most child abuse (physical and sexual) is committed in the home by a family member or acquaintance.

The media picture is skewed and misdirected and misnames the problem by ignoring the predominance of sexual abuse of female children and of physical abuse of male children in the home. This analysis, initially offered in the first edition, is still the base of the analysis used here. However, it is not simply that the media distracts us from the reality of abuse, but that even what is presented is misconstrued. While not wanting to exploit hindsight bias, London and Cornwall should both be reminders to be careful when reading Cashel.

3. *The importance of discourse.* In comparing media patterns with crime patterns we don't want to rest with the feeling that one (social construction) is more true than another. If anything, we should learn from the panics presented in Reading the News that what is important is the fact that for most people most of the time what they have to go by is the stories the hear, listen to and

see in the media. What is important then is to look at these different stories or discourses and to see how closely they attack power or scapegoat the powerless.

In the media coverage of the Mount Cashel Inquiry in the *Globe and Mail* between 1989 and 1991, there is not one but rather competing discourses that define what happened. These discourses can be disarticulated, so as to better see the vector of blaming. These discourses are: 1. blaming homosexuals (e.g., Articles 4.6, and 4.7); 2. blaming the victims (e.g., Article 4.8); 3. blaming power (e.g., Article 4.9); and 4. blaming the system (e.g., Article 5.0). These discourses overlap, disagree and compete for attention. We have to consider to what extent danger was marginalized. Does the media picture skew, misdirect and misname the problem by ignoring prominence of sex abuse of female children and physical abuse of male children in home? Is the crisis of legitimation for Mount Cashel also a crisis of confidence in the criminal justice system itself and its ability to protect children? And, by highlighting homosexuality rather than pedophilia, is attention drawn to a small minority of an already stigmatized group and away from institutional culpability and abuse of power and authority?

Article 4.6 "Newfoundland Roman Catholics vent their rage over sex scandal"

The white-haired Newfoundlander, his voice shaking with anger, denounced the Roman Catholic church as "a haven for homosexuals and perverts." (*Globe and Mail*, June 15, 1989)

Article 4.7 "Painful stories of beatings and neglect"

One by one, Newfoundland's forgotten children are finally telling their painful stories of how they were abused and neglected by those who were supposed to protect them... The revelations are ending years of silence in Newfoundland about homosexuality and child abuse. Many of the victims have kept the stories to themselves for 15 years. (*Globe and Mail*, September 30, 1989, by Kevin Cox)

Blaming the victims. Unlike the previous section, this interpretation, that the victims were somehow complicit in their victimization, is an almost silent, subterranean one. Nonetheless it is important enough that a major newspaper speaks out against it in an editorial.

Article 4.8 "His misguided musings"

In a column for an Antigonish weekly paper and in a radio interview... [the bishop] suggested that the boys at Mount Cashel orphanage who were sexually assaulted by priests and lay brothers in the 1970s might not have been true victims. They might even have been co-operating. If not, why did they stay? (*Globe and Mail*, August 12, 1989, editorial)

Blaming power. On April 26 and 27, *Globe* columnist Michael Valpy lays out a theory that the victimization was caused by an abuse of power. He begins by identifying the institutional players and ends by calling it an abuse of power. On the following day he suggests that the power of the church resulted in the ending of the police investigation.

Article 4.9 "Child sexual abuse is an abuse of power"

The question asked... was how the Royal Newfoundland Constabulary, the Roman Catholic Church and Newfoundland Departments of Justice and Social Services could all have taken part in a cover-up of alleged sexual abuse of boys in the St. John's Mount Cashel Orphanage in the mid-1970s... Until very recently, the relationship between many of the people of rural Newfoundland and their clergy was medieval... Their power in the small communities came to be enormous... It was an unhealthy power, exacerbated by the isolation of so many priests in the outports... Sexual abuse is an abuse of power. It also, until recently in Newfoundland, was the sin that had no name. When the 1975 reports on Mount Cashel surfaced, the power of the church merged with the taboo on talking about child sex abuse... Nothing more was said... until now. (*Globe and Mail*, April 26, 1989: A8)

This attitude that it was power at fault, which appears in other articles as well, feeds into the last discourse.

Blaming the system. In September of 1989, the Newfoundland Constabulary told the Hughes Inquiry that it could not find documents relating to its investigation into allegations of abuse in 1975. More than twenty boys were interviewed by police at the time, but no charges were laid. In addition, key allegations were left out of the complaint and statements were altered, testimony at the Inquiry showed. As Article 4.10 shows, there were also allegations that social workers and politicians neglected their responsibility, leaving more than enough blame to go around.

Article 4.10 "Complaints 'fell on deaf ears,' former Cashel orphan says"

A former resident of the Mount Cashel orphanage told a royal commission yesterday that he and others were abused in the early 1970s at the institution run by the Christian Brothers... [he] said he told several politicians... about problems at the orphanage in 1974 and 1975, but they fell on deaf ears. He said he got the same reaction from police officers, a provincial social worker, and other Christian Brothers when he tried to convince them that the abuse was happening. (*Globe and Mail*, September 20, 1989: A4)

What are we to make of these conflicting yet complementary stories?

Was Mount Cashel a home for orphaned boys and pervert priests? Was the abuse committed by priests a manifestation of their homosexuality, their power or their pedophilia? Was it aided by the disinclination of those who had the power to investigate abrogating their duty because the victims were powerless?

A second issue, which may cast light on the first, is the role commissions of inquiry play in the maintenance of order in a modern society.

4. *Commissions of inquiry.* A cynical view regards royal commissions as a way the state can handle a legitimation crisis. If there's been a problem in the criminal justice system, for example, a commission of inquiry can be given a limited mandate to investigate and make administrative recommendations to the state on how to repair the problem without posing fundamental questions about deeper social relations. Its proposals may be helpful in certain cases but don't necessarily get at the social roots of problems. Given the way commissions function, they inevitably work in the interests of the state and, in establishing consensus, re-establish the legitimacy of the state.

On the other hand, commissions of inquiry have broad powers. They have judicial powers of subpoena and examination and are only limited by not finding criminal responsibility. A royal commission has an authoritative air and is empowered to get at issues that pose a public crisis of confidence. The head of the Hughes Commission of Inquiry, for example, was a retired Ontario Supreme Court judge.

With the Mount Cashel inquiry, the Hughes Commission had to deal with a very emotional and volatile issue. The Hughes Report noted that sexual abuse at the orphanage was known and hushed up in the 1970s. There were also allegations that the abuse went back to the 1940s and 1950s. The deputy justice minister, a police chief and the Canadian head of the Christian Brothers were alleged to have arranged to send two abusers from the province in 1975. The original police investigation lasted less than a week, no charges were laid, and it took until 1989 to reopen the investigation. There were also allegations that reporters were told of the events in 1975 and 1976, but no stories were published about the issue.

A former provincial government lawyer alleged that the former deputy minister of justice concealed from provincial child welfare officials a police report detailing physical and sexual abuse and statements from a former member of the Royal Newfoundland Constabulary that the justice department was active in having the case dropped. Moreover, there was evidence from the former director of public prosecutions that he had briefed the justice minister in 1979 about the suppression of child abuse charges in 1975. There was also evidence that social services workers knew of the abuse of one of the boys in 1976 and returned him to Mount Cashel because the abuse was considered an isolated incident. Similar allegations of cover-ups and collusion to protect offenders at some of the institutions mentioned above were made as well.

It would take a lot more space to go into the history of allegations in the Hughes Inquiry, the recommendations published in the report, the outcome of the subsequent court trials, the media coverage in books and the like. However, the point being made here is that the inquiry was needed so someone could be seen to be doing something about the abuse at Mount Cashel after the incidents had occurred and been known about for years.

The crisis of legitimation for Mount Cashel was also a crisis of confidence in the criminal justice system and its ability to protect children. The inquiry focused attention on a case that was potentially embarrassing to the criminal justice system, especially after the high level of collusion in silencing the victims and protecting the guilty had become apparent. By highlighting the homosexuality of the brothers, rather than the pedophilia, attention could be drawn to an already stigmatized minority group and away from institutional culpability and abuse of power and authority.

This same legerdemain, or sleight of hand, is routinely accomplished as child abuse is topicalized in the media, with attention being drawn away from the family and the relationships of intimacy and gender where abuse routinely occurs. The treatment of the issue of child abuse in general fulfils the same implicit need to preserve the legitimacy of the status quo.

While government officials do not necessarily set up commissions of inquiry to protect themselves from scrutiny and put the blame on homosexuals, the misplacement of blame is not simply a mistake. The misplacement of blame reinstates legitimacy. From a larger point of view, the news media misses the crime but not for lack of trying. First of all, there is a tendency to devote a lot of coverage to institutional abuse and neglect intrafamilial violence, and, second, there is a tendency to focus on marginalizing and individualizing the problem instead of on how structural relations of authority and power make it possible in the first place.

Commissions of inquiry can fall into this trap just as well as the media. In so doing they create a mutually reaffirming myth of blame that leaves most everyone comfortable, thinking that justice has been served, when the very conditions that enabled the violence to occur have not been addressed. In the final analysis, the Hughes Commission needed to re-establish the status quo, restore faith in the criminal justice system and identify dangerous offenders in the community. And the media performed its role of returning affairs to normal as well, although the discourse is fractured with contrasting explanations.

Summary

We see in the media coverage of Mount Cashel that the consequence of airing dirty laundry through the Hughes Inquiry was to focus attention on the physical and sexual abuse of male children by adult males in an institutional setting. Those crimes certainly did happen and deserve to be reported. However, in the process, child abuse, a term originally developed to describe the abuse of female children in families, became inscribed with new meaning, as abuse outside families. Through the inscription of homosexuality and pedophilia, the danger was posed so as to focus blame on an already stigmatized group. This is seen in both the Cornwall case and the events in London, Ontario. Danger was marginalized and legitimation was restored.

The consequence of such inscriptions is to make the violence against female and male children in the home invisible and to miss the point that abuse of power and authority is not about sexual orientation. It also marginalized those very real complaints from within institutions that the problem was a few individuals rather than the organization of power. In these ways both the reporting on the inquiry and media coverage in general keep society safe from the dangerous questions and return us to the status quo, to confidence that things are as they should be.

As for Mount Cashel, in the end some brothers went to jail, several of the former residents went on the *Geraldo* show and the orphanage was torn down. A proposal was made to build a McDonald's on the site but was unsuccessful. All that outrage, and that's what's left.

5

AIDS Fiends and High-Risk Groups
Misrepresenting and Signifying a Disease

Having AIDS is not a crime, but it is often distorted in the news and has been associated with gay men, drug users, prostitutes and other so-called "deviant" groups. Feeding into the hysteria, authorities have called for quarantine and segregation of people infected with the disease, as was done in Haiti and Cuba. Further heightening the fear, in Canada and the United States, people have been charged with criminal offences such as aggravated assault for exposing other people to the human immuno-deficiency virus (HIV).

In his brief presentation, Eric Smith talks about how acquired immune deficiency syndrome (AIDS) is misrepresented in the media. He says that the stereotyping of "AIDS carriers" and the misidentification of who is at risk has created social panic over the disease. This suggestion gives us a model for looking at the media's coverage of disease in the news, that it is associated with the "other." The "other" is a marginal group that can be blamed or scapegoated for a social problem, in this case the spread of a disease.

In the section Reading the News, we look at articles that contain alarmist characterizations of AIDS and portray it as being spread by deviant, marginal groups to the "general population." Although many sensitive and thoughtful articles have been written about AIDS, the news examined here constructs a sense of danger that threatens the broader community. Through the misrepresentation of AIDS in the news, scapegoats are found for the problem, and blame is placed on certain marginalized groups in society. Consequently, many people still do not perceive themselves to be at risk.

The Sample Study looks at a selection of media coverage about AIDS and another one on swine flu. The analysis examines how the theme of demonization is coupled with the metaphor of plague, implying that people who are contagious spread disease through casual contact, either maliciously or through negligence.

In the last section, Analyzing the News, we look at the broader coverage of disease, and focus on how its threat is topicalized as a risk in a way that creates a signification crisis, where the symbolic exaggeration of threat actually makes the problem worse.

Unfortunately, the Krever Inquiry into Canada's blood supply uncovered all too clearly how prejudice and negligence contributed to the spread of AIDS among hemophiliacs in Canada. This chapter suggests that the symbolic misrepresentation of other diseases misconstrues and thus continues to contribute to their spread.

The method featured in this chapter is a content analysis using headlines, accompanied with an analysis of templates or framing. A theme is scapegoating, and while the emotion associated with an epidemic might be fear, I suggest that there is also surprise and doubt. Studies I have found useful for thinking about disease in the news media are Blendon et al. (2004), Eagleton (2004), Eichelberger (2007), Lupton (1993), Sontag (1990), Treichler (1987) and Watney (1987).

Eric Smith's Talk

I have two responses on how I think the media has dealt with AIDS issues. In my own case the media has been very good. If the media is dealing with a person who they see as an underdog, then you'll be treated fairly and they'll run stories that you like. However, if you look at AIDS issues in general, the news media does not do a very good job in covering them. Unfortunately, the media is probably only a couple of steps ahead of the government in the way it deals with AIDS issues in general, and there are several problems that I want to mention that I think tie in a bit.

First of all, as nosey as media people can be, when it comes to AIDS issues, they're very willing to simply accept and print the press releases the government hands out. They don't check to see if what the government is saying is right; they simply run it. There are a number of examples, and if you want to get an idea of the poor job the media's done, the book *And the Band Played On* details some problems with the media.

One of the first news stories on AIDS was done in 1982, and at the time AIDS researchers were trying to get money to increase their research. When the press covered the story, the PR people put out press releases that indicated there wasn't a problem with funding. There were only twelve people in the federal government working on AIDS; however, the PR people issued statements saying that there was a seventy-five-member Centre for Disease Control task force working on the issue. Two weeks later, when *Time* magazine did an article on it, the press releases had increased that to 120 people. The reporters didn't check to see if those numbers were right; they simply ran the story.

Similarly, in Nova Scotia in 1990, the press ran a story saying that the Department of Health declared there were only five AIDS deaths in Nova Scotia in all of 1990. Anybody working in any of the AIDS groups in Nova Scotia will tell you that that's very far off the mark. At our organization

[People Living with AIDS Coalition] we keep a memorial book where we keep track of names of people who have died. We have eleven or twelve names in the book for 1990, plus there are three or four more others who died but we don't know their names. But the press is quite content to run what comes from the government.

Furthermore, when the government is attacked on issues like not doing enough on AIDS education, one of their typical responses is that all the education we need to be giving people is not to have sex with prostitutes. Unfortunately, those are the stories that get printed, that prostitutes are a major problem in spreading AIDS. So it would be nice if reporters could do a bit of follow-up on the things that come from the government.

Secondly, although I think the press is improving, one of the other issues that was especially a problem in the early 1980s, before it was even called AIDS, was the fact that the press simply wouldn't write stories about it. No self-respecting newspaper wanted to print articles about "those kind of people." If you look back you find the stories did not really start until it was white heterosexual males who were becoming infected. Once those acceptable people were becoming infected, then it was okay to print the stories. By and large, however, that attitude is now changing.

The press has done a fair amount of coverage on AIDS issues in the last while, but compare that to how they handle other problems. For instance, in 1982 there was a big scare when several people died from taking Tylenol laced with cyanide. The *New York Times* ran a story every day during October, plus twenty-three stories in the next two months. However, in the first two years of the AIDS epidemic they managed to write six stories. Or compare that with the coverage of the outbreak of Legionnaire's disease. That was in the press every day. But because of the group that was affected — veterans, who are acceptable people for most of society — it was all right to run stories on them.

A third issue the press has a hard time dealing with is appropriate language to use. We keep trying to train media people to use or not use certain words, but some of them just don't get it. It may not be fair to blame the reporters themselves, as I'm not sure who writes the headlines, for that may be the problem of people higher up. One of the words that we don't like is the word victim. Personally, after several years at Cape Sable Island I've been called a lot worse, so the word victim doesn't bother me.

The problem is, though, with AIDS we're moving to a stage where it is a long-term, manageable illness. We're trying to get people who are infected to stop seeing it as a death sentence. They keep seeing these words with negative overtones, and it makes it very hard to convince them, in fact, that they may have a long time ahead of them. In Halifax there was certainly a lot of upset at the headline several years ago, "AIDS fiend strikes again." I think most people in the AIDS community found it inappropriate.

Another phrase that bothers me is "admitted homosexuals." Every time I read my name in the paper, I'm an "admitted homosexual." If they have to discuss my orientation at all, can't they just say "homosexual?" The day I read about the premier being an "admitted heterosexual" I'll accept "admitted." This is a time when reporters are inaccurate in the language they use.

A fourth issue I've complained about is the lack of follow-up. They do a story and you wait to see what the next step is, and you don't hear any more. For example, the Nova Scotia Task Force on AIDS reported in 1988 and the government said it was accepting thirty-nine of forty-seven recommendations. Has anybody gone back to check?

One of the task force recommendations was that HIV and illnesses transmitted the same way be protected in the *Human Rights Act*. In 1988, the minister of health said the government wasn't going to accept that because it was already protected under the disabilities section of the *Human Rights Act*. However, several weeks ago [1991] the attorney general was asked what would happen if I were to take my case to the Human Rights Commission. He said I had the right to do so but he wasn't sure I would win because he didn't think disability included HIV. So you get rather bizarre messages from government, and nobody seems to be there to pick up on them.

The last thing that would be nice is if media outlets could use the same reporter to cover all these issues. For some issues, you get reporters who know as much about AIDS as you do, and within the space of five minutes they've got their story all wrapped up. At other times you get reporters who don't know much more than how to spell the word. Obviously I have my favourites in the press that I prefer to talk to, but there are other press people who come in the door and I think, where can I hide?

Several months ago one of the AIDS groups, ACT-UP, presented a cake to the Advisory Commission on AIDS to let them know they were going to be keeping an eye on what they were doing. ACT-UP was concerned about anonymous testing. The press was there and asked a few questions, so a spokesperson for ACT-UP was talking about why they thought anonymous testing was important, and out of the blue the next question was, "Does this mean you're also going to be protesting against the Gulf War?"

I would like to see the media in general take a bigger role in doing education on AIDS issues. I know some press people don't agree, but if we have to wait for the government to do it there are going to be a hell of a lot of people who are dead.

I'll close with my favourite line from the media. When I'm doing interviews with the CBC I'm usually introduced as "Nova Scotia's most well-known homosexual and carrier of the AIDS virus." If it points out anything, it's certainly shown me that I chose the wrong way to become famous. There must be a better way.

Reading the News

Eric Smith identifies several issues associated with the reporting on AIDS in the news media: inappropriate language such as "victims," an inordinate focus on homosexuals and prostitutes, the media's disinterest in the disease when it was called the "gay plague," a lack of critique and follow-up on government information, and inadequate education on the disease and its prevention. These problems can be grouped together as mistakes in representation, or less charitably as ignorance, but they can also be seen as the representations and significations of disease. They are its metaphors.

From the very earliest days, reporting on AIDS has had its metaphors, usually associated with gay men, as in Article 5.1, which is believed to be the first news article on AIDS published in Canada. The term "gay plague" is referred to as a nickname for a disease that is mysterious, deadly and rare, although more than homosexuals are at risk.

Article 5.1 "15 Canadians reported killed by 'gay plague'"

Kitchener, Ont (CP) — Acquired immune deficiency syndrome a mysterious, often fatal disease known as the gay plague — has claimed the lives of at least 15 Canadians since it was first reported in this country one year ago... other groups — including Haitians, intravenous drug users and their sexual partners and hemophiliacs — have contracted the disease and are considered at risk... [AIDS] breaks down the body's natural defences, leaving victims susceptible to infections such as pneumonia and cancer... It has no known cure and researchers are uncertain of the origin or cause. They have speculated it might be transmitted by sexual contact or through the blood. (*Winnipeg Free Press*, February 19, 1983: 15)

The article is definitive and unequivocal in identifying the groups at risk — male homosexuals, Haitians, hemophiliacs and intravenous drug users and their sexual partners. This characterization makes the disease seem marginal, not affecting most people but only members of minority or deviant groups. In the early media discourse on AIDS, such characterizations structured the difference between what were considered to be high-risk groups and the general population.

Although AIDS is identified in the article as no longer a uniquely gay disease, it is still presented as marginal despite the fact that sexual activity and blood products could imply a threat to anybody. That link for danger is not constructed, as it would break the normalized ideology of how the virus is transmitted. It would be like saying that "mad cow disease" is contracted through eating contaminated meat but that only Rastafarians are at risk.

Although the article expresses uncertainties about transmission, the danger is construed to be for "those people" who are at risk. Regardless of how true the article was in terms of the knowledge at the time, the consequence of characterizing AIDS as a marginal threat does not make it seem like something anyone should be worried about.

Article 5.2 contains an attitude that was not uncommon in the early 1980s but should have been uncommon in 1988. The health minister of Nova Scotia is said to have advocated quarantining "AIDS carriers," conjuring up the image of a contagious plague.

Article 5.2 "Politicians want AIDS carriers in quarantine"

Halifax (CP) — Two Nova Scotia politicians are suggesting that some AIDS carriers be quarantined. Health Minister Joel Matheson and Halifax Mayor Ron Wallace said it is in the best interest of the public to separate from the rest of the community those AIDS carriers who are sexually active and spreading the disease. Matheson said his department and legal experts are investigating whether he has the power to include AIDS carriers among those he can quarantine. Wallace also called for the quarantine of some AIDS sufferers to help stop the spread of the disease. Halifax police are currently looking for a bisexual male who recently infected two women with the AIDS antibody. (*Calgary Herald*, January 13, 1988: B3)

There are several themes here. First, the article constructs the danger as from the outside, from sexually active AIDS carriers who are spreading the disease. Second, the fear of plague sentiment is buoyed by the report that Halifax police are looking for a bisexual male who infected two women, a characterization which borders on calling the person a predator. Third, what started as a health matter is now a police matter, a criminal matter, and not just political grandstanding. The report does not say that there were two cases of HIV transmission during heterosexual sex, but that a bisexual male infected two women. The danger is constructed as one of normal women being contaminated by a sexually deviant man.

The rest of the article, not reproduced here, is written from the point of view of health management and unrelated to specific incidents in Nova Scotia. It quotes the director of Manitoba's communicable disease control office on how to prevent the spread of AIDS to health workers. It again raises the spectre of HIV being present in bodily fluids other than semen or blood; however, it offers no information on how to practise safer sex. The article explicitly deviantizes the transmission of disease, while the subtext anchors the perception that AIDS is a problem for the authorities: politicians, the police and health workers.

The tone of the article is alarmist and at the same time patronizing. The image is one of a bisexual man preying on innocent women, with police and politicians involved. However, with no health or safety information, the public is left to misconstrue the nature of AIDS transmission.

Eight months later, a follow-up article, Article 5.3, has a front-page banner headline: "AIDS fiend strikes again." The article says official concern over the bisexual man infecting women with AIDS has continued and escalated. The health minister, the police chief and the director of the Atlantic Health Unit say there is an AIDS carrier "knowingly" spreading the disease. The man is once again identified as a "bisexual AIDS carrier," who has so far infected three women with the virus. The "public" is being threatened, and it is serious enough that the police are involved. Certain key words are emphasized, establishing the metaphor of threat: "AIDS carrier," "disease" and "virus."

Article 5.3 "AIDS fiend strikes again"

Health Minister Joel Matheson and Halifax Police Chief Blair Jackson knew up to 10 days ago that an AIDS carrier is knowingly spreading the disease in the city, Atlantic Health Unit director Dr. David MacLean said Sunday... He confirmed that a bisexual AIDS carrier linked to two Halifax women who tested positive for AIDS last spring has been linked once again in Halifax to a woman who is six months pregnant and also tested positive for the virus... "My concern of course is that the public is being exposed to a very serious health hazard," Mr. Matheson said. "The police are the appropriate agency to handle the situation and I cannot make any further comment due to the sensitivity of the matter both in legal terms and otherwise."... In addition to the three women, who tested positive for the virus, there is a 60 percent chance the pregnant woman's baby will also contract the virus... Dr. MacLean said efforts to curb the fear associated with AIDS through education programs will suffer a "setback" because of the incident... "I don't have any doubt that this will add fuel to the fire of those who feel that people that carry the virus should be locked up... but when you are dealing with human behaviour it is not surprising that, at some point in time, you would find this." The incubation period for the AIDS virus can be several years and the long-term survival rate for those developing AIDS-related symptoms remains zero, he said. (*Halifax Herald*, September 19, 1988: A1, by Dale Madill)

The first part of the article details the facts of the so-called bisexual AIDS carrier, but the second part ranges more widely to similar situations in the United States, where people have been charged with willfully attempting to injure and with attempted murder, presumably for knowingly spreading the disease, although the article simply mentions AIDS-related charges. The tone of the article is alarmist, painting the picture of a deviant and dangerous bisexual man who has already infected three women and one unborn baby and could be subsequently charged with a criminal offence.

The facts, however, are not simply reported by the article as much as constructed by the words used to describe the case. The authenticity of the account is based on quotations from the health minister and the director of the Atlantic Health Unit. The danger of the bisexual AIDS carrier is linked to past cases in the spring and to a prostitute in Toronto. The director tacitly legitimates the opinion of those who argue for quarantine and expresses the opinion that it is human nature that some people will knowingly act irresponsibly. The conclusion that the disease can remain hidden for several years and the survival rate is zero is unnecessarily alarmist.

Most important is how the article also gives an indication of risk to the general population. This creates a division between threat and threatened, between group and outsider. In addition, typically, authorities have emphasized the notion of who is at risk rather than what activities can put a person at risk. Thus, they are responsible for the fact that most people don't think they themselves are at risk because the embodiment of the disease is literally the deviant "other." There is no discussion of the unsafe sexual behaviour but of the unsafe sexual partner.

More and more cases appeared in the news of people charged with various criminal offences for what could be described as acts of omission. These cases reinforced the criminal character of AIDS. The man identified in the above articles was subsequently found guilty of criminal negligence causing bodily harm and sentenced to three years in prison. In another case in Vancouver, a woman was charged with aggravated sexual assault for not telling two men she had sex with that she was HIV positive. In a civil case in Ontario, a woman sued her divorced husband because he was a practising bisexual who knew his sexual practices put him in a high-risk category for contracting AIDS, but did not tell her.

In a long-standing case, a man was arrested in Vancouver in 1991 on charges laid in Ontario of aggravated assault, criminal negligence causing bodily harm and common nuisance. He was alleged to have infected three unidentified women and of subsequently violating a celibacy order. In 1993 he was tried in Ontario, acquitted of the aggravated sexual assault charges in May and died in July before the judge could deliver a verdict on the remaining charges. In December the judge said he would not deliver a verdict posthumously. A compensation board finally awarded each of three victims $15,000 but ruled that one victim's sexual behaviour had contributed to her acquiring HIV, suggesting that "a reasonable person wouldn't be so quick to hop into bed." Later, a *Toronto Star* editorial pointed out that the only question for the compensation board should have been whether the women were victims of a crime, not whether it approved of their relationships.

Some cases of AIDS transmission have been seen as acts of commission. An HIV-positive prisoner in the United States was convicted of attempted murder for biting a prison guard, and it was ruled that it did not matter whether the virus could be transmitted through a bite as long as he believed it could. In a similar case, a prisoner at the Guelph Correctional Centre in Ontario was sentenced to three months for biting a guard. A man with AIDS in New York was charged with attempted murder and jailed in a state psychiatric centre for biting an emergency services technician, and a man committed robberies in Los Angeles by threatening people with a blood-filled syringe.

In what was continually described as a "bizarre case," a man and a woman were charged with conspiracy to commit murder after injecting an Edmonton man with blood contaminated with the HIV virus. The murder conspiracy charges against the man were subsequently dropped for lack of evidence, but the woman remained charged with aggravated assault and threatening to cause death or serious bodily harm. In another case, the Supreme Court of Canada in 1993 upheld the conviction of a man found guilty in 1989 of committing a common nuisance by endangering the lives or health of the public.

By late 1992, more than twenty-five American states had laws that forbade passing or intentionally exposing others to the AIDS virus. In U.S. cases, victims of sexual assault have gone to court to compel their attackers to have HIV tests but have not always been successful. In Canada, there was no specific law regarding that at the time. In the meantime, while ordinary provisions in the *Criminal Code* such as assault were instead used to charge people, there was no unanimity on how to deal with people who transmit HIV. In 1992 in British Columbia, it was decided to use more caution in dealing with HIV-infected people who are having unprotected sex, in order not to scare off people from being tested for the virus. Deciding to treat the matter as a health issue rather than a criminal one, the state would only consider charges in cases of so-called sexual predators.

And this is the viewpoint of the Canadian HIV/AIDS Legal Network today, that while there is no evidence that criminal law can prevent HIV transmission, it is a criminal offence to expose another person to HIV through unprotected sex. The courts have decided that people with HIV should disclose their status or face being charged with a criminal offence such as aggravated sexual assault. They also point out, however, that a better approach than criminal sanctions is education and health prevention.

In summary, the purpose of citing these cases is not to show that people with HIV or AIDS are dangerous, but rather to begin to see that disease is physical and cultural. The latter overlays the former, as characterizations such as "plague," "carriers," "threat" and so on can easily transform a health care issue to a criminal matter.

However, categories of people are not dangerous, not even terrorists. People are at risk from behaviour that might expose them to the virus, just as they are at risk from what terrorists do. However, as these sensational cases demonstrate, it is easy to invoke the power of criminal law to protect us from them as if identifying "them" will solve the problem. In a case in Oregon, a man was convicted of third-degree assault and reckless endangerment for not telling his girlfriend he was HIV positive. In sentencing him to no sex for five years, the judge said, "How do you fashion a sentence for someone who has a fatal illness?… In one sense, he has already received the ultimate punishment." It seems the judge thought of AIDS not as a disease but as a judgement against people who are already guilty, sinners who then assault innocent people. Such a characterization contributes to the demonization of AIDS.

In this section we have looked at some media coverage, much of it in the early days of the "AIDS epidemic" of the 1980s and the resulting societal response. Various themes emerge, such as disease threatens a population from the "outside," it can attain plague-like proportion quickly, it requires quarantining and can become a criminal matter. Furthermore, it has a literal embodiment in the "other." These are the metaphors, the significations or templates, of disease.

In the next section we look at the representation of AIDS in the media and at a more recent disease and see if these themes apply.

Sample Study

1. *The construction of AIDS.* The *Canadian News Index* first published articles on AIDS in 1983, indexed under "diseases." There were ninety-nine articles in 1983 and 112 in 1984. By 1985, AIDS had its own category with 643 articles. With a 474 percent increase in news articles, HIV/AIDS had gone from being considered a relatively rare disease to being seen as a major health threat. By 1987, there were 1,423 entries, the highest number during the 1980s, dropping to 578 in 1990 as interest perhaps faded in the new-found epidemic.

However, interest in the topic did not completely disappear but became broader and more focused. In 1991, new subcategories, such as "AIDS and women" and "AIDS and health care workers" appeared with an increase in stories. The sheer increase in news articles on AIDS shows it was being seen as more of a general health threat, rather than simply a rare disease affecting a small subgroup of society. (Using Google News Archive is an excellent way to easily track the development of articles over time).

The growth in the number of articles on AIDS reveals the extent to which this disease dominated the news. Writing in the *Globe and Mail* in 1993, Stephen Strauss commented on how some diseases are reported on more than others. In the previous two years, six hundred stories had been published on AIDS, six on arthritis, eleven on prostate cancer, twenty-five on diabetes and forty-four on heart diseases. Cancers killed 50,749 Canadians in 1988 but were written about only 219 times, while 1,097 people died of AIDS in 1991 but the disease received more extensive coverage. The Centre for Disease Control said that less than two hundred women died of AIDS between 1990 and 1992, reported in twenty-five articles, but ten thousand women died of breast cancer, an issue written about thirty-nine times.

The reasons put forward for the preponderance of coverage of AIDS are that it is incurable, strikes a prurient chord and is about sex, death and criminality. A casual news search was recently done along the same lines: breast cancer brought 9,130 stories, AIDS 20,406; diabetes got 17,081, and arthritis 5,523. No conclusion is drawn from this, but it is an echo worth investigation.

Interestingly, similar concerns are raised about the coverage of swine flu, that it is covered far more extensively than other more prevalent diseases, such as tuberculosis or dengue.

While AIDS coverage grew through the 1980s, a second pattern that is important to look at is how "being at risk" is portrayed in the news media. Having AIDS is not a crime, but by being linked to deviant groups, it was certainly treated that way in the early 1980s. Initially, it was linked to the "deviant" lifestyle of gay men, prostitutes and drug users, and not until later was it seen as a threat to other people in society. The unfortunate consequence of the early characterization of AIDS is that it created a way of signifying the disease that persisted long after it became patently untrue. The early deviant signification of AIDS kept people from seeing their own risk, which increased the spread of the virus. This is where we break from a literal reading of the news to create a more analytic, emancipatory reading.

In 1983, the first year the *Index* listed AIDS articles, there were ninety-nine citations, some of which were reproduced on microfilm. The list of headlines in Exhibit 5.1 outlines how the risk was portrayed: who was at risk, what causes the disease and how it is spread. The articles speak of AIDS as a mysterious often fatal disease known as the gay plague, where researchers are uncertain of the origin but that it might be transmitted by sexual contact or through blood. At risk were certain groups, but the vector of contamination was confused: semen, saliva, blood, mosquitoes, bad luck? However, because the virus affected the immune system, leaving the body open to opportunistic diseases, homosexuals were being warned to limit their sexual partners and maintain a healthy lifestyle.

Exhibit 5.1 Representing Risk, AIDS in the News, 1983

"Specialist warns of AIDS epidemic," *Winnipeg Free Press*, January 13, 1983: 18

"15 Canadians reported killed by 'gay plague,'" *Winnipeg Free Press*, February 19, 1983: 15

"Man contracted AIDS through 'plain bad luck,'" *Halifax Herald*, July 2, 1983: 43

"AIDS strikes fear, baffles MDs," *Winnipeg Free Press*, July 4, 1983: 15

"AIDS panic unfounded, experts say," *Vancouver Sun*, July 7, 1983: A15

"AIDS fears unfounded," *Globe and Mail*, November 18, 1983: 5

"AIDS cases doubling every 6 months: Official," *Toronto Star*, November 25, 1983: A14

"AIDS cases on increase," *Halifax Herald*, November 25, 1983: 13

Interestingly, some blamed sensational media coverage and poorly informed doctors for panic about AIDS, suggesting that news stories were too much like horror stories. But overwhelmingly, the media emphasized that people who did not fit into the high risk groups could rest assured they would not contract AIDS and that it was only a particular sub-group of a subculture that was at risk. Because of this misrepresentation, recognition that it might be unsafe practices that put a person at risk was overshadowed by the identification of unsafe people. Researchers described it as one of the most serious health threats in the history of modern medicine but also stressed that the general public had little to fear. This way of signifying the disease would make the symbolic threat greater than the physical.

In the early news articles, AIDS was characterized as a mysterious disease whose cause was inexplicable and baffling for experts, sometimes caught through plain bad luck. Headlines used phrases like "terror," "killer disease," "deadly" and "mysterious illness." Because of the representation of AIDS as caused by unsafe people, a Gallup poll on AIDS awareness reported that while 83 percent of respondents were aware of AIDS, 59 percent knew their chances of getting it were quite small, but some still felt it could be contracted through toilet seats.

Meanwhile, medical experts testified that for the average Canadian, the risk of contracting AIDS from transfusions or blood products was almost zero. The medical director of the B.C. Red Cross Blood Transfusion Service said warnings would not be put on U.S. blood products used by hemophiliacs because it would be insulting to tell hematologists how to use blood products.

By 1984, researchers feared that hundreds of thousands of people could be carrying the virus responsible for AIDS and that AIDS was more extensive than previously thought. While articles were still being published saying that the disease struck promiscuous homosexuals, the Atlanta Centre for Disease Control said that AIDS may be slowly spreading to other sectors of the population. A 1984 *Globe and Mail* article pointed out that AIDS could be spread through conventional sex but that the immune system of gays was different.

As late as 1985, researchers were discussing the concepts of the vulnerable anus and fragile urethra versus the rugged vagina, in a misinformed attempt to explain why AIDS could be transmitted through anal sex but not (supposedly) through vaginal intercourse.

The consequence of associating AIDS with identity rather than behaviour is illustrated by an article published in 1984 that reported that Manitoba's first confirmed case of AIDS was not initially recognized because the victim did not fit into any of the high-risk categories. Through this period, newspaper reports lacked consensus. Some discounted the easy "identity equals disease" link for Haitians, for example, and pointed to the startling conclusion that heterosexuals could not only contract but also spread AIDS. Other articles reaffirmed the old homosexual-AIDS connection. It appeared that the concept of high-risk groups versus the general community would not pass away easily. Several years later, articles were still being printed about Patient Zero, which reinforced the conception that AIDS was spread by sociopathic marginals.

Overall, AIDS is signified in a very particular way in these articles, associated especially with so-called high-risk groups. Although the conspiratorial causes proposed for AIDS have been many and unusual — a plague from King Tut's tomb, a result of genetic mutations caused by mixed marriages, a plot by the U.S. government to undermine the former Soviet Union or destroy American ethnic minorities — the more usual reporting around AIDS is far more mundane. While the conspiracy theories might make for further investigation, first we turn briefly to a more current example.

2. *The construction of swine flu.* In this section we construct a timeline of the spread of a viral disease, the swine flu epidemic of 2009. It is fairly straightforward and factual. At the end of March and into the first week of April, an increase in the number of flu cases was noticed in Veracruz, Mexico, and reported to the World Health Organization and the U.S. Centre for Disease Control. However, the media didn't pick up the story until the week of April 20. On April 24, Canada's Public Health Agency confirmed that it is swine flu (H1N1), and Mexico closed schools, libraries and museums. On April 27, with about six cases in Canada, Canadians were advised to limit travel to Mexico, and the World Health Organization raised the worldwide pandemic alert level to Phase 4.

By April 28, the Centre for Disease Control reported additional international cases of swine influenza, characterized by person-to-person spread of a virus able to cause community-level outbreaks. Mexico closed swimming pools and pool halls, and the WHO said that the 1918 Spanish flu pandemic started out mild but killed more than 20 million people. Online traffic jumped as people looked for information. Facebook posted maps of the geography of discussion and a trendline that showed discussion starting April 23. On

April 29, *Wired* carried a story about how online searches had increased in Mexico for flu symptoms a week earlier than media coverage began.

On April 29, a *New York Times* report on the WHO said the spread of H1N1 had reached Phase 5, meaning there had been sustained human-to-human transmission in at least two countries, Mexico and the U.S., and that there were strong signals that a worldwide outbreak was about to occur. This was one of the top five stories read in the *Times* between April 29 and May 5. The WHO said that a pandemic was imminent and that all of humanity had to join in an urgent battle against the infection. The day began with nineteen cases in Canada, rising to thirty-four by the end of the day, with 185 cases internationally.

The WHO began to refer to the flu as influenza A H1N1 because the organization wanted to make it clear that there was no danger posed by pigs. Nonetheless, Egypt ordered all pigs to be slaughtered even though there were no cases of the virus in the country. On May 1, officials in Hong Kong cordoned off the Metropark hotel after it was discovered that a Mexican staying there had contracted swine flu. About 274 guests and staff were quarantined as a result, even though none tested positive.

By May 4 there were a thousand cases worldwide, 590 in Mexico alone, where twenty-two people had died. On May 5, health officials said that the viral disease was not going to be as bad as SARS in 2003, when it killed forty-four people in the Toronto area. On May 6, the WHO reported that H1N1 was confirmed by laboratory tests in 1,516 patients in twenty-two countries. Mexico reported 942 cases, including twenty-nine deaths, while the U.S. had 403 cases and two deaths, and Canada had 165 cases. On May 7, the WHO said that one-third of the world's population would be infected if the flu became a full pandemic, but also that it was too soon to predict how many would die. The number of confirmed cases was 2,099, with forty-two of forty-four deaths in Mexico.

In an interesting editorial in the *National Post*, an inside story from the WHO briefing commented on how media were cautioned not to exaggerate the projected incidence of the disease. However, as was noted, the following headlines appeared in various venues:

Exhibit 5.2 Headlines

"2 Billion infected? WHO stokes swine flu fear," ABC
"WHO says up to 2B people might get swine flu," Associated Press
"Third of world's population could get swine flu: expert," *Daily Mail*
"Swine flu cases widen reach with 'epidemic curve,'" *Bloomberg*
"Governments prepare for possible flu pandemic," *Voice of America*
"H1N1 flu outbreak may hit 1/3rd of world's population," *Times of India*

Overall, in this recapitulation of swine flu stories the following themes emerge: 1) a disease from outside, 2) which spreads quickly and insidiously, 3) which requires containment and 4) which embodies the "other." There is nothing necessarily wrong with this representation; it is a template for the mediated character of the disease, it is its metaphors. About the only thing missing between the characterization of AIDS and that of H1N1 is the distortions of sexual representation. In the next section we look more closely at some of the mechanics of how mis/representation is done, in both the cases of AIDS and H1NI.

Analyzing the News

In the previous section we looked at a dominant theme in AIDS coverage: the portrayal of a plague-like disease spread by sexual predators to an innocent public. In this section, looking at larger patterns in AIDS reporting, the first striking thing is the simple enormity and intensity of coverage. AIDS has been the subject of extensive reporting in the press, especially since being seen as a disease that threatens the general population.

It is important to recognize this early mis/representation of AIDS, not only because marginal groups were stigmatized through their association with AIDS, but the signification made people who did not identify themselves as members of those groups less likely to see themselves at risk, more likely to engage in unsafe practices and more likely to contract the disease. AIDS has been confused by the metaphors used, but understanding AIDS as a disease requires seeing what the metaphor elides. Though the label has changed, many still saw it as the gay plague, which brings us to the Krever Inquiry.

1. *The Krever Inquiry.* The Commission of Inquiry on the Blood System in Canada began on November 22, 1993. It was named after its chair, a court of appeals judge who had previously conducted an inquiry on the confidentiality of health records in Ontario in 1978–80 and had also served on the Royal Society of Canada study on AIDS in Canada in 1987–88. The inquiry's budget was set at $2.5 million and its mandate was to inquire into how the problems with the blood supply arose and how to reform the system.

More than one million Canadians received transfusions between 1978 and 1985, and, of these, more than one thousand hemophiliacs and blood-transfusion recipients were infected with HIV before the mandatory testing and heat-treatment of blood was begun by the Red Cross in 1985. Amidst allegations that Red Cross officials knew of the contaminated blood and yet refused to release safer products, an inquiry was timely and necessary.

In testimony at the inquiry, people recounted inadequate or incomplete advice from physicians and the common assumption that only certain people got AIDS. For example, in testimony in Toronto, a hemophiliac said that when he asked his doctor in 1983–84 about AIDS, he was told he didn't have anything to worry about. At that same day's hearings a woman testified, "I thought AIDS was something going around and killing gay men. I never thought it could be in the blood. It never hit me." Witnesses said doctors and nurses had failed to inform them about safer-sex practices, told them their partners were at no risk of contracting HIV, refused them treatment, left their meals outside hospital room doors but said HIV was no worse than the common cold or chicken pox.

In testimony at the inquiry, the chief medical officer for the city of Toronto from 1981 to 1988 made the point that it was impossible to apply the hindsight of 1994 to events of 1983. However, a report from the Centre for Disease Control in Atlanta on July 16, 1982, had said that the occurrence of AIDS among the three hemophiliac cases suggested the possible transmission of an agent through blood products. So though judging by hindsight might be unfair, clear warning signs were being ignored at the time. Although that chief medical officer was among the first to see the possible risk to hemophiliacs from contaminated blood, he had formed a committee that did not see contact-tracing of gay and bisexual men as important. Anonymous testing is now preferred to contact-tracing, because the latter discourages people from being tested, but at the time there was simply no interest in tracking down people to inform them that they might be at risk.

Although the Krever Inquiry's mandate was to look into how blood-transfusion recipients contracted HIV, sexual orientation still arose as an issue. By characterizing transfusion recipients as innocent victims, a line was drawn differentiating them from others who had contracted HIV, the implication being that the others had done so because of their lifestyle, by choice.

Homophobia is an important issue, because it created an image of what type of person was at risk of contracting the disease and what type wasn't. In hearings in Toronto, Vancouver, Edmonton, Regina and Winnipeg, witnesses accused government officials of joking about reopening leper colonies for gay AIDS sufferers and of denying funding to gay groups and hindering AIDS education.

In hearings in Halifax, witnesses testified how the gay community had been ignored when AIDS first appeared and how health authorities were only interested in the threat to the general public. The founder of the Nova Scotia Persons with AIDS Coalition testified that the former administrator of community health services had told him that "likely all the people at risk of contracting the AIDS virus were infected and would soon die, so there was no urgency to have a public health campaign," that the provincial epidemiologist felt that no more than twenty Nova Scotians would be affected by AIDS and that a government official was rumoured to want to quarantine people with AIDS on an island in Halifax Harbour. Gaetan Dugas, thought to be the first AIDS sufferer in North America, lived in Dartmouth between 1979 and

1983 but no one knew if he had the disease. He was subsequently dubbed Patient Zero.

The inquiry also heard how Red Cross officials felt it wasn't their job to warn hemophiliacs of contamination in blood products, and that national guidelines that allowed contaminated blood products to be sent to hospitals to be used by hemophiliacs were followed in 1985, while safe products were withheld. In commenting on his lack of action, the provincial epidemiologist in Nova Scotia from 1980 to 1988 said, "We were trying to find out more information about how the disease was spread. It appeared to be associated primarily with a certain type of lifestyle, mainly homosexuals." While he said that in 1984 he had "changed his mind that 'AIDS was something that was over there and not coming to Nova Scotia,'" the community health services administrator said "that he wasn't worried AIDS would soon be sweeping Nova Scotia. He believed only five percent of the population was homosexual and the group of intravenous drug users was relatively small." In testimony in New Brunswick, the medical director of the provincial Red Cross said he had ignored a national directive to contact and warn the gay community and that blood donated by men who appeared and acted gay was discarded by nurses. In commenting, he said their action was entirely correct, moral, ethical, rational and sensible. In testimony after testimony, the Krever Inquiry heard how officials withheld safe blood products and knowingly distributed contaminated blood. The national organization was said to be inflexible, to have disregarded suggestions from provincial officials whom they accused of overstepping their authority and to have saved heat-treated products for "virgin" hemophiliacs.

The Krever Inquiry highlighted the existence of a double standard: a special category of "innocent" victims, who deserved an answer as to why they got infected, unlike gays, who were thought to have contracted AIDS through deviant sex. However, what is evident in the inquiry is that many people, including heterosexuals, contracted AIDS through sex. Moreover, many people contracted HIV through lack of accurate information and stereotyping on the part of authorities, who felt that AIDS was a gay disease. If the attitude toward the gay community was "It'll get rid of them, gays, and the intravenous [drug] users," the alarm bells were not raised until it was too late. It is clear that institutionalized homophobia reinforced through the media which assisted in spreading the disease.

At the beginning of 1993, the Atlanta Centres for Disease Control and Prevention revised the definition of acquired immune deficiency syndrome to include tuberculosis of the lungs, recurring pneumonia and invasive cervical cancer. These, along with twenty-three other conditions and a new laboratory test for the immune system, define AIDS. One consequence of the redefinition of the disease was increased recognition of how it affected women;

the definition had originally been based on how it affected gay men. AIDS was one of the three main causes of death for women between fifteen and forty-four in the U.S. And even though the media still reported cases where men contract HIV from prostitutes, studies indicated women were twelve to seventeen times more likely to have contracted the disease from a man than the reverse, and 80 percent of cases involved women of childbearing age. By 1993, heterosexual sex accounted for 75 percent of AIDS infection cases worldwide and was estimated by the World Health Organization to account for 90 percent of new cases.

2. *Enter H1N1*. In this section we construct a timeline of the spread of a viral panic, the mediated swine flu epidemic of 2009. It illustrates how a disease is socially constructed and also introduces some complexity in the analysis.

Inevitably, in the coverage of swine flu, concerns arose that the media was exaggerating or panicking the issue. Some commentators attributed most of the panic to the need to get ratings, calling it flu-coverage fever and a web-born virus. There were hundreds and sometimes thousands of articles cited in Google News on many topics every day. Other writers commented on the contradictory advice on whether or not to eat pork, if the outbreak could be a form of germ warfare and how spammers were cashing in on people's fears by sending millions of e-mails peddling counterfeit drugs as remedies.

The media monitoring firm Influence Communication said the news coverage of the swine flu outbreak was feeding a collective hysteria: the 2005 avian flu outbreak had 0.4 per cent of media coverage in Canada while the swine flu outbreak was at 4 percent of news content in the country, with coverage jumping 930 percent since it erupted on April 23. Between April 27 to May 4, the coverage of swine flu was 7 percent of front-page news in Canada, 8 percent in the U.S., and 14 percent in China. From May 3 to May 10, swine flu appeared as 4 percent of all front-page news stories in Mexico, 2 percent in the U.S., and less than 1 percent in Canada, according to geographicalmedia.com.

On April 28, *Hitwise* reported that the search term "swine flu" ranked number 133 among the more than 1.5 million unique search terms in the week ending on April 25. Another way of looking at it was that more than 1 in every 8,000 U.S. Internet searches that week was for swine flu.

On April 28, Frank Furedi, a sociologist at Kent University, wrote in *spiked.online* that "what we are faced with is a health crisis that has been transformed into a moral drama." He went on to outline how current outbreaks of the flu are linked to historical catastrophes, global catastrophes are characterized as inevitable, fears are constructed about the "weaponisation" of disease, and conspiracy theories arise. He said that the swine flu outbreak has infected our imaginations, giving shape and tangibility to our anxieties about everyday life.

Michael Fumento, writing in *Forbes.com* on May 1 on the "price of a porcine panic," reminded us how in 1976 the projection was that the flu epidemic would kill one million people, but didn't. The annual flu in America infects up to 20 percent of the population and kills about 36,000, while about half a million people are killed worldwide by the flu. In comparison, the 2003 SARS epidemic caused 8,096 cases and killed 774 people. The danger posed by the swine flu was called a "hysteria outbreak," given the relatively small number of cases.

On May 5, it was reported that at Paris airports baggage handlers refused to offload bags that came from Spain or Mexico. In the U.S., anti-immigrant activists were advising people to stay away from Mexicans to prevent swine flu; Japan stiffened entry requirements for Mexican visitors; and in Shanghai, seventy-one Mexican nationals were quarantined in a hotel. Singapore quarantined all passengers from Mexico, requiring them to stay in isolation for seven days, and several hundred guests were quarantined at the Metropark hotel in Hong Kong. Mexico continued to shoulder the symbolic weight of the disease.

By May 6, the media could hardly be said to be exaggerating. However, it was not uncommon to see articles that said that the disease was declining and milder than expected, which was then followed by a warning to stay on alert and not be complacent. The news is not that we are safe or that we are in danger, but rather both.

3. *Reading headlines*. This is a more specific way to construct a timeline of the spread of a viral panic. The analysis relies on the assumption that headlines are constructed from an understanding of the readers and are designed to provide a balance of context and novelty to make the news un/familiar at the same time as minimizing the work readers are required to do. Headlines negotiate the news for readers' understanding the context of events being followed. In this reading of headlines we see a gamut of emotions: shock, fear and even surprise.

The time period selected is approximately four weeks, between April 21 to May 19. Hundreds of articles found under a search for "swine flu" were collected from the *National Post*, supplemented by over two hundred from the *Globe and Mail*. A selection of headlines are reproduced in Exhibit 5.3.

Exhibit 5.3 Headline Coverage, *National Post*

April 24, "WHO confirms 60 dead, 800 sick with flu-like illness"
April 25, "Mexico, US scramble to contain swine flu"
April 26, "Flu scare empties Mexican streets, churches, bars"
April 27, "Flu fears could throw economic recovery off course"; "Virus not the

deadly pandemic first feared, Canadian experts say"; "Obama: Swine flu 'no cause for alarm'"; "Canadian officials brace for more swine flu illnesses"

April 28, "What the #!%*? is the deal with swine flu?"; "Pandemic fears may complicate stock markets, tourism sector"; "WHO raises alert level as virus risks going worldwide"; "Swine flu pandemic not inevitable: WHO"

April 29, "Mexico pandemic bunk"; "Don't call it a pandemic"; "Early hyper-alarm misplaced"; "Prepare for pandemic, WHO warns countries"; "US reports first swine flu death"; "Swine flu isn't so scary"

April 30, "Mexico winds down to slow spread of flu"; "Doubt cast on Mexican flu toll"

May 1, "257 People infected worldwide"

May 2, "21st century world better prepared for pandemic: experts"; "Hysteria seems to be spreading faster than swine flu itself"

May 3, "Flu cases rising in Canada, Alberta pigs infected"

May 4, "WHO to declare full flu pandemic"; "Global flu cases surge past 1,000"; "Swine flu: Blame ducks and people, not pigs"; "Snowmobile avalanche deaths: Deadlier than swine flu, and..."

May 5, "Afghanistan quarantines its pig. That's right, the only hog in..."; "Mexicans return home as flu fears ease"; "Pork bans unjustified, illegal: Mexico"; "Mexican banned after using hysteria over swine flu to intimi-date..."

May 6, "Let's avoid a porcine panic"

May 7, "Mexico gets back to normal, China eases flu quarantine"; "Swine flu: People, you're not panicking enough!"

May 8, "WHO's credibility questioned as pandemic fears fade"; "WHO changes tune, now says pork safe to eat"

May 10, "Flu tally climbs in Canada, worldwide"

May 11, "Flu death tally continues to climb"; "Swine flu shows no sign of major spread outside North America, WHO..."

May 12, "Flu could still mutate, says World Health Organization"

May 13, "WHO confirms flu spreads to Cuba, Finland, Thailand"; "No need to kill Alberta pig herd with swine flu: officials"

May 14, "H1N1 flu cases, death toll rises worldwide"

May 18, "Canada lifts flu-based travel limits for Mexico"

May 19, "Don't panic, prepare"

The initial concern over swine flu began in the media around April 20, plus or minus a couple of days. While initially there was a lot of "panic" over the spread of the disease, by April 28, more or less, the emotion had faded to doubt and perhaps even surprise over the slow rate of the spread of infection.

The mis/representation over AIDS, which was largely misconstrued over the vector of the disease, was here seemingly misconstrued more in terms of the magnitude of infection. The first was a mis/representation of kind, while the latter was a mis/representation of degree. However, the fear of epidemic, the concern over the "other" and the need for quarantine were present in both: H1N1 was a disease from Mexico that afflicted the unwary, it had the potential to kill millions of people and authorities warned of a pending pandemic. To analyze the spread of the signification of a disease and to see how the disease is represented, however, gives us more control in an uncertain world.

Articles that located the source of infection on a pig farm in Mexico and the original first child victim, and the first case on a pig farm in Alberta, which was infected by a worker travelling from Mexico, literally embodied the disease. We could conduct a similar analysis for SARS perhaps, or Ebola or bird flu and see how discourses mutate as a disease progresses. SARS had a patient zero, as did AIDS and H1N1. Initial fears of contagion are replaced by reassurances of containment, while disease has superceded nuclear annihilation as the fear of how the world will end.

However, as seen from the headlines, there is a lot of equivocation over what the epidemic means. The confusion becomes exaggerated in the extreme in the form of doubts over whether to believe any of the coverage, which leads us to a brief comment on conspiracy theories.

4. *Conspiracy theories*. A blog in the *New York Times* commented on the difficulty of communicating "risk," that is the potential that something might happen even if it doesn't. The blogger commented on how the media was looking for expert advice on media exaggeration. The doubt and surprise over the lack of a real pandemic got to the point that media stories started to appear about how the swine flu was a conspiracy and not in fact an actual disease. The stories themselves were referred to as viral. In Mexico the explanations ranged from a conspiracy by the Mexican president in order to get votes, to a ploy by the CIA to plant a weapons-grade virus in Mexico City to test its effectiveness, generate profits for multinational pharmaceutical companies and ruin Mexico's economy so that the U.S. could bail it out but demand the privatization of the oil industry. One website identified the following top ten conspiracy theories, presented in order of importance and likelihood:

Exhibit 5.4 Conspiracy Theories
1. Drug manufacturers facing layoffs and red ink are behind the plot
2. TV networks facing low ratings and revenues spread the virus
3. Anti-immigration forces resisting legalization of aliens are behind it
4. PETA launched the outbreak, along with mad cow and bird flu
5. Al Qaeda attacked Mexico so its workers would spread the plague

6. Surgical mask producers saw a chance to sell off surplus stock
7. Mexican drug cartels trying to overthrow the Mexican army
8. Labor unions trying to mitigate the lower prices of foreign workers
9. Anti-Catholic forces seeking to weaken the Mexican Catholic church
10. Doctors facing a recession boost patient load for treatable disease

These conspiracy theories are, in a sense, corrupted versions of social constructionist theories, trying to debunk the veracity of the epidemic and introduce the real reasons to account for what has happened. They are spoofs, of course, but how much do they stray from more legitimate explanations? The difference is that social constructionist theories are framed from above, while conspiracy theories are framed below. Both rely on the idea that truth is constructed and try to find meaning in and behind the headlines.

Both legitimate and conspiracy explanations also trade on the analysis of power. While constructionists look at the social representation of a disease in order to unveil the influence of authorities, conspiracy theorists want to re/locate power as an issue in the medical discourse that elides it. When it was suggested in Haiti that AIDS was a weapon of western domination, there was an attempt to see power in an otherwise benign medical equation. Similarly, the WHO can track the progress of the spread of H1N1, but what is missing from this equation is the location of transnational farming operations in poorer countries with weak environmental legislation, coupled with the international movement of people from rich countries on business and travel.

Summary

A shift in social thinking occurred over AIDS in a fairly short period of time. In slightly more than a decade, society progressed beyond thinking that AIDS was just a gay or otherwise marginal disease to see how it affected (sexual) bodies not (social) identities. However, the early stereotyping created a long-lasting stigma, and many people contracted HIV because they felt and were treated as if they were not at risk, as documented by the Krever Inquiry. This stigma continues today through the shame and embarrassment associated with HIV testing and education. The disease itself does not care about a person's identity or sexual orientation. Although it is now known to be spread through high-risk behaviours rather than by high-risk people, it is the sad example of a disease that has been contracted in a climate of ignorance created by distorted social messages. The way the disease was signified contributed to its spread, and this misinformation was spread through the media.

In our second example, H1N1 or swine flu, we also see how the disease is as much constructed through the media as it exists as a disease. There are various similarities in the media coverage of the two: 1) a disease from outside,

2) which spreads quickly and insidiously, 3) which requires containment and 4) which embodies the "other."

As well, after the initial fear and shock comes surprise and doubt over the severity of the disease. The key difference between the two diseases is that one is sexualized and the other is racialized; however, both are discourses of power. The media that challenges this power is conspiracy theories, but that is another story.

6

The Halifax Race Riot
Extralocality and Racism in the News

Ethnocentrism means seeing the world only from one's own ethnic or cultural point of view, thinking that other people should share that point of view and judging them by one's own cultural standards. Ethnocentrism can result in prejudice and discrimination, and when displayed in the media can reinforce a slanted view of the world.

This chapter takes up the issue of ethnic sensitivity in the portrayal of "race relations" in the news. Joy Mannette recounts three cases and discusses how race and ethnic issues are portrayed in the news in ways that reinforce ethnic bias and display a lack of ethnic sensitivity. Although the examples used are from Nova Scotia, the analysis can be applied to events in other parts of Canada, such as Oka, Davis Inlet or Caledonia, or to other countries as well, such as the L.A. riot, the Crown Heights riot, conflict in Lebanon or the Gaza Strip, the Gulf War, the restoration of democracy in Haiti or the invasion of Panama. Ethnic bias is not always easy to see in news coverage, but that is part of the problem.

In Reading the News, specific examples are reproduced to show how lack of ethnic sensitivity and sometimes overt ethnocentrism play a part in the discussion of race and ethnic issues in the press. The main topic discussed here is the so-called 1991 Halifax race riot, with articles drawn largely from local papers. However, the underlying theme is that these messages are unaffected by distance and can be reproduced miles from the event.

The example chosen for more extended analysis in the Sample Study is a riot that took place in Montreal in 2008 after police shot a youth during an incident in a park. It is alleged that the youth was a victim of racism. The analytic issue of extralocality is used to describe how distance is inconsequential in modern society, as we receive news of events far from where they occur.

In Analyzing the News, this process of disseminating news and reproducing particular ethnic relations is examined through the allied concept of diffusion. Given that much of what we know of the world comes through the media, we need to question how the news interprets the world in such a way that it comes to stand in for direct experience.

The theme explored in this chapter is extralocality, and the emotions are panic and hatred. Studies I have found useful for thinking about race and riots are Ash (2003), Chiricos and Escholz (2002), Dixon (2008), Entman (1994), Escholz (2002) and Myers (2000).

Joy Mannette's Talk

There is a Mi'kmaq word, *"napite'lsit,"* that offers a nice orientation to some of the things that I want to talk about in relation to the way in which race and ethnic issues get taken up and treated in the media. If I were proceeding in a typical Mi'kmaq fashion, I wouldn't tell you what it translates into in English, I would just leave you with this whole metaphoric presentation and let you figure it out for yourself.

The treatment of race and ethnic issues in media coverage involves intolerable carelessness, and I'll elaborate how the politics of race gets treated in three particular race and ethnic incidents within the Nova Scotia context. The first was in the fall of 1968 in Halifax. We had a moral panic on the issue of black power centred around the October 1968 first human rights conference that was held there, and then in November and early December of 1968 in the formation of the Black United Front of Nova Scotia.

The second topic is a bit more contemporary, and that has to do with a Weymouth Falls case. On June 8, 1985, a black man who lived in Weymouth Falls, Digby County, Graham Jarvis, sometimes known as Graham Cromwell, was shot and died as a result of a gunshot wound. The perpetrator of the shooting was accused of manslaughter and was acquitted.

The third topic is the recent Mi'kmaq treaty trials here in Nova Scotia, beginning with the Mi'kmaq treaty moose harvest in the fall of 1988 and the ensuing trial process in Sydney, which focused on the thorny issue of whether provisions under the 1752 treaty between the Crown and the Mi'kmaq nation are sustained today. Those are the incidents I'll talk about in terms of the politics of the special status of race.

If we look back at 1968, what we see is the creation of a moral panic in Halifax. We see a very deliberately orchestrated media campaign that transformed a series of relatively innocuous events within the black community into something close to insurrection. The media coverage focused on the threat attendant to the visit to Halifax of Stokely Carmichael. The *Chronicle-Herald* had an interview with him at the airport when he was leaving but no coverage of what ensued while he was here.

It's interesting to find the kind of stories that the *Chronicle-Herald* pulled from the wire during the fall of 1968 as it began to shape its sense of the politics within the local black community. One of the stories it used was a benchmark speech for people who look at the way in which the media treats race relations. Enid Powell, speaking in London, England, in the spring of

1968, prophesied that rivers of blood would run in the streets of Britain if black migration was to continue. That story showed up in the *Herald's* coverage at the same time that the Black Panthers were in Halifax. That's the kind of wire service selection going on at the time.

The result was a construction of possible insurrection by the black Nova Scotia community which was simply not supported by the events going on within that community at the time. And the October 1968 human rights conference was a liberal action, yet it too was seen as radical activity.

If we look at the question of unusual care being taken in relation to coverage of race issues, we certainly couldn't apply that to the Weymouth Falls case. Indeed, the dominant media in Nova Scotia dealt with that issue by effectively silencing it. It was the tabloid format of the *Daily News*, which covered the Weymouth Falls case through January of 1986; and the *Toronto Star* broke the case on December 27, 1985, with very sustained coverage. Excessive care was taken in how that particular medium sought to examine the shooting of this black man and the attendant circumstances around it.

If we look at the question of carelessness, however, we can see that widely represented in all media coverage of the Weymouth Falls case, for example, in confusion over people's names. It seemed very difficult for the media to understand that someone might be known popularly within a community in a way that's not reflected on their birth certificate; after all, the only kind of people who go by aliases are criminals. Also, persistent problems surrounded the identification of various spokespersons who were agitating within the black community for a re-examination into Graham Jarvis's death.

In the more recent case of the Mi'kmaq treaty trials, reporters were assigned to cover situations about which they knew very little. It was an on-the-job learning experience. Coverage of the Mi'kmaq treaty trials would have been much more prominently displayed had they taken place in Halifax, because in Sydney, a subregional bias entered into media coverage. The Halifax-based media, in accessing legitimate spokespersons for the Mi'kmaq community, oriented to the Confederacy of Mainland Micmacs, located at Schubenacadie [Truro]. Given that the Union of Nova Scotia Indians, which was pivotal in organizing the treaty trial initiative, is located in Sydney, this represents a carelessness in media attention to race issues.

What can we say about the characterization of race that emerged from these three incidents? There were various strategies designed to deflect attention from the issues the communities in question wanted to pursue and to refocus attention on issues that lent themselves to a more reformist approach.

In the first instance, if you peruse the dominant media coverage, we were given an understanding of race borrowed from the American context. The characterization of race relations that we received was violent, a threat to the established order and of organizational instability within the minority organizations. That, I think, has been a persistent theme in the coverage of race and ethnic issues from the mid-1960s. We don't have a lot of reference within the Nova Scotia context to the racial politics of central Canada; instead we have remained stuck in this rut of referencing the American context. How that got played out in the sixties was equating black politics in Nova Scotia with what was going on in the U.S.

By the 1980s, there is a different effect taking place which revolves around the myth of black progress, which has been widely disseminated in the media. As a result, in the Canadian context it is assumed that the kind of problems that were associated with black communities in the 1960s no longer existed in the 1980s, that affirmative action initiatives had corrected those problems. That certainly is the tone that underpins the situation of the 1985 Weymouth Falls case.

Now, it becomes difficult to talk about the overall understanding of race that comes out of the Mi'kmaq treaty trials because we have all had our racial consciousness raised as a result of the events at Kahnawake and Akwesasne in 1991. It's often tempting to look at the Mi'kmaq treaty moose harvest in 1988–89 and the ensuing trials in light of those events, but that would be fallacious. The Mi'kmaq treaty trials were a revelation within the Nova Scotia context, and they put the whole issue of aboriginal rights quite firmly on the agenda. Moreover, the Mi'kmaq treaty trials came on the heels of the Marshall inquiry, which also put the issue of race on the public agenda even though it was based on an understanding of race as biogenetic, not culture or power.

So when we try to understand what it is that we learn about racism and race issues from media coverage, we must also understand that we are learning through the media about situations we never encounter in our daily lives. We vicariously interact in a symbolic way through media coverage with ethnic communities that we know nothing about. We come to understand them as violent, we understand that their lives are messy and ill organized, and that they are increasingly making extravagant demands on the social order that is unprepared to deal with those demands.

The metaphor *"napite'lsit"* translates into English as: When you look at a situation or a person and you look at it with ill intentions in your mind, you attribute to that situation or that person the same ill intentions that you direct towards it."

Reading the News

Joy Mannette says the media does not handle race relations very well but works in such a way as to reinforce ethnic prejudices. This can happen because when we get information about the world from what we read and watch in the media, we have very little control over these symbolic representations.

This process of relying on externally produced, mediated information is called "extralocality," and the spread of information at a distance is sometimes called "diffusion."

On July 19, 1991, the front-page banner headline of the afternoon edition of a Nova Scotia provincial paper read: "Race riot rocks downtown." The article said a local minister, a black community leader, pleaded with rioters and police to stay calm. Officials were quoted as saying that the violence was not surprising, and representatives of the black community said they would be planning boycotts and marches to combat racism and discrimination. The shocked headline, therefore, indicated deeper underlying problems.

As can be seen in Article 6.1, the riot at the centre of the controversy concerned a group of blacks who had been turned away from a bar. They then went through downtown streets assaulting white bystanders, vandalizing storefronts and getting involved in a confrontation with the police. The incident was later explained as sparked by door policies at a bar that allegedly discriminated against blacks, but in this article it is said to have originated when a group of whites had attacked a black man.

Article 6.1 "15 hurt in early morning rampage"

Racial tensions in Halifax's nightclub district burst into violence early yesterday morning when a group made up mostly of blacks rioted in the downtown core, assaulting bystanders, fighting with police and smashing windows.

Police said yesterday 15 people were injured and eight (four blacks and four whites) were arrested. Four people have been charged so far. Six people were treated and released from hospital. As many as 150 people may have been involved before the incident ended around 5 a.m.... [The police chief] said yesterday about 35 police, including two car-loads of Dartmouth officers, responded in full riot gear, using nightsticks to quell the riot. Here is a breakdown of the events based on accounts of witnesses and police officials:

On Wednesday night a black man was attacked by a group of whites in Rosa's Cantina on Argyle Street... [the owner] saw a group of about 50 black men coming toward them... a group in the rear began randomly assaulting whites... Police then confronted the crowd for about an hour near the Derby tavern... still in riot gear... The group moved to Uniacke and Gottingen Streets where it remained for about an hour, vandalizing the area until police and community leaders successfully intervened. Businesses had plate glass windows smashed and the "Charlie Zone" police sub office lost a window when a white youth threw a trash can through it. At a news conference yesterday [the police chief] acknowledged the riot was racially motivated. (*Daily News*, July 20, 1991: 4, by Charlene Sadler)

The news media very quickly labelled the rioting on the streets as racial tension. It involved a violent confrontation between blacks and whites, the alleged perpetrators were black, the police say the incident was racially motivated, and (to a local reader) they came from the "black area" of town. While perhaps there is no obvious reason to conclude that racial tension was the best explanation for events, the article and successive media coverage forcefully constructed this interpretation as the best one, particularly through the use of racial references and shocking words such as "rampage."

An editorial the following day used emotionally charged words such as "war zone...chaos...rampage...devastation...destruction...racial tensions... swarmed...rebellion...disorder...outrage...and malaise." It is arguable whether similar actions by whites would be labelled in the same way. Among the sources used in the editorial were the director of the Black United Front and a local minister in the black community. This introduced a confusing element to the story: was the event motivated by (racial) discrimination (with blacks as victims); was it a (racially motivated) attack (with blacks as perpetrators); or was it simply a series of violent criminal acts? The editorial provided for ambiguity in that the event was not portrayed as merely a race riot, but neither were the racial tensions underlying it discounted.

Coverage of the violence was extensive. There were innumerable front-page stories and editorials in the provincial *Halifax Herald* and *Daily News* on the riot, its causes, subsequent events and solutions. The riot, the anti-racism march, the vow to crack down on racism by the mayor and the inquiry into police relations all received intensive coverage. Many of the articles, like Article 6.1, provided a concise version of the conflict.

A reader can get much of the picture of what happened by reading any one of these articles. Smaller articles, such as Article 6.2, presented parts of what happened but depended on other articles "intratextually" to make sense, but because media coverage was prominent and extensive that was unlikely to pose a problem.

Article 6.2 "Man 'couldn't talk to them'"

Esmain Ahmadvand, 25, was walking home... [at] 2 a.m.... he was suddenly caught in the middle of a group of 40 to 50 black males who were punching everybody who got in their way. Ahmadvand... who immigrated from Iran 15 months ago to escape the turmoil there, suffered a broken nose in the beating. He said he didn't understand why he was the victim of a seemingly random attack. (*Daily News*, July 20, 1991: 5, by staff)

A sense of the capriciousness of the violence was conveyed by this article describing one small incident in the riot. A man walking home from work (doing nothing out of the ordinary) was suddenly surrounded by a crowd of black men beating people at random (with no provocation) who attacked him even though he hadn't done anything (which was totally unfair) and they wouldn't listen to reason (which makes it even worse). The article, short as it is, anchored the categories of "vicious attackers" and "innocent victim." It is an account that can be read both intralocally, in the context of other accounts of the incident, and extralocally, as an instance of what happens in such situations (i.e., riot, random). Reading an article about an event (which makes no sense) in order to create sense (of it as an event) is tacitly located in the organizational practices of reading.

Article 6.1, and to a lesser extent Article 6.2, were offered as a typical "riot account." Headlines such as "Blacks say bars at centre of riot, Halifax police beef up patrols" were typical. However, there were also stories of how police officers taunted the mob and that the group were on their way home when confronted by the police. This introduced a more troublesome interpretation, which constructed an alternate version of the events. The subversive theme of police provocation disrupted the race riot theme and eventually became an overarching criticism of the ethnic makeup of police personnel.

A report in the national news filed from Halifax included what had become the official version of events and of the racism that sparked it, and also the concern that the police had exacerbated the situation. However a story two days later, filed from Halifax by the same reporter, explained the problem as stemming from a racial confrontation at a local high school two years earlier. The charge of police provocation was relegated to the last paragraph and the idea was attributed to blacks who turned out for a weekend community meeting.

The specific theme of police provocation gradually faded from view as days passed, but was replaced with the more general idea that more minority representation was needed on the police force, a criticism some tried to stymie by saying too few blacks apply in the first place. Thus, competing interpretations of the riot could be read in the news.

The *Toronto Star* carried the story on the front page for four days, each article written by the same reporter in Halifax. The first appeared on Saturday and got several facts wrong, including the night of the riot. It did report the insinuation of police provocation, but this was a small item in a story that started with "generations of racism exploded into violence... building just like a powder keg, like a volcano and it has erupted."

The Sunday front-page article in the *Toronto Star* gave details of several confrontations between blacks and whites. People involved in fights were quoted, vowing revenge for harm done to them or their friends. The lead paragraph read: "A crowd of angry blacks — estimated as at least 30 — attacked a group of whites in a north-end housing project last night, breaking an uneasy calm after two nights of racial violence." On Monday the lead paragraph read: "People in the neighbourhood where a white man was badly beaten Saturday night by angry black youths are calling for an end to the accelerating cycle of madness." The news detailed attacks against various people near housing projects.

Surprisingly, the fourth front-page article, on Tuesday, did not focus on violence, specific acts of discrimination or possible racist actions by police but on systemic poverty: "From the concrete alleys that are children's playgrounds in Halifax's north-end housing projects to the dilapidated houses in remote rural areas, high drop-out rates and double-digit unemployment are the norm in Nova Scotia's black communities."

By July 24, 1991, the *Toronto Star* had dropped its coverage of the race riot to page 4, where it was placed alongside an article about a "near riot" in Montreal occasioned by a confrontation between police and a group of blacks outside a bar. So, competing readings of the event occurred in this extralocal newspaper as well, which however also shows how articles are placed and can be read "intertextually."

The importance of the riot to the national media was highlighted by the fact that a week later, when a man was assaulted in a small Nova Scotia town, it made the *Globe and Mail* solely through its link, real or perceived, with the earlier racial violence in Halifax. This article described a white man beaten by a black in a racially motivated attack and stands on its own as a crime report but makes sense extralocally because of earlier articles in the *Globe and Mail*. The two articles are read in their intersection with each other.

As for the original riot, after the initial flurry of shocked articles in the local papers, the media began looking to the past for causes. This retrospection continued as a dominant theme in later articles and raised the issues of discrimination, poverty, economic recession, previous incidents, racism in the police force, racism in the criminal justice system and so on.

But in less than a week, the retrospective search for causes took a twist — there were concerns that the media itself had exaggerated or even contributed to the problem. The local media looked at how the national papers were treating the story, and the Halifax police chief was quoted as saying that "the weekend was in fact pretty quiet." An editorial a day later suggested that the violence may not have been as widespread or as bad as the media had conveyed. In an accompanying article, a tourism industry spokesperson said that television cameras can actually invite trouble. A local columnist wrote that the media exaggerated the racial element, and in a newspaper poll published the same day, some suggested there wouldn't have been as much trouble if the media had just ignored bad news. Two days later an article in the *Herald* worried about the effects on tourism. However, an editorial the next day slammed those who had said the media had exaggerated the problem, accusing them of buck-passing and finger-pointing.

Over time the theme continually changed. By the first of August the new story was the anti-racism march, where both whites and blacks marched to protest racism. By December the reports on the riot were out. The police report found that the police had not acted with brutality or racial slurs. The report of a civilian group, however, charged that the police did not interview all witnesses and that police themselves did not know about car-to-car police tapes. An editorial suggested that the civilian report "seems more in touch with the real world," and the front-page banner headline of the provincial paper, "Race reports worlds apart" stressed the gap between the two reports. By February the attorney general vowed action on race relations, and there were comparisons with the Los Angeles riot.

To conclude, the coverage of the Halifax race riot was overwhelming and complicated. The initial barrage of articles eventually diminished in number, but the issue continued to be reported for months. The description of what had happened was at issue because interpretations of events were continually shifting and being debated. It was like a palimpsest, a parchment that was continuously being written, erased and rewritten. The story of the riot was continually being rewritten as interpretations were inserted into a reading of the event. The surprise was that the event retained any coherence as such.

Sample Study

Montreal race riot. On August 11, 2008, the *Montreal Gazette* published a front-page account of a riot that erupted after the shooting of a youth by police.

Article 6.3 "Fury erupts over police killing; Teen shot.
Montreal North streets ablaze as youths riot"

The mother of an 18-year-old shot and killed by a police officer in broad daylight is demanding explanations from the Montreal police force. But people in the neighbourhood where Fredy Villenueva was fatally wounded weren't waiting for explanations last night. Their fury erupted into a riot in Montreal North, with knots of protesters roaming the streets and setting fire to cars and garbage barricades.

The Montreal riot police squad was called out, and hundreds of officers formed a perimeter four or five blocks away from the Ground Zero... Rioters vandalized the local fire station and set several cars outside ablaze... Onlookers cheered as a van went up in flames... "I just don't understand why the police took my son's life," Lilian Villanueva said yesterday as tears streamed down her face. She could barely speak between sobs... Their son, Fredy, died at Sacré Coeur hospital Saturday night after a confrontation with officers near Henri Bourassa Park in Montreal North.

A Montreal police statement said officers felt threatened by Fredy, his brother Dany and a number of friends, which is why they reacted with force. But Fredy's sisters said they couldn't figure out how anybody could have felt threatened by their younger brother. They said Fredy was a low-key kid whose favourite activity was playing video games. "He was shy. He wasn't the type of guy who would antagonize a police officer."…

Witnesses said police arrived while the group was calmly throwing dice behind the arena, next to a field where children were playing soccer. The witnesses said the police officers singled out Dany Villanueva. They tried to search him and when he resisted, a male officer pushed him to the ground and arrested him, some teens said… one of the young people involved in the incident said no one in the group made physical contact with the police officers. [He] said the officers became aggressive within 30 seconds of getting out of their car…

A statement issued by… police said the officers were surrounded by youths when they tried to arrest one suspect. "At one point, the group began to move and a good number of individuals charged toward the police and threatened them," the statement said. "One of the police officers present then fired in the direction of the suspects, striking three of them."…

Members of an impromptu gathering last night… said they felt police are too aggressive with young people. "This wasn't a street gang. He was a child," said Johanne, who did not want to provide her last name. A woman called Nancy added: "When kids see that, they're going to hate police. I'm going to tell my kids, 'If you see a police car, go away.' I don't trust them." Julissa said Fredy was on a waiting list to enroll in technical school. He kept himself busy helping out around the house. "We have a sister who is disabled, so he spent a lot of time at home taking care of her."

Fredy wanted to become an electrical mechanic like his father, who works in an auto garage in Montreal North. The Villanuevas immigrated from Honduras in 1998… Yesterday, they said their faith in their adoptive country had been shaken to its core. "We thought we were going to be better off," Julissa said. "We thought there was justice here. We thought the police were supposed to protect us." (*Montreal Gazette*, August 11, 2008: A1, by Amy Luft, Christopher Maughan and Julia Kilpatrick)

Over the following days articles developed the story.

1. *First day of coverage following riot article.* On August 12, a columnist criticized the "failure of Montreal police to contain a crisis before it spirals out of control." Another criticized the public security ministry for a series of systemic cover-ups of police shootings of unarmed civilians. A news article said while people are angry with the rioters others are angry with police for abusing their power; quoting: "we're a peaceful people, but if we're treated

like wild animals, we'll start acting like wild animals. It's time for this to change. We work hard. We should be treated the same way as everyone else." Another article the same day criticized police practices for exacerbating tensions with minority groups. Racial profiling and a crackdown on incivilities are criticized. The provincial public security critic calls for an independent inquiry rather than the police investigation. The first editorial published on the topic began:

Article 6.4 "Police must win the trust of minority communities"
A man is dead. At least five others are injured. Stores were looted. Cars were burned. Buildings were set alight. This is the poisoned harvest of the Montreal police department's troubled record in relation with minority communities. After a police officer shot and killed blameless 18-year-old Fredy Villanueva on Saturday, the neighbourhood boiled over Sunday night. (*Montreal Gazette*, August 12, 2008: A14, editorial)

2. *Second day of coverage.* An article "Stories from the 'hood,'" reported speaking with residents about the riot. Some said they were afraid of their neighbours, but most said they were afraid of police. A young black man said that police are not used to black people. A middle-aged white woman said the police are constantly harassing youths who are not doing anything wrong. A young black man said they are always stopping him when he is on his bike, asking him where the reflectors are; an older black man said they don't show common respect in talking to him. A photo was published with kids wearing t-shirts which said, "Stop killing our kids." One article speculated that the reason police singled out Villanueva was because of previous convictions, while another quoted a former sergeant and veteran officer saying that an officer who feels threatened will reach for a gun: "It's just a fact." Meanwhile, a criminologist criticized the secrecy of the police investigation, saying that it undermines public confidence.

3. *Third day of coverage.* As family and friends gathered to pay their respects, police stepped up patrols in "trouble areas." Mourners expressed anger at the way police handled the shooting. There were more details about Fredy's brother, Dany, and his imputed links to a criminal gang. A columnist criticized the police investigation for failing to interview the officers involved in the shooting and suggested that this had been systemic over the years. A news report said that 28 percent of those killed by police were visible minorities (in a city where minorities make up 17 percent of the population). In 86 percent of forty-two cases between 1987 and 2008, the police were exonerated.

4. *Fourth day of coverage.* For the first time, a veteran officer "with intimate knowledge of the case" (who was not at the scene) spoke up. He said that

one of the two officers at the scene (of the shooting) was being beaten up by youths. This was going to become a key point of contention.

5. *Fifth day of coverage.* In a third opinion column by the same author, the mayor was criticized for contributing to Sunday's riot by not reassuring the public that justice would be done, thus leaving a "vacuum in public discourse" to be filled by the protest, and ultimately the riot. Surprisingly perhaps, an editorial reiterated the need for independent investigations of police shootings. This also became an important point of contention. The mayor announced that he has been meeting with community workers, government officials, and that his administration might build a new sports facility in the area where the riot occurred.

6. *Second week of coverage.* Two articles criticized the police investigation.

7. *The following months of coverage.* From the riot in August 2008 to the end of May, 2009, there were over ninety articles published, seven in September. There were repeated promises of openness and calls for better police/community liaison. Seventy-one people were arrested for offences committed during the riot. On September 30, the report of the investigation was submitted and three prosecutors were assigned to determine if charges should be laid. In October, six articles appeared. The mayor announced over 2 million dollars in social programs, and 600 people marched to call for a pubic inquiry. In November there was one article, where the two other youths shot with Fredy reiterate they did not attack the police officers and did nothing to instigate the shooting. Police interviewed the victims within hours, while they were sedated in hospital and without lawyers, and while they said they waited five days before interviewing the officers, they later admitted they hadn't even done that.

In December it was announced that no criminal charges would be laid. Twenty articles were published. The report said the police acted in self-defence, and the police chief said he's satisfied with the transparency of the process. Police presence was stepped up. The reaction from youths and other members of the public was a lack of surprise, as the police were criticized as not being a credible force. A coroner's inquiry was announced, and an editorial expressed the belief that questions will be answered. However, it is more in the nature of an inquest, held to determine circumstances surrounding death but with no responsibility to assign blame. The prosecutor who speaks at the press conference says:

Article 6.5: "Inquiry judge will have 'all the latitude he wants'"
One of the three crown prosecutors who reviewed the hefty file… announced [the police officer] and his partner acted as any reasonable person would under similar circumstances. The officers, patrolling in the area at about 7 pm, noticed six people playing dice in the parking lot… a violation of a municipal

bylaw. When they went to investigate, they recognized one of the group, Dany Villanueva, a known member of the Bloods. But when they asked for identification, Dany refused to show any, which led to an altercation. As the officers were trying to handcuff Dany, his brother, Fredy, approached and began taunting the police, telling them to leave his brother alone. Other members of the group grabbed Lapointe's partner around the neck.

"I saw four young individuals in good shape all capable of taking away my service gun..." [the officer] told investigators. "I saw no alternative but using my gun to protect myself and my partner." The whole incident unfolded in just two minutes... One voice can be heard on the [surveillance] video saying: "He had no choice but to shoot the guy, the guy was threatening him," [the prosecutor] said. (*Montreal Gazette*, December 2, 2008, by Sue Montgomery)

A criminologist said that the announcement of an inquiry was an effort to pacify public opinion, rather than to get at the underlying issues, for example. In addition, an editorial column pointed out that neither videos of the incident had been made public, and that neither officer was interviewed directly by the police. It concludes: "The problem is not citizens playing dice; it's the perception that the law-enforcement system is using loaded dice." In December 2009 one of the original police officers was asked why they approached the young men in the park, if they were really interested in policing dice or if they were engaged in racial profiling because they had been told to put pressure on street gangs.

In January 2009, offers of legal representation for key non-police witnesses was withdrawn. In February, two lawsuits against the police were announced. In March, lawyers acting for the police officers asked for a publication ban. In May, the (upcoming) inquest was criticized for not considering police-ethnic relations and for having too restrictive a mandate. Several groups began to call for a boycott of the inquiry. The public security minister was criticized in the provincial assembly. On January 27, the judge announced that he had no choice but to suspend the proceedings. On January 28, it was announced that legal representation would be provided to the victims.

Given that accounts of outrage and outrageous events are represented in the media for consumption at a distance, what do we read at a distance in these reports?

Analyzing the News

The fact that the media could offer readers different interpretations of the same event shows how different points of view can be brought to bear on an issue. The idea that the news can simply be reported, unadorned and without slant seems simplistic, when one event can be characterized as a riot,

135

as provoked by the police, the result of systemic poverty or reflecting racial inequality in the criminal justice system.

The different interpretations are not a problem, and it would be a mistake to think they can simply be sorted to find which one makes the best fit. Rather, the multiplicity of accounts opens up the (dangerous?) idea that issues in the media are open to debate and that it is this public debate that might be of interest. At their very base, news articles are interpreted by an active reader, who locates them intralocally and extralocally in the context of other accounts and events, creating interpretations at the same time.

Two issues are taken up in this section: how a racial incident was discursively constructed and the phenomenon of the news's extralocality and its consequences. In this second edition I enlarge the discussion of how the diffusion of knowledge about an event away from the centre influences police-race relations. The sample here centres around the shooting and race riot in Montreal in August 2008.

1. *Race riots.* Race riots are both events in the world and events constructed in the news. The media can create social panic by sensationalizing and exaggerating an event, so from a reporter's point of view it is important to get the facts straight. But what are facts and what would getting them straight look like? For readers who did not directly experience an event (which is most of us most of the time), the media's account stands in for that experience.

Most people experience crime vicariously through the news. They are not where the news happens, and they cannot determine how factual the media accounts are. They are at an effective distance from the event, where it is too soon to know what happened and too late to change it. The report of a race riot, then, is not simply a report of an event in the world, it is an extralocal report written by people one will never meet, of events one will never witness in person, of events that one cannot change. The report is treated as being one of an actual event, but it is at heart a social construction accomplished through discourse, that is, a story. The symbolic iteration of the event is newsworthy and informative, but it is a story, nonetheless real and real in its reading.

The structural organization of the accounts is shown in the following analysis. Article 6.1, "15 hurt in early morning rampage," is not simply a factual account. The facts in the account may or may not be factual. And in fact, there was subsequently controversy over what had really happened. If we suspend our usual view that the account is about an actual event, a transparent (re)presentation, it can also be read as a set of instructions, a prescription. This suspending or putting aside of the question of facticity for a moment is interesting because the account constructs a description of events retrospectively. The account tells the reader how it is to be read as a report about a riot, after the fact. The chronological order, the apparently literal description of what happened as time passed, the use of authoritative sources, quotes from people who should know what happened, descriptions of the criminal charges and their disposition — all provide the reader with rules for the warrantability of the claim that a race riot indeed happened.

Racial tensions are named as the cause of the violence at the very beginning of the article, providing a strong interpretation of what follows. By beginning in this way, the article directs the reader to read an account of a race riot, it provides rules for that reading, and it is difficult to construct an alternate reading from the account. The opening phrase is not equivocal or ambiguous; there is a place, a time, an action and an explanation. The criminal acts then mentioned throughout the article — rioting, assaults and vandalism — all reinforce the sense that a race riot actually occurred, rather than, say, a group of people leaving the theatre.

The initial summary indicates that a large number of people were involved, the riot police were dispatched, and there were a number of arrests and people charged. This section serves as a preface for the account within an account that follows. The account of events even reiterates the preface, which does not make the article repetitive but reinforces the facticity of the account.

There are then the personal accounts: A black man was attacked; a minister was called by the bar manager who was concerned about the tension; a group of about fifty black men were coming toward them; police officers were present in anticipation of trouble; a group in the rear began randomly assaulting whites; police ran with the crowd, picking up those that were injured; police confronted the crowd in riot gear; the group vandalized the area until police and community leaders successfully intervened.

These accounts are chronological, as an account of a happening has to be, detailing the initial incident, the subsequent tension, attempts to defuse the situation and the interwoven street violence and actions of the police. Such articles bracket the account of the "event" with phrases promising that the account is a description of what happened, based on trustworthy reports from eyewitnesses and the authorities, reinforced by the admission from the police chief that racial violence is the reason for the incident. While it is obvious that the facts are only facts through being labelled as such, it nonetheless provides for a preferred reading.

All these various elements, such as the tensions, the violence and the police, work together to create the interpretation that a "race riot" actually occurred. Explicit references are to race, and there are more subtle references to "black areas" of the city.

These elements are more than simply factual descriptions of what happened; they are facts by virtue of being embedded into a rendition of an event, and the event recursively becomes real through the inclusion of such facts: various people had been charged with assaulting an officer, disturbing the peace, obstruction and resisting arrest, and causing a disturbance, further substantiating the events, make no mistake.

Subsequent media accounts used expressions such as "race riot, racial violence, violence not surprising, racial tensions, street violence, renewed violence, rampage, rage" and so on. Through the use of such terms the incident was further reified as an event, linked to past events and deeper underlying problems and made to meet the description of a racial problem. The riot was a thing in the world but the race riot was constructed through the news. The question of whether there was a race riot was a source of contention, because there were those who said the media had focused unfairly on racial violence, failing to see it as evidence of deeper problems and exaggerating it in a way that was harmful, for example, to tourism. Both criticisms point to the effect that words can have.

A consequent criticism of how the riot was handled in the media was that "black" was used as a defining term in a way that "white" never is. In a parallel incident in Sydney, Nova Scotia, for example, approximately seven hundred people clashed in the street and, even though it was reported that racial epithets were used, it was not termed a race riot in the headline and that interpretation was specifically denied in the text. Months later, in a similar incident in Shelburne, N.S., a police chief was quoted as saying that racial names were used by both sides but there was no indication of a racial problem. In neither case did the media use the term "race riot," even though there was evidence that racism was involved; perhaps the difference was that most of the protagonists were white.

2. *Extralocality*. There are various other situations where the media has been criticized as contributing to ethnic discrimination. It is difficult to cover news stories of the ethnic groups in Canada today, especially when the structure of news gathering relies on reporters sitting in meetings, deciding on stories and then going out to gather information. The problem with that scenario is that news is not defined within these communities themselves. It is easy to reinvest time-honoured stereotypes linking ethnicity to drug trafficking or violent crime. As witness to this, Chapter 7 looks at concerns over immigrant crime that flamed up after the shootings of Georgina Leimonis at the Just Desserts Cafe and of Constable Todd Baylis of the metropolitan police force, both in Toronto. These shootings, and more importantly their media coverage, led to concern that immigrants were committing a disproportionate amount of crime and that crime statistics should be collected by race, an idea that was entertained by Statistics Canada and then abandoned.

The construction of the race riot in Halifax had a national existence, accomplished extralocally through the news. The story was picked up by such papers as the *Globe and Mail*, the *Montreal Gazette* and the *Toronto Star*. Given the medium of newswires and on-the-spot reporters, it is no accident that the portrayal of events in the out-of-province newspapers was similar to that in the Nova Scotia media.

Place doesn't matter in a mediated world. People with no direct experience of the event get the facts in the news, and the event takes on a surreal symbolic existence. The initial riot, the subsequent interpretation of events and the eventual findings of the committees to investigate the police handling of the incident are all available through the news network. In many places and for most readers, extralocality replaces experience. If the story of the event corresponds intertextually with events the reader is familiar with they resonate even more strongly. For cities with large minority components this story must have seemed all too plausible, and the actions of the people described all too reasonable.

We can also look at how interpretations of events change over time. Explanations for the riot shifted from mob violence to provocative actions by the police, to discriminatory policies at local bars, to years of discrimination, to poverty and recession, to racism in general and so on. The final note that concluded media coverage of the riot months later was that the problem can be solved through minority hiring by the police force. These interpretations are neither superficial nor insightful, and while it would be simplistic to say they provide closure, they do close off interpretations.

The key thing is that extralocality is a feature of the news that provides readers with interpretations of events far from the original. This is an issue for those who attempt to determine who controls the information that creates the dominant interpretations. However, the accounts of the Halifax race riot in the local and national papers highlight the problem of extralocality in a different way; the credibility of the information that readers use in the course of their everyday lives becomes questionable. The events were said to be reported in a way that made the situation seem "worse than it really was." Canadian and American newspapers both repeated the erroneous information that a man was stabbed. The Halifax police chief topicalized the problem: "'If I was in another part of this county and read what I had read, I would be wondering whether I should call my relatives in Halifax to see if they were OK down there,' MacDonald said. 'It just sounded so intense — "Another night of racial tension, a black man gets his throat slit."... [the message] it sends out about our community that I don't think is really the truth of the matter.' The weekend was in fact pretty quiet, [the police chief] said."

It is not simply that papers outside Nova Scotia got some details wrong, reporting erroneous information and exaggerating the scope and the seriousness of the problem. It is not simply that perhaps many of the accounts were factually correct. This reporting highlights the fact that our news is secondhand, channelled through the medium of news reporting. Even for people living in Halifax, the main source of information about the events was the news. The local media's analysis of the reporting at the national level makes it seem that if the media could only get its facts straight, there wouldn't be a problem. However, extralocality is an issue whether the facts are straight or not.

3. *Diffusion.* Ruling relations in modern society need not be direct or in person, although they often are. Ruling can be achieved by professional organizations that transcend any particular location and experience and manage at a distance. And since the media is by nature extralocal, it is able to take up and transform our experiences through the form of accounts available to it, while those very experiences are informed through the knowledge that we live in a mediated world. The media transforms experiences into news, and, at the same time, experiences are informed by the news. The knowledge we have of the world is put together from myriad bits of information about far-flung places we'll never see, by people we'll never meet. This is a diffuse ideology.

In the last exhibit, we see verbatim accounts of incivilities by the police against the public reported by members of the Montreal community. Minorities are more likely to report negative interactions with the police. Part of this is because minorities are more likely to live in high-crime neighbourhoods where policing is contentious. The important thing that has been little researched is that, if those same minorities are exposed to media reports of police misconduct, are perceptions of police wrongdoing increased? Ironically, the police were reportedly targeting incivilities on the part of the public, that is, minor offences at the time of the shooting, a practice that exacerbates neighbourhood tensions with the police.

Exhibit 6.6 Reports of Police Incivilities

"People need to have a bit of respect... We're a peaceful people, but if we're treated like wild animals, we'll start acing like wild animals. It's time for this to change. We work hard. We should be treated the same way as everyone else." ("'No to violence, yes to peace'," *Montreal Gazette*, August 12, 2008: A3)

"If you are male, a member of a visible minority and drive a sports car, you can be targeted... One youth told me he was stopped 10 times in one day. That is a lot, and I think the young people are fed up... The people of this community are complaining about how they are treated." ("Youth resentment sparked by police profiling," *Montreal Gazette*, August 12, 2008: A6)

"The cops here don't treat people well. I was born and raised here, but you know how they call me? With a megaphone. And I've only ever had one ticket in my life… Usually, they're sitting just over there, playing dice, talking and smoking cigarettes, not harming anyone. But as soon as the police see them, they go right over to hassle them. That's what really stinks. I think it's terrible. They're always telling the group to separate, but they're never doing anything wrong… Every time I'm riding this bike, they always come over and ask me if I have my reflectors, where I got it, as if I'm a criminal… It's like if you're black or Latino in Montreal North, you're automatically a member of a street gang… They come and search us for no reason. If they need to justify it, they says it's because they thought we were armed… [The police told people] Don't hang out with this guy because pretty soon, we're going to arrest him and his whole family. Is that a normal thing to say?… The other day, I was coming out of the barber's and [the police] said, 'Hey! Come here,' just like that. That's not how you talk to a stranger. How about: 'Sir, can we talk to you for a second?' That's police. If you're always telling me to f-off, do you think I'm going to say hi to you? No. But if you're polite with me, I'll be polite with you." ("Stories from the 'hood'," *Montreal Gazette*, August 13, 2008: A4)

"Excuse me, but I feel like if they were whites sitting on the ground, they never would have been targeted. But because it's a group of blacks, they treat us like that. Don't we have the right to live like everyone else? We're human beings, too, you know. You can't say colour doesn't matter." ("Community turns out to support family in grief," *Montreal Gazette*, August 14, 2008: A3)

"What we think is that behind the police there are lawyers and people who have a lot of money and power who are telling them what to do and what to say to cover up what happened here. We are immigrants, we are poor, and they think that because of the colour of our skin or because we don't speak the language very well we are going to let it happen. Racism and brutality is an everyday thing for us. In Spanish we say *basta* – enough is enough." ("Vigil for slain teen," *Montreal Gazette*, September 10, 2008: A6)

These are examples of direct incivilities allegedly experienced and reported by members of the public in the media. They become part of a "discourse of incivility," which came to stand in for police-public relations in Montreal North at the time. They are experienced directly, expressed locally and reported extralocally. The discourse of incivility actually creates a way of understanding events from the point of view of the powerless.

With two decades of police shootings, most of which exonerate the police and have minorities over-represented as victims, the crackdown on incivilities by the police just inflamed matters. The riot was predictable as an expression of resentment against the police, who are seen as an agent of dominant power. The riot, from this point of view, was also thoroughly preventable, but once it happened it was blamed on the public. When the dominant discourse backs up the police, it is surprising that there are as many direct expressions of public discontent appearing in the media as there are.

But once the stories of incivilities appear, they become (intratextually) available for local readers, as well as extralocally available for readers at a distance who may or may not be able to connect to events. This is how riots can travel. In this case, the media can diffuse blame or assign it.

Citizen contacts with police can involve procedural injustices, which include unwarranted stops, verbal and physical abuse. These are perceived as unfair, especially to members of minority groups, who perceive the police as part of the dominant group in society. If people with less power read that other people with less power also have difficulties with the police, a multiplier effect occurs. There is an event reported in the media, read by an experienced reader who understands (intralocally and intertextually) the event as that type.

In Montreal there is a history of police conflict with minorities, especially in high crime neighbourhoods. People exposed to media reports of police abuse are more prone to believe that police misconduct is widespread, a resonance effect that is not helped by the perception that the police protect themselves. So even for people who lived the event, the riot was occasioned and interpreted through mediated experience. But it lives beyond their experience as well. And the significance of the mediated experience of the discourse of incivilities is that extralocally race relations are highlighted, as is the credibility of the police.

Summary

This chapter began with the idea that the news sometimes puts an ethnic spin on race issues. Joy Mannette mentioned several examples that bear out this idea. Ethnocentrism and racism are said to inform such media accounts, and the media can reproduce a dominant, discriminatory point of view.

A reading of the Halifax race riot of 1991 was provided to see how reporting developed on that event. Race was highlighted in the papers as at the root of the problem, in a variety of ways: racism in bars, racism by the police, racism and poverty, and so on. The shifting accounts of what happened bring home the idea that interpretation is central to the understanding of an event, and not simply extraneous. Reading those accounts both locally and away requires making them make sense through being related to other stories of similar events.

The media takes up experience and transforms it into factual accounts;

we then experience the world as secondhand but immediate. As an example of this dual aspect of the news, I came upon a massive car pile-up on a main highway outside the city of Halifax late one night. The traffic had suddenly slowed and stopped and, after a long wait, tow trucks and police cars slowly moved through the lanes of traffic.

After more than an hour the traffic slowly resumed, and less than a kilometre ahead there were dozens of cars off the road with broken lights, crumpled fenders and so on. The area was lit with the flashing lights of tow trucks, police cars and ambulances; people were milling around, television crews were in the middle of the road. I had the feeling that I was in the middle of something exciting, and it was clear what had happened, but I also felt that I should get home as quickly as possible to turn on the television and find out what had really happened. I didn't find the story on the television, but I did see it in the newspapers the next day. It wasn't nearly as exciting as the real thing.

The issue of interpretation was taken apart further in the analysis section, where we looked at an initial account of the event to see how it was constructed through discourse. The account was found to have a structure that enables an interpretation of what happened as a race riot. Not every news article on racial conflict is going to have such a structure, of course, but the structure of this one leads a reasonable reader to see that a race riot occurred. The importance of looking at how media discourse portrays the world becomes more apparent when we realize the extent to which our knowledge of the world is extralocal and known only through the news. More than one person, myself included, had relatives phone from Toronto because they thought Halifax was in flames, burning in a racial conflagration.

In the example of media reports of the shooting in Montreal, the consequent riot and the months leading to the establishment of an inquiry we see reports of a police crackdown on incivilities. We also see reports in the media of police incivilities experienced by citizens. People of minority groups who live in high crime neighbourhoods characterized by aggressive policing are more likely to perceive the police as corrupt, especially if they are exposed to media accounts of police misconduct.

Interest in race relations and the criminal justice system is increasing and, although much has been written, much more work needs to be done. Those in the media are themselves part of the problem when they unreflectingly reproduce dominant ways of thinking about minority groups. However they can also be in the position to reflect interpretations that subvert power and expose inequality.

7

Crime Rates and Crime Fear
Portraying Crime as Out of Control

Carjackings and home invasions show that crime is out of control; the crime rate is up; violent crime is on the increase; young offenders laugh at the law — these are all contemporary ways of expressing what is becoming an everyday fear about crime. Is crime really on the increase, or is it just media hype? This chapter begins with a talk by Paul MacDonald, now retired from the Halifax city police, who had been their media relations officer. He describes some of the difficulties inherent in the job: releasing information about crimes that have been committed, dealing with reporters who are unfamiliar with police procedures and making sure the public gets the correct impression of crime.

Reading the News looks at examples of how crime is reported in the news, focusing specifically on stories about the increase in crime and crime rates and the need to "do something about crime." During 1994, several highly publicized violent crimes occurred in Canada, and many asked whether there had been an increase in crime or not. Some suggested the media was sensationalizing and exaggerating crime out of proportion to its actual incidence, exactly one of the problems identified by Constable MacDonald.

The topic is further explored in the Sample Study, which focuses on the events and aftermath of the 2005 Boxing Day shooting that resulted in the death of Jane Creba. This topic most clearly illustrates the place of fear and anger as dominant reactions to crime news and sets the stage for a law-and-order agenda.

Analyzing the News takes up the idea that the newspapers have to 'get the story right.' However, what would that look like when the media does not simply take a subservient role in representing reality, but has to choose stories, slant and perspective? In addition what would getting it right look like when the media can't control the authorities it uses or how consumers read. They are many variables upon which the news is contingent when it creates its knowledge about the world that it doesn't control.

It is simplistic to expect the media to mirror reality, and perhaps not even the issue. Since people get their knowledge about crime from the media, if they get a distorted view that crime is out of control, their fear of crime might not reflect their actual possibility of victimization. However, although an unreasonable fear has unfortunate consequences for how people live their lives, it is still very real and reflects how a knowledge of the world constructed and obtained through the media is practical knowledge "for all intents and purposes" — fear is discursively produced.

The topic of this chapter is fear of crime, but the underlying theme is that fear of crime is constructed socially, through the media. A social panic unfounded in reality may not simply be a media exaggeration, but it can serve a real purpose in society. A media relations person may have a very difficult job helping reporters "get it right" if there are strong pressures to present a picture of crime out of control and the need for new laws to do something about it. Studies I have found useful in thinking about crime rates and fear are Altheide (1997), Banks (2005), Chadee and Dixon (2005), D'Arcy (2007) and Wortley, Hagan and MacMillan (1997).

Paul MacDonald's Talk

I'm the media relations officer with the Halifax police, and I've been on the force since 1966. Approximately six years ago we got involved with community-based policing, and I ended up in the job I'm doing now. To start, I had on-the-job training from people who were in this job before. Then I was sent off to Ottawa to the RCMP school media relations course. When I first came back, I had a phone and a little desk, and I sat there waiting for the phone to ring. But unless there was actually a news-breaking story, I was never getting any phone calls. Today, about three years later, the phone is ringing continuously, there are always people coming in to see me, and I created a very, very busy position. I must ask some of the media people what they did before because they seem to be using me continuously for stories.

Police stories are a main staple of the media because they make good reading. A good story is where you have conflict, a hero, a villain, and somebody overcoming obstacles. I believe quite often most people, and probably myself included, have read a book or read a story where we empathize with the criminal. The person was smarter than the system, he was victorious in the end, and this makes a very interesting type of newspaper story. So what we have to do as police departments is realize that we are going to be featured, that we have to be able to communicate with the media and try to get our point across, so that the general public understands what police work is all about.

Last week we had a one-day police-media workshop with members from the local media attending. We focused on police policies but also the need for police management to understand where the media are coming from. The media today is the watchdog for all of us. People today are just too busy;

they don't have time to watch what's going on with government, industry, with the environment, pollution or wrongdoing.

The police realize that we have an enormous responsibility and along with that goes accountability. One of the main areas where you're going to get accountability is through the media. The hardest thing is if a police officer is involved in some type of wrongdoing, having made either a human error or a criminal error. To stand up and say, "Oh yes, we did that. That's one of our people," is hard. It's human nature to think maybe this'll go away. But what we're attempting to do is become more forthcoming, more outward. If something leaks to the media and it ends up on page seven today, two days later it's on page three, and by Saturday it's a front-page story. Each day people are following it as it progressively gets worse and worse, instead having your whole front-page story that day, and letting everybody judge what happened.

There are incidents where you'll get sympathy from the public, "Oh, I see why this happened." But if you just stonewall and say "no comment," and pretend it doesn't exist, then you're going to end up putting in the mind of the investigating reporter that there is more to this than meets the eye. But if you give everything out, then you're going to end up with a front-page story, but it's going to come and go. You try to get into your story why this happened, and what's going to be done to prevent it from happening again.

I don't know why anybody in the world wants to be a reporter. I mean how do you go to work and be a police reporter today, tomorrow you're working on pollution in the harbour, the next day you're talking to some lawyers about some fraud cases, and the next you're talking to somebody about the environment. You have to be an expert in every field that I can think of, and one of my main jobs is clarity. I have to explain everything. Because quite often what they'll do, they'll put a junior person on as a police reporter, especially when you're busy.

I'll give you an example that happened just the other day. A reporter asked me about a certain case, and I said, "Yes, the person will be arraigned in court tomorrow morning on weapons charges." And the reporter said, "What do you mean?" I said "What do you mean what do I mean?" And they said, "Arraigned, what's that?" And I said "Oh." And you have to go back and explain.

In another example, a reporter called and said, "Do you have any suspects in the motorcycle-rapist incident?" This was about three months into the investigation. And I can't say, "Yes, we have a suspect," because if we do the person may flee the area. If we say we don't have a suspect, the person says, "Oh they don't know who I am," and maybe do it again. So I don't say if we do have or don't have suspects. Instead I said, "We do not have any warrants out, there has been no arrest, it's still under investigation."

The headline the next day said, "Police have no suspects in motorcycle-rapist case." In fact we did have a suspect and we were preparing the case to go to court, so the investigator comes in with the newspaper and demanding, "Why did you tell them there was no suspect, I'm going to lay charges, you know." So I called the reporter and I said, "Well, I didn't tell you there was no suspect." "Well, you said there were no warrants. And you said there were no charges. So there can't be any suspects."

So how does a person be a reporter and talk to me one day, and talk to somebody from the Power Commission the next day about gridlocks and power lines, and try to understand exactly what that person's talking about?

I think one of the main issues is who is going to make the decision on what information is going to be used. The media would like to come in and look at all the police reports and say, "OK, we'll use this and this." However, the police say to the media, "You can't have this, but we'll give you that." So we're trying to come to some type of a compromise. We have the responsibility to the person who made the complaint not to identify that person. We also have the responsibility to the person charged, that they have a fair trial. We have to stay away from opinions and from past records of people, and other issues. And I am the person that ends up making the press release.

In the media structure also, you have the news editors and the assignment editors who receive the information from the reporter. If there is a suicide, somebody has made the decision whether to report that. Let's say this person tied up 5,000 people going home on the bridge. If they're going to use his name, somebody in their hierarchy makes that decision. And that's where I think it's important that the police and the media try to understand each other. Not so much for the fact that, yes, we want a better image.

If I send out a press release to every media outlet and say we have a great new crime prevention campaign, and would you meet us here tomorrow morning and we'll reveal it, we'd have maybe three or four reporters. However, if a major crime happened, you wouldn't even have to call the reporters. You would have every reporter dying to get into the place because crime prevention programs aren't really that interesting.

To sum it up, what we have to get back to with community-based policing is our relation with the media. The media gives a perspective on crime, and sometimes they're right, but sometimes they're wrong. The media can give a perspective that every house in the south end is a potential target. You better lock your doors and put chains and get guard dogs. They can heighten fear or they can lessen fear.

And the police have to be very careful how we deal with the media, as we can heighten the fear of crime or take it down to lower than it actually is.

Reading the News

Paul MacDonald raises several concerns about the interaction between police and reporters, echoing some of the points that will be brought up later. He says it is important to make sure the media gets the information right, to avoid misinterpretations and misinforming the public. The risk of sensationalizing crime, for example, is that it can both feed into and increase the fear of crime in the community.

Here we look at how the media topicalizes concern about crime and what should be done about it. Articles 7.1 and 7.2 announce a new omnibus crime bill.

Article 7.1 "Crime legislation has priority: Prentice"

The Conservatives say the new crime bill outlined in the throne speech is their main priority, and will be the first piece of legislation introduced in Parliament this fall ...

"It is the priority of Canadians, that's what we've heard over the course of the summer months," [the minister] told CBC News... "We don't feel we were able to get the criminal justice legislation that Canadians asked for through the House of Commons in the last session. We're going to hold the opposition's feet to the fire to get it through this time."

The new crime bill... will include measures on impaired driving, age of sexual consent, stricter bail conditions and mandatory prison terms for gun crimes. Discussions about the bill came as Statistics Canada released its latest crime numbers... finding that the national homicide rate fell by 10 per cent in 2006, in keeping with a 30-year downward trend...

All of the measures [were]... brought forward during the first session of Parliament, but never passed. Prime Minister Stephen Harper... accused opposition parties of stalling the crime bills in committee and trying to water them down... the former legislation will be revived as one omnibus crime bill. (*CBC News*, October 17, 2007)

The so-called Tackling Violent Crime bill was contentious, not simply because of its provisions, but because it was a political bluff. The bill included tough measures as part of a law-and-order agenda, but it was clear that if the opposition defeated the bill it would trigger an election. The government also announced a toughening of the *Youth Criminal Justice Act*. As can be seen in Article 7.2, the rhetoric of community and safety, violence and danger is invoked to create a consensus on the need for action.

Article 7.2 "Omnibus crime bill first challenge for opposition"

Ottawa — The Conservative government tabled its omnibus crime bill... Tackling Violent Crime... [which was] stalled in the last session of Parliament...

[which] would stiffen penalties for impaired driving, raise the age of sexual consent to 16 from 14, impose stricter bail conditions for those who commit crimes with guns, and also impose mandatory prison terms for gun crimes. The most controversial proposal, opposed last session by all three opposition parties, amends the *Criminal Code* so that those found guilty of three violent or sexual offences would have to convince a judge that they shouldn't be branded dangerous offenders.

At a news conference... Public Safety Minister Stockwell Day made the case for the crime package... "Brought together, all these measures... will result in a safer community for all of us, locally and across the country and we're asking for the support of opposition members in moving this through." [He] said the initiatives in the bill were requested by police officers and they will help alleviate their frustrations in dealing with violent, repeat offenders. "This legislation is going to help immensely," he said... Mr. Harper accused the... opposition parties of dragging their feet... [and] that Canadians are impatient for action to make their homes and streets safer... "If they are serious about fighting crime then they should have no problem in expediting this bill"... [He said] Canadians are correctly asking "how on Earth" a person who has repeatedly committed violent crimes is let out on bail. "Our bill will make sure they will remain behind bars, where they belong." (*Montreal Gazette*, October 18, 2007, by Meagan Fitzpatrick, CanWest News)

The legislation passed in the Senate in February 2008, after the Liberal caucus walked out of the Senate. In June 2009, tough drug-crime legislation in the form of Bill C15 was debated and passed. It was designed to give people convicted of serious drug crimes automatic prison terms of six months or longer, otherwise called mandatory minimum sentences. The federal justice minister was quoted as saying that the tougher sentences were aimed at "serious drug traffickers, the people who are basically out to destroy our society." Critics argued that the law did nothing to rehabilitate drug users and would simply mean more crowding in prisons. Some suggested the Liberals supported the bill in order to avoid seeming soft on crime.

Mandatory minimum sentences are more associated with criminal justice legislation in the U.S., where they have been used since the early 1980s. While mandatory minimums are often politically attractive, they have been criticized for being ineffective in reducing drug use and incarcerating more than 1 percent of the adult population. Currently, many U.S. states are repealing their mandatory minimums legislations because of the associated high cost of more people held in pre-trial detention and more trials.

The Supreme Court of Canada struck down a mandatory minimum sentence of seven years for importing or exporting narcotics in 1987, calling it cruel and unusual punishment because it didn't take into account the nature and quantity of the drug or whether the person charged had any previous convictions. However, in 2000, the mandatory minimum sentence of four years for criminal negligence causing death involving a firearm was upheld. Clearly public opinion is shifting to the right. For example, public-opinion surveys show that Canadians believe that sentencing practices are too lenient. In 2005, 74 percent of people surveyed believed sentencing is too lenient. On the other hand, there was strong public support for restorative sentencing, which promotes a sense of responsibility in the offender and secures reparation for the crime victim. There was less support for deterrence and incapacitation, a turnaround from attitudes surveyed in 1985. Slightly more than half the sample in 2005 expressed support for mandatory sentencing. One conclusion is that the public is aware of the dangers of absolute mandatory sentences and instead want courts to impose lesser sentences where exceptional circumstances exist.

The legislation was also condemned by the John Howard Society. They argued that community-based correctional programs keep offenders connected to positive social networks. In addition, they argued, the best approach is to prevent crime through social development by ensuring quality education and health care, jobs and other social supports. However, in 2009, the government passed a bill providing mandatory minimum sentences of six months for those convicted of growing as few as five marijuana plants.

In 2009, the federal government also introduced legislation making it a crime to flee a jurisdiction to avoid prosecution, a move praised by police. The justice minister also announced that new legislation would allow police to photograph and fingerprint people who had been arrested by the police. Under current law this is only possible after a person has been charged for an offence. These two new measures were part of proposed "modernization" legislation, which would make forty amendments to Canadian law. In 2009, it was also announced that the federal government wanted to curtail the "faint hope legislation," which allows convicted murderers to apply for early parole. Again, as with drug crime measures, there is opposition to the legislation.

Article 7.3 "Tory bill targets early parole. Feds aim to cut faint-hope clause allowing murderers to bid for freedom"

The Conservatives tabled a bill yesterday aimed at repealing the controversial clause which... would leave first- or second-degree murderers no longer able to apply for earlier parole eligibility at the 15-year mark of a sentence. "Our government believes murderers must serve serious time for the most serious crime," [the justice minister said]...

But one Calgary defence lawyer said the tough-on-crime stance is a bid by the Tories to bolster political popularity. "They are marching to this constant drumbeat of tough-on-crime rhetoric... It is politically expedient but not good for society." [She] said the faint-hope clause isn't so much about freeing criminals but giving prisoners incentive to rehabilitate so they aren't simply warehoused and turned loose on the streets. "It's always easy to cloak themselves in a tough-on-crime mantra, but I think our government is being irresponsible and looking for short-term fixes that don't fix any problems," she said. (*Canoe News*, June 6, 2009, by Nadia Moharib, Sun Media)

These proposals, mandatory minimum sentences for drug crime, making it an offence to flee prosecution, abolishing early parole for convicted murderers, and tougher measures to deal with drug crime, are all generic issues. That is, they are unconnected to specific events that might give them added urgency. The news articles reproduced here presume that there is a problem with street crime that is currently not adequately dealt with by the criminal justice system. However, the articles gloss over deeper questions of whether there has been an increase in crime and whether increasing penalties would increase deterrence. Independent of other evidence, a reader could be lead to the conclusion that there is a problem and that it is necessary to do something about it.

Much editorializing, especially, conveys the intractability of gun crime, saying the criminal justice system is seriously flawed. The perception that street crime is escalating in our society and that the law is too soft on offenders is created by news articles, commentaries and opinion and editorial pieces. However, it is not easy to know whether the problem they describe is exaggerated or not. Consider the following article. Does it increase fear of crime?

Article 7.4 "Lack of motive in SUV double homicide 'troubling': police"

A gunman killed two young men in a parked sport utility vehicle in downtown Toronto last year, and [police say] a motive for the shootings remains "completely unclear"... [a third person] made a "frantic call to 911" after a gunman approached the Range Rover and fired directly into it, killing the two men... shortly after midnight on June 13, 2008. The lack of motive for the shooting is "troubling" and the "most challenging" part of the year-long investigation, [police] said... "Absolutely no one would have known that they were returning to that address, and that's hugely significant to us in our investigation"... [Police say] when the "precipitating event" to the murders is determined... it could very well prove to be "hugely insignificant," indicating it was a random killing. (*CBC News*, June 10, 2009)

This article has several thematic elements: 1) otherwise innocent victims are 2) killed in public by a 3) young man 4) unrelated to them 5) with a gun 6) in a manner that seems random 7) in the city. While in the *CBC News* it is made to seem random, in the *Toronto Star* a police detective says that is one thing he cannot believe. The *Toronto Sun* said it was a young man on a bike and CTV said it was a young black man. Comments on the CBC site ranged from it being a gang initiation rite to a case of mistaken identity. Comments at the *Star* said that the gun registry was useless and that the killer should be put to death.

Placement is no longer an easy way to gauge the relative importance of a news story. Unless a person actually reads a newspaper, much news is read online. So it is more the amount of coverage in multiple publications and the content of the articles that gets attention. The event might not rank alongside international terrorism, corporate crime or political corruption, but it trades on and reinforces a concern about the link between (black) youths and (gun) crime. Relying on the police as the main source of information reinforces the seriousness of the crimes.

One way of measuring concern is to contrast it with the likelihood of a crime occurring. For example, in the first edition of this book, the article "Crime not up, but concern is — StatsCan" was used to topicalize how the public can have a sense that crime is out of control even if they are not any more likely to be victims of violent crime than they were in the past. The problem is the different realities of victimization surveys and mediated crime. The former is a survey on personal risk, part of the General Social Survey program, while the latter is not designed to be representative. If we have the impression that crime has increased even when the likelihood of victimization has remained unchanged, those of us who thought crime had increased must simply be wrong, victims of distorted information.

When people have concerns about crime, and yet it is clear based on people's own reports of victimization, that the feeling has no empirical justification, no consideration is given to the idea that there may be other good reasons for people to think that crime has increased: that people could be more aware of crime, people could be concerned that the criminal justice system is not dealing adequately with crime, or the media may have created the concern in the first place. And of course there is the possibility that a personal sense of victimization can change over time, as people become more desensitized to crime. And, finally, if concern is fear, why should fear be rational? It is difficult to know what is being measured here, but this is a traditional criminological concern, that fear is created by news.

That story was printed as a national front-page story, and in smaller papers as well. The articles were similar, citing various statistics to buoy the claim that victimization rates had not increased, even though people had the apparently erroneous perception that crime had increased. Another article in the *Globe and Mail* proclaimed that light had been shed on Canadian crime, and its draw read "Law and Order. Canadians' growing fears of assault and intrusion result from increased reporting of anti-social acts. In fact, the numbers show that violent crimes such as murder are not on the increase."

A similar article from the United States compared public fear of crime with police crime statistics. This report was not based on a victimization survey but on police statistics, which are based upon people's willingness to report incidents to the police in the first place and thus are generally felt to be underreported. The article began with "Contradicting a widespread perception that New York City is more violent than ever, the Police Department released its official 1993 crime statistics yesterday, which show that reported incidents of violent crime decreased modestly for the third year in a row." This is the only reference to public fear, while the rest of the article deals solely with the statistics.

The question of whether crime has actually decreased or reports to the police have simply dropped is not addressed. No reference is made to who said there was widespread fear, what evidence this statement was based on or what could account for it. The notion that public fear is widespread yet groundless seems to be a common theme in the media, just like the contradictory theme, that crime is increasing. It is puzzling.

The 1992–93 period witnessed a spate of articles on the fear of crime. A *Globe and Mail* editorial cartoon even showed Santa Claus in an army surplus store holding a newspaper headlined "Fear of Violent Crime Growing," asking for a red bulletproof vest with white fur trim! At the same time as official surveys were being published showing that victimization trends were unchanged or decreasing, there were reports that Canadians were not only afraid but angry. The results of an Angus Reid poll reflected a growing approval of a law-and-order approach to crime. Respondents were quoted as favouring the return of the death penalty in certain cases, tougher rules on parole and manual labour for young offenders. Not only does the public seem to want tougher measures against crime, politicians are taking those measures.

The shooting of metropolitan Toronto police constable Todd Baylis in June 1994 became a focus of concern about immigration. Editorials called for changes to the process, because the accused had been able to stay in Canada for two years after he had been ordered deported following a criminal conviction for drugs and weapons. When arrested, he was found to have two loaded semi-automatic handguns in his possession.

This event, combined with the murder in April 1994 of Georgina Leimonis at the Just Desserts cafe in Toronto during a "crash robbery," further reinforced the demands for a review of immigration policies. The immigration minister responded with a policy to deport immigrant criminal offenders and was quoted as saying, "I will not allow people to make a mockery of our laws and I will not put Canadians at risk."

The immigration minister was quickly criticized for assigning only a twenty-member RCMP task force to the job of tracking down and deporting immigrant criminals, for indicating confusion in immigration policies in general, for contributing to members of minority ethnic groups being unfairly targeted as criminals, for unfairly targeting immigrants who have been on welfare perhaps through no fault of their own and for allowing failed claimants to become landed immigrants if they can avoid deportation for three years.

In an unusually public statement, a metropolitan Toronto police officer said there should be better controls on immigrants who come to Canada — controls that in any other situation would be considered an infringement of a person's constitutional rights, an invasion of privacy and a violation of the right to be presumed innocent. In one report a retiring police officer came out in support of fingerprinting immigrants, a conservative law-and-order approach.

A study conducted by Statistics Canada and released in July 1994 showed that immigrants were more hardworking, better educated and more stable than native-born Canadians, countering the view that the immigration system lets in criminals. The "immigrant" who killed Constable Baylis had come to Canada from Jamaica at age eight and was only in a narrowly bureaucratic sense Jamaica's problem. In July 1994, the prime minister of Jamaica said in a speech in Ottawa that the deportation of immigrants would be no solution for Canada's social problems and that the number of deportees returning to Jamaica was contributing to a rising crime rate there.

Getting tough on crime, then, seems on the surface to be a response to a failure to control crime, especially crime committed by immigrants, minorities or youths. But at the same time as measures are being introduced against these groups, Statistics Canada was saying that crime rates are actually not increasing. Why was a National Crime Prevention Council formed to combat the social causes of crime if there was no crime epidemic? Why not set up a National Crime Fear Prevention Council to reassure the public that the government is doing its utmost to protect them from harm?

While it is easy to blame the media and to criticize readers who are unable to put it all into perspective, reporting and reading are not apprentice activities, where what is reported and what is read are objective realities that simply have to be transmitted in the right way. However, perhaps something else is going on. Let's look at a more recent example.

Sample Study

The Boxing Day shooting in 2005 was all too like the one in 1994, when Georgina Leimonis was shot in a crash robbery at the Just Desserts cafe by the son of a Jamaican immigrant who was later deported. In Toronto, after the senseless Boxing Day murder of teenager Jane Creba, law and order

CRIME RATES AND CRIME FEAR

became a central issue again and was then reprised in the federal election campaign. While there were those who said that unemployment, a lack of community-based programs, racism and so on were the real problems plaguing the black community, politicians began saying enough is enough and started demanding tough justice for anyone caught with a gun, as in this editorial published in the *Toronto Sun*.

Article 7.4 "We must take back the streets"

On this, the first day of 2006, let us all make this resolution: That this will be the year we take back our streets from the gangs, guns and drug dealers... We must demand... a mandatory minimum 10-year prison sentence... for anyone who uses a gun in the commission of a crime... that bail be denied... [and that] Crown attorneys refuse plea bargains for all offences involving gun crimes... [and stop giving] convicted criminals "credit"... [for] time they spend in jail awaiting trial... [that] Ontario hire 1,000 more police officers... that Ottawa scrap its useless $2-billion gun registry, along with the Grits' absurd election promise to "ban handguns,"... [and] city council give Police Chief Bill Blair the resources and support he will need to break up Toronto's estimated 70 street gangs... In many cases, the laws we already have on the books to fight gun crime are adequate... if the sentences... were being vigorously applied by the courts... This is the heart of the problem and fixing it is going to be an enormous job. (*Toronto Sun*, January 1, 2006, editorial)

The first edition of this book focused on the concern about youth crime, but it seems that the issues fifteen years later are more about street crime. Beyond that, some things remain the same. For example, stories are even now more broadly available than they were then. Through newswire services, homogenized news is universally available and extralocally produced.

The headline in the late online edition of the *Toronto Star* read "Boxing Day horror downtown." The first paragraph told the whole story: "Shots rang out on busy Toronto streets crowded with Boxing Day shoppers today, killing one person and wounding seven others." The headlines on the succeeding days from the *Star* are reproduced in Exhibit 7.1. Inside the article we have description, opinion and of course in online news, readers' comments.

Exhibit 7.1 Boxing Day Topic Headlines, *Toronto Star*, December 26, 2005 to January 3, 2006

"Boxing Day horror downtown" — 12.26.05, 9:55pm
"'Bang, bang, bang, bang!'" — 12.27.05, 01.00 am
"1 critical after Yonge shooting" — 12.27.05, 11.32 am
"T.O. like any big American city" — 12.27.05, 07:38 am
"City has 'lost its innocence'" — 12.27.05, 06:50 pm
"There's no going back to what we once were" — 12.28.05, 01:00 am

"Slain teen a top student, athlete" — 12.28.05, 05:28 am
"'Knives and .45s' in Doomstown" — 12.28.05, 05:28 am
"Gunshot victim recovering" — 12.28.05, 07:07 am
"Editorial: Taking right steps to stop gun crime" — 12.28.05, 09:13 am
"Slain teen was 'bright light'" — 12.28.05, 05:37 pm
"Opponents of gun ban press on" — 12.29.05, 06:13 am
"'We're going to lock them up': Police" — 12.29.05, 06:29 am
"No time to say goodbye" — 12.29.05, 08:46 am
"Toronto had no innocence to lose" — 12.30.05, 01:00 am
"John Tory backs street cameras" — 12.30.05, 08:02 am
"Seized gun linked to shootout" — 12.30.05, 05:58pm
"Miller 'stunned' by shooting" — 12.30.05, 06:06 pm
"Girl's slaying has 'touched each of us'" — 12.31.05, 07:40 am
"Scholars fight arms flow, violent culture" — 12.31.05, 07:41 am
"Bullets are usually very selective" — 12.31.05, 07:45 am
"We all have to act to push for change" — 12.31.05, 08:13 am
"A letter to readers" — 12.31.05, 08:55 am
"Leaders trade shots over solution to crisis in Toronto" — 01.03.06, 01:00 am
"Lawyers doubt tougher bail rules" — 01.03.06, 10:30 am

An initial reading of these headlines shows concern, anger and the feeling that what happened was despicable. This led to a reading for quotations, especially those expressing emotion, displayed in the next exhibit.

Exhibit 7.2 Comments in the *Toronto Star*, December 27

"In Toronto I've always felt I could walk anywhere. But there's people getting shot all the time now and it's getting kind of ridiculous."

"I've seen this kind of violence before because I used to live in the States… It's really bad ere now. Toronto — for me, it's just like any big American city. There's no difference. You can get killed just by walking down the street."

"Nobody is surprised anymore. This is what Toronto is like. But you can't be afraid. You live once, you die once… Maybe Toronto used to be a safe city, but it's not anymore."

"Everywhere you go you're going to find crime. It's unfortunate that it had to happen on Boxing Day at 5 o'clock in the afternoon, but it happens. But this scares m a little bit more because I love Yonge Street and I love walking up and down here. I'll definitely be a little more careful but I will still walk up and down here."

"It's something that comes with being in a big city," one person said, but it was a police officer who used the line that would be repeated in various media: "Toronto has finally lost its innocence." The homicide detective said "I think we're going to feel this day for a long time to come."

These comments are not angry ones and not even sad or fearful. In trying to characterize them I would say they're fatalistic, stoically accepting of what happened.

The police chief said, "They don't care about themselves, they don't care about others, it is absolutely critical that they be brought to justice." The police promised an increased presence; the premier said he would continue to press Ottawa for a ban on handguns; and a summit on gun safety was promised. Stephen Harper, campaigning for the federal election, was quickly featured in media coverage about the (Liberal) government's failure to control handguns.

But it was an article that appeared on December 30 that cast things in a different light. It alleged that the reaction to the shooting was heightened because the victim was white and that Toronto had not in fact lost its innocence because there had been plenty of victims over the years. This time, however, the victim was white, not black, and the killer a young black urban male. The first man convicted in the shooting was deserted by his father when he was young and brought up by a mother with substance abuse issues, facts the judge refused to take into account in sentencing him.

The last word on the case will be left to a letter to the editor after Creba's killer is sentenced.

Article 7.5 "Creba case shows need for change"

Regarding Jane Creba's murderer pleading guilty... so how's the Canadian legal system working for you now? As we learn the details of Jeremiah Valentine's confession, we find that he really had no respect for the laws of this country, and no number of anti-gun laws passed would have changed the situation one bit. We learn he was prohibited from not only owning, but possessing, a firearm, but he still had one. He was carrying a snub-nosed revolver (prohibited). He was carrying a revolver in a place other than his home or a licensed shooting range (illegal). He pointed a firearm at a person (illegal). He didn't have an authorization to transport the handgun (illegal). He attempted to shoot, and likely kill, someone (illegal). He fired the handgun in an unsafe manner (illegal)... He broke probation by being in a liquor store and possessing a handgun. He was arrested twice in two weeks for trafficking cocaine. He was a proven violent and dangerous criminal, and yet the court system let him roam the streets enabling him to kill an innocent teenager.

What's wrong with this picture?... One definition of insanity is doing the same thing over and over again and expecting a different result. Clearly, what was done here didn't work. It's time for an overhaul of both police procedures and court actions. We can't afford not to. (*Barrie Examiner*, January 2, 2010, letter to the editor, Douglas Barrie)

In summary, when one reads the newspapers, listens to the radio and watches the television, it seems difficult to ascertain if the public's fear of crime is misplaced or well-founded. It is also difficult to tell if there really is an escalating crime problem that requires tough solutions. If there is such an urgent problem to require tougher legislation, then perhaps the public perception is correct. But if the fear of crime is simply exaggerated, then what are new crime control measures designed to correct?

Sometimes the media seems to be sending out contradictory messages, that crime is on the rise, but the public's fears are unreasonable. However, asking such questions presupposes that the framework of "crime rate stable but fear rises" is the correct one. These questions are taken up in the next section.

Analyzing the News

One wonders what an unreasonable fear of crime would look like. Would it look like an article with the phrase, "Canada has not become more violent and crime against individuals is not on the upswing, but many Canadians nevertheless believe the crime rate is rising, a Statistics Canada report says"? This very real *Globe and Mail* article went on to say there was no greater risk of crimes such as robbery, assault, theft and sexual assault in 1993 than in 1988. The public's fear of crime was made to seem exaggerated in comparison to the objective reality of crime statistics, and a co-author of the report was quoted as saying: "There is still a crime problem... but let's not be hysterical about it." The explanation for the hysteria was presented as follows: politicians and the media are to blame for the public perception that the crime rate is escalating.

I have two problems with this. First, there is a tendency to think that a perception that crime is higher than the reality indicates a fear. It could indicate concern, anger or outrage, for example. Second, contrasting the two, the biased subjective opinion and the objective scientific fact simply ignores the reality that people are asked to estimate the likelihood of an event occurring despite not having the resources to accurately do so.

1. *The frustration calculus.* People estimate their likelihood of being victimized by crime fairly accurately at the local level even though they might overestimate the crime rate nationally. However, they also employ two contradictory heuristics or cognitive biases in assessing the likelihood of crime: the longer an event goes without happening the more likely it is going to occur;

and if something bad happens the odds are that it is more likely to happen again. These lay heuristics are used in the estimation of crime. They might be fallacious, but they are nonetheless convenient and available, if rather gloomy.

Results from the 2004 General Social Survey (GSS) indicate that 28 percent of Canadians aged fifteen years and older reported being victimized one or more times in the previous twelve months. This is up slightly from 26 percent in 1999, when the victimization survey was last conducted. When this information is broken down, we can see that three offence types increased: theft of personal property, theft of household property and vandalism. These are all crimes that are relatively common and that affect a person's sense of integrity. There were no increases in rates of sexual assault, robbery, physical assault and motor vehicle theft, and break-and-enter decreased.

As mentioned above, household victimization offences were the most frequently occurring criminal incidents (34 percent), followed by violent victimization (29 percent) and thefts of personal property (25 percent). Residents of western provinces generally reported higher rates of victimization than residents living in the east. The risk of violent victimization was highest among those aged fifteen to twenty-four years. Being single, living in an urban area, going out in the evening and having a low household income (under $15,000) also increased the likelihood of violent victimization. For household victimization, rates were highest among renters, those living in semi-detached, row or duplex homes and urban dwellers.

Violent victimizations were most likely to occur in commercial institutions, which were usually a person's place of work. Public places were the second most frequent locations of violent victimization, including sidewalks, streets or highways. These might be near or outside the victim's neighbourhood (18 percent), in parking garages or parking lots (3 percent), rural areas or parks (3 percent) or on public transportation (2 percent).

Obviously, there are variations in where violent crime occurs depending on the offence. Robbery incidents were most likely to take place on the street (43 percent), physical and sexual assaults were most likely to occur in commercial establishments (39 percent and 49 percent, respectively). The most common commercial establishment where a sexual assault occurred was a bar or restaurant (20 percent), while a physical assault most frequently occurred in an office building, factory, store or shopping mall (14 percent).

One thing that was consistent between police (75 percent) and victimization statistics (69 percent) was the absence of a weapon. Additionally, only one in five violent incidents involved more than one accused (22 percent), and the majority of violent crime (76 percent) was committed by one person. The majority of accused are male (87 percent), and young.

What is perhaps surprising is that in about one-quarter of the crimes, victims said the incident did not affect them much. Among those victims who were found to have difficulty carrying out their main activity, 37 percent said that it was for one day, 39 percent for two to seven days, and 16 percent for more than two weeks. The emotions that the incidents evoked in victims were anger (32 percent), being upset, confused or frustrated (20 percent) and feeling fearful (18 percent).

It appears from victims' own accounts that people were not traumatized for a long time. Moreover, the GSS shows that most people never even report criminal incidents to police and that the rate of reporting has gone down over time, not increased. In 2004, only about 34 percent of criminal incidents came to the attention of police, down from 37 percent in 1999 and 48 percent in 1993. Household victimization incidents had the highest report rate (37 percent, where there's insurance), while thefts of personal property had the lowest (31 percent).

While there were various reasons given for not reporting incidents to the police, 28 percent of violent incidents were not reported by victims because they were "dealt with in another way" and 28 percent were not reported because the victim felt that they were "not important enough" to bring to the attention of the police.

Given the relatively low incidence of crime, the lack of long-term trauma, the dominant emotional reaction being angry or upset rather than afraid and the low and decreasing report rate, it seems clear that the "crime news equals crime fear equals public paralysis" equation needs to be rethought.

2. *The fear calculus.* In the first edition a comparison was made of crime statistics between 1988 and 1993. Although these numbers are obviously out of date now, there is a lesson to be learned from the past.

The news report at the time stated that, comparing 1988 and 1993, the assault rate remained the same, robbery declined and theft of personal property also dropped. No other comparative numbers on criminal victimization are given. The rate of urban household victimization was about 70 percent higher than the rural rate, and the urban victimization rate for women was 20 percent higher than for men. The report suggested that underreporting in the past probably made current numbers seem artificially high in comparison.

The study the newspaper report was based on was the national victimization survey, which measured crime and the fear of crime. This first measure, the rate of victimization reported to researchers, shows not much overall increase. However, the second measure used at the time showed that the official rate of crime reported to the police had increased. Sexual assault and theft increased, and other categories of crime exhibited similar modest increases. Rather than attributing these numbers to an increase in crime, which would contradict the previous results, the researchers explain them as resulting from a simple increase in reporting, a conclusion which is defensible, but arguable because it is difficult to know whether reporting really goes up or not.

Where it gets interesting is that the news report says that 46 percent of people surveyed thought that crime has increased, and that women were four times as likely as men to say they felt unsafe walking in their neighbourhoods alone after dark. This was called unfounded, because it was not supported by the victimization survey or with evidence gathered from official statistics. This is the classic dichotomy, where criminal justice research criticizes lay interpretations as irrational.

In terms of the perceived change in the level of crime, while 46 percent of Canadians thought crime had increased, 43 percent believed crime had stayed the same, and 4 percent thought it decreased! The highest perception of an increase was in urban areas, with 48 percent believing crime had increased, while in rural areas 56 percent believed it had decreased or stayed the same. This is certainly not hysteria, as some (the media, criminology researchers, politicians) would have us believe.

Another fear fact cited in the news then was that the number of women who felt unsafe increased, but it is difficult to see this as hysteria because if we look at violence against women there is good evidence to justify women being afraid to walk alone at night. Perhaps the level of fear increased because of greater awareness, women being less likely to think it can't happen to them or even the realization that the criminal justice system has not always acted in the interests of women.

Other news articles pointed out at the time that the percentage of people who felt very safe walking alone in their neighbourhood after dark decreased. This decline in confidence is not the same as a rise in fear, but what exactly did the justice minister mean at the time when he said media coverage may be to blame, and that we should keep it in perspective? The whole problem is not knowing what to believe about crime. The resulting heightened law-and-order attitude on crime may have signalled frustration with the criminal justice system more than fear. Are both frustration and fear supposed to mirror the rate of criminal victimization? Are emotions supposed to be reasonable and match official statistics?

The official crime rate generated by the police and reflected in the Uniform Crime Reporting (UCR) statistics depends on crime reported by the public. The victimization rate generated by the General Social Survey depends on crime reported to researchers. The second will reflect a higher incidence of crime in society than the official rate simply because people are often reluctant to step forward and report crime to the police. However, there is a third crime rate, people's subjective perceptions. To compare this with objective information collected from the GSS or UCR statistics is both unfair and misleading. Although police and government researchers know more about victims and criminals than most of us, they do not necessarily know more about being a victim or a criminal, and their knowledge that crime is not increasing does not mean that the public's perception that it is, is false. The crime and victimization rates do not tell the whole story.

The crime (UCR) and victimization (GSS) rates and the fear/frustration rate (FFR) need not be the same — they are all social constructions. First, even the best statistics reflect the quality of the questions researchers ask or the character of police work. Second, people can have a general perception that crime has increased, even though their direct experiences do not bear this out, because they also have a mediated experience of crime in society obtained extralocally through the media. The fear of crime and the perception that the criminal justice system needs to do something about it is a socially constructed experience refracted through the media.

Crime coverage at the time was prominent. The *Toronto Star*, for example, increased its coverage of crime 37 percent between 1991 and 1993. The coverage of young offenders increased as well, 453 percent in the same time period! Articles on young offenders were prominent in the Canadian news in 1993, available across Canada through the *Canadian Press* and published virtually unchanged in newspapers as geographically diverse as the *Vancouver Sun* and the *Chronicle-Herald*. And although there was some equivocation about whether the rate of youth crime was increasing or not, the overall perception in 1993 seems to have been that it was out of control, a perception enhanced in no small measure by the crime-control platforms adopted by the national political parties in the fall election.

It is difficult to keep things in perspective when the news constantly reflects the fear that crime is on the increase. There are stories about violent youths, the growing use of guns in violent crimes and the new crimes of home invasion and carjacking, and there is continual debate over whether crime rates are really going up or not.

Immigration policy was revised as part of a growing turn towards a law-and-order approach to crime. The federal and provincial governments had also tabled changes to the Young Offenders Act (YOA) to double the sentence for first-degree murder; to try sixteen-year-olds charged with serious violent crimes in adult court; to share information on young offenders with police, school officials and child welfare agencies; to use victim impact statements in court; and to publicize information on young offenders where there was a perceived threat to public safety. The issue of lowering the minimum age of responsibility to ten years of age was even referred to a Commons committee for further study.

However, as Kenneth Whyte pointed out in a column for the *Globe and Mail* (June 4, 1994) at the time, "the facts argue against an increase in teen criminality... the rise in the number of charges laid is due to nothing so much

CRIME RATES AND CRIME FEAR

as society's increasing reliance on the courts and constabulary... the number of youths convicted of truly violent crime is stable... fighting a phantom crime wave can be quite expensive."

Whether crime was actually out of control and on the rise or not was arguable, and probably irrelevant, for there was a general concern internationally that crime was out of control in the 1990s. The U.S. passed a $30-billion anti-crime bill that included extending the death penalty to fifty federal offences, adding 100,000 new police officers to city streets, banning the sale and possession of certain assault weapons, building state prisons and boot camps, and increasing the range of life sentences. The British government proposed that in the interests of curbing rising crime it was necessary to restrict the traditional right of the individual to be silent in the face of police questioning. The German government tabled a package of laws to combat violent crime, and Canada proposed changes in immigration policy, for young offenders and to toughen penalties for certain drug crimes.

The last word on the Creba case will be given to this letter to the editor, published after her shooter was found guilty of the offence and news broadcasts were saying that he was on the street despite numerous offences because he was a police informant:

Article 7.6 "Crime and punishment redux"
When horrible acts take place in civilized society, we have to do better than cry out for revenge. The [U.N. Convention on the Rights of the Child]... is an international covenant that protects children from the hot anger of the mob. People are too quick to throw out the basic human rights that protect us and our families when they seem to be an inconvenience to the act of revenge. We are perpetually paying a heavy price because fear and anger rule our responses to youth crime. (*Toronto Star*, December 27, 2009, by Les Horne)

Given the negative news on crime, conservative changes in the law and a political law-and-order agenda, the mediated perception (FFR) that crime was increasing would necessarily be out of synch with official statistics (UCR). The fact that it was out of synch with experience (GSS) as well is surprising, but only to the mundane. However, I would like to suggest that it is easy to inflame fear, anger and outrage when it is politically expedient and convenient to do so.

Summary
This chapter began with a police media relations officer describing the work of dealing with the media on a day-to-day basis. This is not an easy job, given the practical difficulties of dealing with reporters who might not be crime-literate or who inadvertently distort or exaggerate crime news.

Then news articles on crime were examined to see how they might contribute to an unreasonable fear on the part of the public and how crime concerns might be detached from both official statistics and peoples' direct experience. What people believe about crime affects their day-to-day living in the world. Fear of crime drives people to lock their doors, buy security equipment and take self-defence courses. And while these are all very understandable responses to a fear of crime, they might not be based in any actual possibility of victimization. But that doesn't matter.

Concern about crime serves the interest of a law-and-order agenda. It is irrelevant whether crime is really increasing or not, because if crime is perceived to be out of control, then there is pressure to do something about it. Protestations that crime is actually stable or decreasing have little effect because the tendency of the media is to highlight dramatic and violent crimes. Politicians appear to be quite willing to climb onto the law-and-order bandwagon and pledge to "do something about crime" as a political manoeuvre, all of which unfolds through the discursive reality of the media. So whether the topic is "crime out of control" or the "fear of crime is exaggerated," the images displayed in the media promote the same reformist strategy — something has to be done to control crime and assuage concern.

Canada often passes crime bills that promise tougher sentences for offenders, more minimum mandatory sentences, more use of incarceration, more prisons, more police on the streets, more investment in surveillance technologies, more restrictions on the rights of the individual and so on. People are willing to go along with these measures because they believe crime is on the increase and/or they believe not enough is being done about it. Does the tail wag the dog, or vice versa; are law reforms driven by public perception or the other way around? They certainly go together.

News reports fit into a textually constructed reality, where public perception and official policy are part of a loop. The more stories people read about crime, especially of events they can't control, the more likely they are to think crime is out of control, which will produce more stories and generate interest in legal reform, a condition promoting the production of crime news in the first place. This can actually lead to apathy, not fear.

So, the work of "getting it right" is a lot harder than at first sight, whether one is a police media relations officer, a reporter or a reader.

8

Crime Stoppers and the Police
The Ideological Construction of Community

Crime Stoppers is a relatively innocuous form of crime reporting, where the police publish the particulars of a crime and solicit the assistance of the public to solve it. It unfortunately is not known to be a glamorous form of policing either. However, we examine these items in this chapter in the context of the relationship between the police and the media in modern society.

Tony Thomson introduces the issue by looking at how the police have come to be interested in the media as a vehicle for public relations and crime control. He sees the growing use of the media by the police as a way to enhance their own image and extend their control into the community. The point he makes is a critical one, that the police are interested in using the media to their own advantage, not simply in providing a public service. Historically, the police have shied away from being too open with the media, but in modern society they tend to use the media to solicit help from the public, to warn people about crime in their community and to promote the need for more police resources around budget time.

In Reading the News, some examples of the use of Crime Stoppers are reproduced to show how the police have used this form of crime reporting for crime control. The Crime Stoppers program has been prominent in soliciting public help in solving crimes, and there has been much publicity surrounding its successes. In these examples the emphasis is on the types of discourse police employ and the types of crime they publicize.

In the Sample Study, the analysis of the Crime Stoppers articles from the first edition is reproduced. The overall impression is of violent crimes committed in public by strangers. This is contrasted with crimes in Toronto in 2008 on video in the next section.

In Analyzing the News, the Crime Stoppers program is linked to other efforts to extend the role of the police, such as a trend broadly known as community policing, a movement that promised to reform the character of police-community relations. Community policing arises from a broad-based social movement that has criticized the police for not being responsive to the diverse needs of all groups in society. It has also become a way for the police to defuse criticism and increase their effectiveness. This section considers the more critical issue of who defines community and threats to its safety.

Overall, crime is as much an ideological construction as a real threat, and whoever controls the definition of crime is in a powerful position to manipulate public opinion. Crime Stoppers gives us a very particular representation of crime, one that emphasizes public, violent crime committed by strangers, with the unfortunate consequence of increasing fear and apathy in the very community the police help define. Studies I have found useful in thinking about Crime Stoppers and community policing are Carriere and Ericson (1989), Ericson (1991), Fishman (1978), Lippert (2002) and Young (2003).

Tony Thomson's Talk

I'm not much of an expert, certainly not on the media, but I want to relate to you a particular kind of interest in the subject. What I've been doing for the last little while is studying policing, that is, RCMP and small town policing. I haven't particularly focused on the relations of the police to the media. I want to come at it from the other way. I want to look at how the police use the media. So it's more from the point of view of the interests of the police than of the media.

I want to present an overview first of the traditional image of the RCMP and the process which led to the undermining of respect and admiration for the force. In the 1970s, the RCMP became more conscious of the need to manipulate public opinion in their favour, to create a positive public image. The relationship between the police and the media changed, and I think it's inherently problematic.

The RCMP had in the past distanced itself from the public and the media. They didn't have a conscious strategy aimed at influencing the public to their benefit. In large measure this was because the desired effect was actually being achieved without their trying to do it. The RCMP had become a national symbol quite early in the century, with the beaver and the maple leaf. The myth of the RCMP had its origins in the taming of the west and the Arctic, in exotic locales and the clash of cultures. Some of this positive propaganda was consciously created: the musical ride, Mounties in red serge, hagiographies written by Mounties about what it was like to police at the turn of the century. This created a positive public image of the police propagated by the media.

Similarly, in the U.S. under J. Edgar Hoover the FBI was reorganized in the 1920s, and he was astute in his political use of the media to depict criminals and the FBI agents who rounded them up. And in Nova Scotia in the 1920s there were a series of break-ins in Colchester and Pictou counties by an automobile gang, which was depicted in the media as terrorizing the rural population in the summer. This made headlines and was very similar to the kind of crime stories that were coming out of the U.S. After the automobile gang is captured the *Halifax Herald* says it was keeping quiet about RCMP involvement in the investigation, and the RCMP was given the credit for breaking this rural terror.

Support for the RCMP was not unanimous; for example, liquor laws were being violated in small communities but many people did not see this as immoral. And in Cape Breton when the RCMP move in to replace the provincial police trying to control militant workers' strikes in the 1920s, the RCMP is seen as worse than the local alternative because they're outsiders, they don't represent the community, and they're seen as at the beck and call of the politicians of Ottawa and Halifax, and therefore of the business interests behind them.

The RCMP wanted a different image of themselves. They wanted the outsider image, apart from society, that was the construction that they were trying to cultivate. A view of equitable law enforcement, an end to favouritism, this is the image the RCMP wanted to present, and the mainstream media was willing to go along. This was seen as an end to favouritism and corruption, a police force which would not be run by the mayor or his cronies in a small town. Close ties with people in the community was not the norm in the RCMP; frequent transfers were. Get them out of the community, don't let them develop close ties. The force was highly militaristic in its discipline: young recruits who have to be unmarried when they join, unmarried for a certain length of time, who lived in barracks. The RCMP were an occupying army, and the Northwest Mounted Police were modelled after the Royal Irish Constabulary.

The myth was unmade temporarily in the 1960s, and south of the border civil rights workers were being harassed and murdered by local police officers, minorities in the north were trying to defend themselves against police attacks, municipal policing earning the epitaph "pig."

Minorities in Canada were less demonstrative in support of their rights and against the police. There was one exception in Canada, the FLQ. In the process of repressing the liberation movement in Quebec, the RCMP shattered their own mythology. Within the mandate of the RCMP was a domestic spying division. Shortly after the attempted insurrection details began to leak out about RCMP wrongdoing in the press. It took a royal commission to detail these particular crimes, the arson, the break-ins, the mail openings and the other illegal activities. It was very damaging to the RCMP in terms of its reputation for incorruptibility and efficiency. Its reputation was badly tattered.

In response to this debacle there were several processes. First, the reputation of the entire force had been tarnished by a single division. So the decision was made to civilianize the spy force and remove it from the RCMP, creating a more autonomous organization. It may contain the same personnel, but it has a different letterhead. And more importantly, any blunders cannot be placed at the foot of the RCMP.

Second, the RCMP had to become more proactive in the manipulation of its own image. A new posting was created called the police-community relations crime-prevention officer.

There was a third equally important development outside the force to which the RCMP had to respond and that was the advent of community groups demanding more local control over the police. So the important social issue that emerges in the early 1970s regarding the police is accountability. To whom are the police accountable? The RCMP were accountable to the attorney general, to their supervisors, and in general they were accountable to the philosophy of equitable policing.

So there's several models of policing. There's the RCMP occupying-force model. The alternative model appeared to be municipal policing and that was worse. Municipal policing was at the beck and call of local elites of the time. There's a story in one small town that every morning the mayor walked into the police station to give the police chief his orders for the day. In contrast to this model of policing, the RCMP were better.

There is also a third model beyond the occupying force or three-tiered policing which is what you had in the towns, and that's community control, police accountability to the community. This is what emerged in the 1970s, but there's a real sociological problem with this third model. The problem as I see it is that "the community" is very hard to define. Who is the community? If the community is composed of divergent groups and different class interests, who represents the community? These were very important political issues which emerged in the 1970s and certainly had to work themselves out in the development of community-based policing.

From the point of view of the RCMP, who also turned to community-based policing, it meant a new relationship with the media. The RCMP's relationship with the media up to this point had been minimalist: they wanted to give the least possible information, especially about particular crimes. From the point of view of the media what sells newspapers is crime stories, but what the media wanted, the RCMP didn't want to give. However, when the RCMP and other police got into community-based policing, they wanted to use the media for their own image because a positive public perception of the police force makes policing more effective.

So, on the one hand, you have the media wanting dramatic crime stories, but you have the police force not wanting to give many details. On the other hand, you have the police force wanting to give positive crime prevention stories which would boost their image in the communities, and yet the reporters and the newspapers had very little interest in crime prevention. When the cop on the street asks the crime prevention officer, "How many crimes have been prevented today?" the answer is "Who knows?" When a reporter is asked the same question, the answer is "Who cares?" Crime prevention is not newsworthy and it doesn't make good coverage. That is a fundamental problem.

I want to raise one other issue very quickly, and that is the media's desire to show crimes. In its desire to show crimes and traumatization, it's not going to stop at where the badge is. It's just as interested in showing police misconduct, police deviance, maybe more so. Maybe that's an even hotter crime story. And the police are feeding into it.

There's a firearms training system that comes out of Los Angeles, where small-town Nova Scotia officers learn from videos with scenarios of crimes, and they're supposed to role-play in them. They're all Spanish-speaking, and the video inhabits a violent world where guns are everywhere, where no one is to be trusted, where every casual encounter is fraught with danger. The philosophy is street survival, and you have to approach every situation as if it is imminently dangerous. Now, this might be appropriate for LA but I'm not so sure it's appropriate in small towns. I think it goes completely contrary to community-based policing. You approach citizens in every situation suspiciously. You stop a car and you have to assume it's a high-risk stop. Maybe once in their lifetime the police officers are going to have a life-threatening situation, and maybe that justifies it. But I'm not so sure it does. And it certainly doesn't justify it in community-based policing.

My last remark here is this: this kind of firearms training system is actually going to feed into the media because it's going to lead to civilians being killed. It's going to lead to civilians with three in the chest or one in the forehead, even in a small town.

Reading the News

Tony Thomson raises several issues concerning the relationship between the police and the media. One is that traditionally the police have had an adversarial relationship with the fourth estate, perhaps because they saw the press as interfering with the role of the police in fighting crime. Reporters ask nosey questions, sometimes embarrassing the police about unsolved crimes, and could release information that would interfere with an investigation. In this way, reporting can get in the way of policing.

The police, however, have come to see that creating a positive media image can actually aid them in their job. Although it is to the advantage of the police to have a positive image in and of itself, on a deeper level it could also aid in law enforcement. An image of a professional, autonomous, independent police force, for example, builds trust and confidence among the public. At one level the police have to repair the damage created by a traditional image of corruption and political interference in policing; on another level, however, the police can actually turn manipulation of their media image to their advantage. Add to this the modern development of community policing, and there is accountability, independence and news control.

The police departments have had success in partnering with the media to achieve crime-fighting objectives. For example, Crime Stoppers programs are media segments involving a collaboration between the public, the police, business and the media. The media's role in fighting crime by publicizing re-enactments of unsolved crimes to generate additional leads and information has been quite successful. Since they began in the early 1980s, the number of Crime Stoppers programs has grown dramatically, they are highly visible and successful in the recovery of stolen property and have increased citizen awareness of anti-crime efforts. In addition, research has found that programs that have the most cooperative relationship with the media enjoyed greater success and productivity.

The police and the media exist in a mutually supportive relationship. Police information officers play an important role in disseminating information to the public through the media, especially on new policing initiatives. The media also relies on the police for a majority of its information on crime news. The police then use the news to serve their interests in policing. Crime Stoppers news articles can broaden the sources of information available to the police to solve a crime and represent a movement of the police back out into the community, represented by projects such as Neighbourhood Watch, Community Policing and Coastal Watch, where tips from people are used to detect drug smugglers. However, research shows that the police still spend most of their time filling requests for information on incidents and a very small amount explaining crime control initiatives.

The police see the media as something that can be used towards the broader goal of crime detection and prevention, but this can be difficult given the relationship between the police and reporters: crime prevention does not necessarily interest reporters. However, underneath these various programs is a deeper issue: the use of the media by the police to control and prevent crime. These programs are quite successful, but one criticism is that the police should not be in the business of controlling the news, that this is too high a cost to pay in order to control crime and that perhaps crime cannot be so easily controlled in the first place.

1. *Crime Stoppers articles.* Exhibit 8.1 is a reconstruction of a typical Crime Stoppers article. Because they are typically small, it is easy to convey a sense of how they work through constructing an exemplar. In this fictional article, the police are soliciting the public to help them in the investigation of an

armed robbery. The crime occurred late at night and involved three youths. The article is predominantly factual, with a crime, a location, a victim and description of the perpetrators. More important, assistance of the public in solving the crime is solicited by asking anyone with information to call the number given.

Exhibit 8.1 Police Seek Help Finding Suspects

Police are asking for the public's help in finding three teenagers suspected of robbing a man in Fredericton at knifepoint last month. The Oct. 15 robbery occurred on Beaverbrook Drive at 11:15 p.m. One of the suspects was wearing a baseball cap, and the other two hooded sweatshirts. Anyone with information on the crime is asked to call police at 452-0000 or Crime Stoppers at 452-STOP. Calls are anonymous and cash rewards are offered for information leading to a conviction. (Crime Stoppers wants your information and not your identity.)

This Crime Stoppers article is an open solicitation for information coupled with the brief description of a crime. The crime is framed in official terms as a robbery. A robbery is not simply the action of stealing or taking through force, it is also a bureaucratic category that enables the processing of an action as a crime and identifies it for the public as against the law. The described event is not framed as a disagreement, a lost wager or a loan, but as a robbery. The crime also violates the sense of fair play because three assailants have attacked one person, and it feeds into the fear that youth crime is out of control. The article presents a normal version of a crime through the discourse used to describe the event. This discourse anticipates and creates an unequivocal interpretation for the reader that a crime has been committed. This item is similar to many such articles that appear in local and provincial newspapers.

The second exhibit describes a type of crime that the police and military investigate and for which public assistance is always welcome. Whereas Exhibit 8.1 was a request for information on a particular crime, Exhibit 8.2 explains more the results of a police-community anti-crime initiative.

Exhibit 8.2 RCMP Crack Down on Drugs in Kings County

Kings County RCMP are continuing efforts this summer to crack down on marijuana grow operations. Police information officer Constable Wright said last week RCMP executed a search warrant in the Berwick area and seized almost 1,000 marijuana plants, or enough marijuana to produce 500,000 cigarettes. Several hand guns were also seized, and police expect to press charges of illegal possession. Police say the drug problem is not getting worse in Kings County, but police are increasing their efforts to address it. Last year, RCMP intervened in 10 drug production sites in the region, and logged 50 drug trafficking incidents. Cst. Wright said RCMP will partner with the Department of National Defence to conduct patrols over the area this summer to detect marijuana farms. He also said the transformation of marijuana remains a concern in the area, with cannabis extraction labs making marijuana oil or hash oil. Wright encouraged residents who have witnessed suspicious behaviour to contact local RCMP or Crime Stoppers at 1-800-000-TIPS."

Article 8.1, below, is also typical of the type of Crime Stoppers article usually published. What is interesting about this item is that Peel Region also uses it to showcase their community policing message, which reads in part: "Peel Regional Police, in partnership with the community will strive to create a safe environment in which to live, work, and visit."

Article 8.1 "Further Arrests in Peel Region's 8th Homicide of 2009"

Mississauga — Peel Regional Police homicide investigators have made two further arrests in Peel Region's eighth murder of 2009… officers responded to the rear of an apartment building on Shipp Drive, regarding a report of a man who had been shot. Upon arrival, officers found the victim… suffering from a gun shot injury. He was transported to a local hospital, where he was pronounced dead. On Thursday, June 4, 2009, investigators arrested… a 45-year-old Brampton man. He has been charged with Second Degree Murder and has been remanded into custody… Information may be left anonymously by calling Peel Crime Stoppers at 1-800-222-TIPS. (*Brampton News.com*, June 12, 2009)

So we start to see different types of Crime Stoppers articles: Exhibit 8.1 is a request for public assistance, Exhibit 8.2 is more of an information piece on police effectiveness, and Article 8.1 is a combination of the two. Article 8.2 also combines the effectiveness of police work with the affectiveness of the crime chosen to publicize.

Article 8.2 "Murderous domestic rampage in Mississauga"

A man wanted for the brutal slaying of a senior and critically injuring his estranged common-law wife has been captured in Mississauga… [he is] the lone suspect in the case and early this morning [police] had made a public appeal to help find him. The man who is known to police for violence was captured and the murder weapon was recovered. Police found the woman dead at the scene when they responded to a 911 call…

Two other victims were taken to hospital with serious injuries. A 44-year-old woman… is in Sunnybrook hospital in critical condition while her 25-year-old daughter… was treated and released of her defensive injuries… [the woman] had a restraining order on the accused, which he apparently violated a month ago, neighbours said... It's believed the daughter and the dead woman tried to intervene in the attack.

Police urged anyone with any knowledge of the murder to contact Peel Crime Stoppers at 1-800-222-TIPS or online at peelcrimestoppers.ca. (*Toronto Sun*, May 30, 2009, by Rob Lamberti and Don Peat)

2. *Patterns.* Crime Stoppers articles are usually short, contain the barest of information and represent requests on the part of the police for information from the public that may help solve crimes. That seems pretty straightforward. The articles assume that citizens will be willing to help the police. They don't usually tell the reader much about the work of Crime Stoppers itself, but they follow the standard pattern of reporting a crime and its location and requesting information.

When articles contain more affective, emotional information, there are more details to draw in the reader. In Article 8.2, the story is all too familiar. The victim has been estranged from the offender. She is with two other women, her daughter and a friend at the time she is attacked. They are all injured, one of them fatally. It appears the investigation is pretty much wrapped up, although there is still the request for any information the public might have.

In general, Crime Stoppers articles are not extensive but reflect and create the relative seriousness of the crime. They contain requests for assistance, the date and type of crime, a description of the crime, a description of the perpetrator, a number to call with information and the assurance of anonymity. Because the articles often contain both a description of a crime and a request for assistance, they are police advertisements.

The information in the article is strictly controlled: there is nothing about the stage of the investigation or possible suspects not released by police. There are no interviews with neighbours and no pictures. No experts have been consulted to comment on the crime or to argue over its seriousness. There is no contextual information to determine whether this crime fits into a pattern or not. The articles are solely about the crimes in question and give us enough information to form a basis for assistance. They are very unlike most newspaper articles on crime.

Many Crime Stoppers articles appear in local newspapers. An electronic news index showed the *Halifax Herald* to have almost a hundred articles on Crime Stoppers over the previous year. The *Canadian Business and Current Affairs* index listed over 600 items, most of them from *Canada News Wire*. Using an internet search engine, over 3,000 results were found for Crime Stoppers at the *Toronto Star*. Using another, comprehensive index of many different newspapers, over 17,000 items were found, in some cases going back over twenty years.

By themselves such articles do not enhance or detract from the reputation or image of the police; there is no reason to think they tell the reader the police are or are not doing their job. Crime Stoppers does, however, represent a way the media can be used by the police to their advantage. The public can be enlisted to detect criminals and solve crimes, and to affirm that crime exists and something must be done about it. Researchers define these advertisements as a practical effort to reduce loss along property lines rather than with solving violent crimes. A recent comprehensive study of Crime Stoppers programs showed that property crimes constituted 75 percent of Crime Stoppers ads in one week.

An editorial in the *Toronto Sun* in May 2009 reported that since its inception in 1984 Crime Stoppers has resulted in more than 7,000 people being charged with more than 34,000 offences, more than 15,000 crimes have been solved, $47-million worth of stolen property has been recovered and $228-million worth of illegal drugs have been taken off the streets.

Such articles applaud the success of the Crime Stoppers program and praise the police for their efforts. Articles celebrate open lines of communication between the community and the public, how the police are involved with the community and how crimes cannot be solved without the public's assistance. These "advertorials" overview the success of the Crime Stoppers program and are a common feature in the newspapers. The language often builds an image of citizens and police battling crime in crime-fighting partnerships. They construct the sense of a community that is united in fighting crime. This construction of community creates a boundary between the law-abiding and the law-breaking, and readers can identify with those who are doing something about crime.

Crime rates decrease for all kinds of reasons, some of them very mundane: crime may be reported less, police activity may be down because of decreases in funding and staffing, or crime may have actually fallen. Editorials that celebrate the effectiveness of Crime Stoppers ads praise effort rather than coincidence, public goodwill rather than just police work. The articles present the police in a positive light in partnership with the community.

Crime Stoppers has been helpful in solving many cases and has recovered much more in stolen property than it paid out in awards. The awards are funded by local organizations, and many are not even claimed (especially in the Maritimes), a testimony to public altruism.

Sample Study

In the first edition of this book, an informal analysis of fifty-two Crime Stoppers articles was conducted. The sample consisted of cases of the police asking for help from the public in solving crime in a variety of newspapers: the *Edmonton Journal, Ottawa Citizen* and *Halifax Herald,* among others. After screening out articles that editorialized on the success of the programs, the items were categorized by type of criminal offence, location and perpetrator-victim relationship. The main categories of offences depicted in the Crime Stoppers articles were armed robbery (35 percent), sexual assault (15 percent) and break and enter with theft (15 percent). Most of the offences took place in public places (67 percent), such as the street or parking lots, convenience stores and banks. The perpetrators for which information was available were predominantly strangers, usually white males in their teens or early twenties. The articles generally received prominent placement, appearing on average before page five of the newspaper.

The overall impression created by these items is of public, violent crime committed by strangers. In order to do a more extensive analysis, the complete set of Crime Stoppers citations for 1992–93 in the *Halifax Herald* was downloaded, a total of 332 articles. In the results, several patterns were found. When "other" and "advertorials" were factored out, break and en-ter/theft accounted for 51 percent of the offences, with armed robbery (38 percent) and sexual assaults (10 percent) coming after. Of the total offences indexed by location (172), 36 percent (61) were public and 53 percent (91) were private. However, of the public offences, 77 percent (47) were armed robberies, 71 percent (65) of the private offences were break and enter/theft crimes, and in 12 percent (20) of the cases the location was not known. Of the total selected offences indexed by relationship (172), 45 percent (78) were committed by strangers, 3 percent (6) were committed by someone known, and in 51 percent (98) of the cases the identity of the perpetrator was not available.

The overall impression is that crimes are being committed by strangers in our community all the time, and that these can be solved through public assistance. Consistent with other research, corporate or white collar crimes are not mentioned, and domestic violence is not included. Assistance is not sought for conflicts between police and public, and civilian complaints with the police are not aired. Other research compares inconclusively with this in terms of whether the majority of ads are non-violent. Some research has found that a majority (80 percent) of so-called crimes of the week contained violence, whereas other research has found only about 20 percent contained violence. What is more important, perhaps, is that most ads of this sort are about property crime, which are arguably lower-class crimes.

From a criminological standpoint, what drives these statistics is criminal activity and the nature of police work. Armed robberies make up a significant percentage of public crimes, but break and enters by their nature tend to occur in private. The identity of the perpetrators in either of these groups is usually unknown or they are strangers to the victim; these are not generally acquaintance-victimization types of crimes. Both of these types of crimes are

175

more likely to be good candidates to appear in Crime Stoppers than sexual assault, precisely because there are less likely to be independent leads for the police to go on.

It is less apparent, however, that these crimes do not represent all crime but only crimes for which Crime Stoppers is a useful venue. Crime Stoppers is not intended to be a public information service but is a service for the police. Crime Stoppers articles present a skewed representation of crime because they advertise only crimes for which the police require assistance.

At face value, the impression created by these articles is of violence committed in public places and invasions of homes by strangers. The victims are largely faceless and could be anyone going about their lives. There is no sense that the victims precipitated the offences in any way, that these were not real offences, that the perpetrators were objects of discrimination and so on. The message readers get is that dangerous people threaten normal law-abiding people and thus constitute a threat to the community. The explicit message of the Crime Stoppers items, that people in the community can help solve these crimes, is thus anchored by the implicit message that crime is an outside force that threatens the community itself.

This was the original analysis, and it still stands the test of time, except that now a new wrinkle has been added: online videos. The traditional print ads probably sensitized people to crime in their neighbourhoods and increased their role in crime detection, and also possibly made people more afraid of crime as well. However, now Crime Stoppers videos are publicized online and available to a generalized, placeless audience.

Some people are already afraid to walk in their own neighbourhoods at night, and certainly the perception is that crime is growing. Fear of victimization is linked to perceived vulnerability and is not necessarily connected to actual risk. An unintended consequence of raising awareness, especially through videos, may be increasing fear of crime and concerns about personal safety even more. This is especially probable since the majority of Crime Stoppers articles are about violent public crimes committed by strangers, because these are the types of crimes for which it is most useful to ask for public assistance.

This is a traditional concern, that crime news reinforces a sense of public alienation and increase fear. However, many of the online Crime Stoppers articles surveyed were not long and did not contain extensive descriptions of violent offences. Their abbreviated and technical air added to their official character, but it's difficult to see how they increased fear.

Perhaps there is something more subtle at work.

Analyzing the News

Let us examine more critically the discursive work that Crime Stoppers ads do. Crime Stoppers is an institutional response to the problem of crime control and is sponsored by dominant institutions — the mass media, the police and private corporations. Crime Stoppers is not based on an official fear that crime is out of control or on the desire of people at the community level to develop a local initiative to fight crime: it is part of a broader effort on the part of the police to enlist citizens' aid. This new crime-fighting partnership is one engineered by the police.

Primary Crime Stoppers articles, ads and videos are emotional portrayals that generate sympathy for the victim and moral outrage against the offender. There are also secondary stories about the program's success, embodied in "discourses of effectiveness and affectiveness." Some examples of primary ads were re/created above.

An example of a "discourse of effectiveness" is an item where the media, independently or by quoting the police, comments on the success of a Crime Stoppers program. Such articles are often self-congratulatory, offer little empirical evidence for claims made and praise the efforts of police to reach out to the community and generate support for fighting crime. These articles validate the success of the programs and thus legitimate the work of the police. Questions are not asked about the moral rightness of the programs, the police are not blamed for not doing their job well, and criticisms are not raised about issues such as using citizens as informants.

It is not the issue of effectiveness that I am concerned with here but rather the "discourse of affectiveness." In Article 8.2, the public can easily identify with the victim and sympathetically see her as the victim of a violent attack by an estranged partner. People should be able to live without the fear of becoming the victim of violent crime. There is no suggestion of sympathy for the offender or of mitigating circumstances, just the portrayal of a vicious act. Let's look at a more modern solicitation for information.

1. *Police release video.* In March 2008, Toronto police released a videotape of Toronto's eleventh homicide of the year, showing a man calmly firing into a group of young men, called "Security Video of a Murder in Progress (Toronto)." It is also available as "Abdikarim Ahmed Abdikarim Murder — GTA's Most Wanted." Commenting on the video, a police spokesperson says: "This is very disturbing. It speaks for itself... He simply walked up within 10 feet of the group, got their attention and without warning opened fire. His actions were discriminate and it is obvious that he intended to inflict maximum damage."

The video was released March 17, 2008, and thirteen months later it had over 56,000 views, with 640 comments. The comments were not sympathetic or shocked, but vengeful: "I swear my bullets are coming from all directions

177

when i find this bitch his family can get it as well fuck if the cops don't find him fuck i will and when i do NO COMMENT" and blaming: "But don't anybody dare point out that he's BLACK (gasp), lest you be labeled racist." The release of the video was credited with leading to an arrest.

In Article 8.3 we see the discussion of the release of a separate video.

Article 8.3 "Shocked by Toronto police murder video? That was the point"

More than two years ago, an anonymous person sent police a video of a man dying… his navy shirt pulled up, his eyes closed. A police officer turns him onto his side. Blood soaks the young man's back and the pavement.

This week, detectives… released the unsettling footage to the public. They acknowledged their goal was to shock people… [However] experts warn both police and media they should proceed carefully. "It was horrifying to watch," [a professor of cultural studies said]… "This poor man's last minutes were a spectacle."…

Last year, police released security camera footage of a gunman opening fire and killing 18-year-old Abdikarim Ahmed Abdikarim. Each muzzle flash could be seen in the clip and its graphic nature elicited some concerns from the public… "That's reality. If we're going to hide reality then people are not going to know what we're up against," said [police]… [A sociology professor said] "Police have to weigh any positive benefits to the investigation against the negative aspects of exposing people to sensational images and making people who knew the victim possibly relive the crime." (*National Post*, February 13, 2009, by Melissa Leong)

In the article, police say that they released the video in order to elicit public assistance. While this might be their purpose, there are also consequences in the publics' exposure to the video. Video footage, whether it is retrieved from passive surveillance systems or recorded on amateur videotape, has a real-time character. New theorizing shows that it is more emotionally charged than a newspaper story, as it literally embodies the crime, it calls on the public as voyeur to inform the spectacle, and it easily lends itself to a punitive orientation to crime in the beginning rather than at the end of the justice transaction.

The police of course do not wish to cater to voyeurism. And in fact the victim's mother said: "It's very graphic but at the same time, the purpose of it is to help police… Hopefully, people are not just looking at it for the wrong reasons. Hopefully, they're looking at it and they can help. It is devastating. It brings out a lot of what happened that day. But it's a modest sacrifice just to get a little disclosure."

However, the public brings their own agenda to the viewing and their own interpretation to the reading. Perhaps a few will have information, but for the many this is a highly violent crime committed in public, an unsolved and thus apparently random crime involving strangers.

Most crime reporting can never aspire to such immediacy. But Crime Stoppers ads can and do become video wanted posters, soliciting the surveillance of the impotent many. They are not a democratic tool in this form, because they are produced by the police. They offer a view of crime that is evil and random, and since they are offered by the police we as viewers align ourselves with the police. But of course, why would we identify with criminals. Ah, but they're not criminals, they're suspects in events that are putative crimes.

The spectacle is individualized, it is physical, it is public surveillance. Whereas the spectacle used to be at the time of the punishment, now it is in the crime. Especially when it comes to video surveillance, the raw footage mimics reality TV.

2. *Public responds.* To determine how these features become visible, a selection of Crime Stoppers ads produced by Metropolitan Toronto police were viewed. The first one was called "Toronto Break and Enter — Guns now in the Wrong Hands." It had received 3919 views. The video clip is about sixteen seconds long and loops five times, with a voiceover that describes how the suspect entered the front door and left the premises with ten handguns and two long guns. The suspect is described as a black male with a husky build, about five ten, twenty to twenty-five years old, wearing dark baggy blue jeans and a white hoody.

On Youtube.com there were thirty-five comments, such as: "What is the probability that this character is out on bail or probation for earlier crimes?" or the string in Exhibit 8.3:

Exhibit 8.3 Guns Now in the Wrong Hands

"good luck dude the guns are probley sold to a crack dealer."

"yo b how u noe dey b jamaican how u bringin up dem stereotype crapp... mayynnee."

"deportation. any nigga that commit a crime should be sent back to jamaica along with their irresponsible mother."

"capital punishment — plain and simple... in some states in the U.S. motherfuckers go to PRISON for not paying two jaywalking fines! That's jaywalking! Assaults = felony charges. This is a crime heaven with lax laws that give 2-for-1 or 3-for-1 time served... let's not talk about the joke of the young offenders law."

The immediacy of the video reality makes it easy to judge the crime. Not many who view the video will be able to make a contribution to its solving, but many are now involved in judging: judging the crime, its motives and what to do with the suspect. The punitive attitude is apparent in deciding that deportation or execution are suitable punishments.

While Crime Stoppers is part of a broader effort to bring police and citizens together in what is generally called community policing, one criticism is that there is no one community, as society is very diverse and divided along class, ethnic and gender lines. Since much of police work consists of reactive calls for service, Crime Stoppers programs are unique in making the public more willing to help the police, allegedly resulting in more effective policing and crime control. However, the shift from a professional to a community-based model is as much ideological as practical, and the effectiveness of its results are mixed.

In the above example, the option of posting a comment on Youtube enables the expression of racist stereotypes. This is an important issue to explore, because rather than the ads orienting to a common community, they appeal to and isolate different sectors of that same community.

In another example, this one called "Toronto Robbery," Toronto Crime Stoppers is asking for the assistance of the public to identify persons of interest and suspects in relation to a robbery in the Wilson Avenue/Keele Street area. Three men are shown entering a building through a stairwell, where it is alleged they don masks and force their way into a secure area, bind the employees and steal cash. They are then shown leaving and the public is asked for assistance in identifying the suspects. There are 27 posted comments, such as the string in Exhibit 8.4.

Exhibit 8.4 Toronto Robbery
"Great… something always new in the city of Toronto."

"stupid always creating problems, these kind of people should receive life in prison."

"ya just throe all the nigger in jail aka nigger college."

"is it possible to watch ANY of these videos without seeing a racist mother fucking comment??"

"thats because its always a black person commiting the crime."

In a third video from the series, "Two Toronto TTC Armed Robberies with Shotgun," three young men are shown trying to rob a transit station booth. There are thirty-six posted comments (Exhibit 8.5).

Exhibit 8.5: Two Toronto TTC Armed Robberies

"I don't understand why people have to steal? Damn those idiots!"

"cuz niggers r too lazy to go and make something of their life without stealing and mooching off the govt."

"I can't wait to join the Toronto Police and lock up criminals! :D"
"they deserved to get their money taken."

"u must be a dumb hoodnigger to say that. their making honest living to provide their family. they never did nothing to those niggers. govt will give them a job right away if they wanted it."

"like what does ttc people do all day really they sit their ass all day stopin for coffee break, ripping off people money like c'mon people."

"Your an idiot."

"Its an honest living unlike these dirtballs."

"wow, this is fucking nuts, and really stupid. fuckin stupid punks need to get a job."

These videos provide immediate, raw footage of crime in the making. The suspects are shown, the details of the crime are simply described, and bring the many to become surveillance of the few (in this modern synopticon). The fact that readers bring to bear their own racism as an interpretive tool is unsurprising and allows for judgments through the media.

It is difficult, however, to see how such videos empower members of the community. The few who might be able to contribute information crucial to solving the crimes might or might not inform. For most people, it is reality TV that mimics the entertainment of crime drama. One released video showed the work of an arsonist, and one of the posted comments called it urban terrorism.

The risk of such video ads is of alienating the very community the ads seek to interest. The stoics among us will find the visuals confirm the meanness of the world they already suspected. They are fatalistic. The compassionate cannot watch or grieve, as the emotional requirement is too great. Those who believe that video surveillance will mean greater safety will praise the release of video footage in the quest to deter crime and catch criminals. They are the conventional, but they are unlikely to have relevant information to offer.

The critical analysis of the media leads us to see how there is construction of a difference between us and other: they commit crimes and harm us. They are violent, commit crimes for shallow reasons like gang initiations or drugs, are difficult to catch and are usually of the lower class ethnic poor. This is the picture we get as we judge the crime in the public panopticon that is video crime surveillance.

3. *Techniques of governance.* Overall, any new policing initiative can involve some reorganization of police structures and duties. These programs might be effective in deterring or preventing crime, but there are possible public relations benefits as well. The police benefit from a positive public image and from managing their image as crimefighters. A program like Crime Stoppers does not necessarily require much change in the traditional method of policing, and it is overseen by the police. These initiatives do not challenge police authority or the overall definition of crime.

Crime Stoppers is reactive in nature. The police select the crimes to be published, which are then written up by newspapers to fit their publishing requirements. As media events, these items remain under the control of the police. In that sense, they are exercises in news control. This is not news reported after the fact, but immediate because it often includes raw footage. A view of the world is constructed that serves the interests of the institutional powers behind the Crime Stoppers program: the police, the media and the businesses that provide support.

The function of the Crime Stoppers advertisements is to reduce property crime loss through offering rewards and anonymity. It also is used in an attempt to solve violent crimes and can be used to promote a law-and-order ideology, although that seems less practical. Creating an anonymous system reduces risk to tipsters and yet also allows tipsters to be good citizen. The manipulation of risk and morality in Crime Stoppers works as an extension of traditional policing. It's a way of doing better work without much more work.

Inserting surveillance footage into the equation brings governance and policing even closer together than is traditionally possible. We are all watched all the time, and while only criminals have any need to worry, as the saying goes, the watching counts us all. As a technique of governance, however, the release of surveillance footage does not simply aid law enforcement but reinforces stereotypes of crime that are incredibly visual and punitive.

The view of the world constructed by these Crime Stoppers reports is explicitly one of anonymous violent offenders committing crimes in public; the implicit message is that the media can enlist the public's help to aid the police, who are best equipped to deal with these threats to personal safety and property. Those who are in a position to benefit from influencing public opinion, the police, retain their legitimacy as agents of social control, and members of the public are placed into a secondary role as unpaid informants through the vehicle of crime discourse. Most of us, moreover, are in a tertiary role — not police, criminals, tipsters, but voyeurs.

The program reinvents the dominant relation between the police and citizens, through media construction of the law-abiding "community" and the portrayal of crime as a threat. The notion of community and the definition of crime are thus constructed by the news articles. In this way, an ideological view of the world is created by texts that create interpretations about safety and danger for the reader, and social control is reinforced.

Summary

The notion that news control is crime control does not mean the police actually control the news media — there is no need. In general the police are in a position to control the flow of information to the media about crime: the description of each crime, the stages of criminal investigation, the laying of charges and so on. Reporters are dependent on good relationships with the police so they are not likely to provoke what is often their sole source of crime information. It is only when a case enters the court system that the police lose their power to define it, as the press turns to lawyers and court reporters for information on judicial proceedings. Fortunately for the police, perhaps, most interest in crime reporting is at the beginning stages. Coverage of subsequent stages of a crime is less common than of initial crime reports and investigations.

The police have come to use the media in their own interests, as can be seen in the specific topics of Crime Stoppers reports. The notion of community is explicitly invoked as a way to involve citizens in detecting crime and as a way to enhance the image of the police as crimefighters. This creation of a crimefighting partnership between the police and the community is possible in a society where the media constructs social relations and is the dominant source of information about crime in the world.

In an internet age, one that was barely imagined when the first edition of this book appeared, video footage can now supplement the request for the publics' assistance, with the unintended consequence of inflaming vengeful attitudes and racist stereotypes.

There is nothing inherently wrong with programs such as Crime Stoppers, but we need to see them in the context of broader historical developments. The police have moved into a much less antagonistic relationship with the media. The consequence has been a subtle distortion of crime news to ideologically reflect the point of view of the police, who are then able to further extend themselves into the community they discursively construct. The other consequence is a remaking of citizenship and what it means, with an attendant fracturing of the community and the cultivation of apathy.

9

Lawyers and Serial Killers
The Press and Sensationalism

Death, doom and destruction — this chapter deals with sensationalism in the news. The media is constantly full of disturbing stories of tragedy and violence in the world. People become sensitized and callous to it at the same time; news of disasters, genocide, war all bring the world closer to home while exposing events that, after all, are happening to "them." One of the most chilling examples in modern society has to be the theme of the serial killer, which captures the alienated urban imagination in a way that many other crimes cannot. The disgust and fear that accompanies this crime is the emotional aspect of that alienation.

As background on the issue of press sensationalism, Darrel Pink describes some of his difficulties as a lawyer in dealing with the media. In his position he routinely issues press releases and fields requests from the media to provide information on criminal proceedings. One of the difficulties he has found in interfacing with the media is that journalists often lack much of the specialized knowledge of criminal proceedings that is necessary to report on them. His criticism is that reporters are more oriented towards the "thirty-second bite" than to an in-depth analysis of crime issues. This criticism has come up in other chapters as well.

Reporters are not inept, but they are perhaps more oriented towards sensationalism than education, which is unfortunate when a story involves something as serious as informing the public about legal issues. In Reading the News, examples of sensationalism, specifically on serial killers, are provided to ground that point. It may seem extreme to focus on such horrific crimes, but these stories are selected to make the strongest case possible. In these articles readers see horrific details sensationalized, exaggerated and glamourized. Such articles do not educate us about the law or about crime but are simply gruesomely "entertaining" in some macabre fashion.

In the Sample Study, articles on "serial killer" were selected from the *Globe and Mail* for the 1980s to see what appears. Interestingly, there is just as much (if not more) use of the term in "popular theatre" as there is in crime reporting. In Analyzing the News, the idea of sensationalism is discussed at a deeper level. Whereas Pink advances the idea that sensationalism gets in the way of good reporting, I suggest that it depends on what purpose reporting has in society. The premise that the media has done a bad job means that they could do a better job.

Perhaps the problem is not that reporters simply cannot represent the complexities of lawyering (which privileges one form of knowledge over another), but that the purpose of the media is something other than to educate us about the law. Studies I have found useful in thinking about serial homicide are Fleming (2007), Guillen (2002), Haggerty (2009), Jarvis (2007) and Warwick (2006) for her discussion of "gothic criminology."

Darrel Pink's Talk

I'd like to pose a series of questions from the perspective of dealing with the media. As executive director of the Barrister's Society, I deal with the media on a regular basis. In terms of the legal system, the courts and lawyers, interest in the media is really heightened at the present time, and whatever is happening in the courts is fair game. But there's somewhat of a paradox in saying that, because five years ago the number of reporters assigned to the courts in Halifax was about four times as great as it is today. In other words, what's happened is the economy has declined and there's increased pressure on the media outlets. They have taken reporters who were formerly assigned the court as a regular beat and have taken them out of that system. So rather than developing a pool of expert reporters who have knowledge about the justice system through its entire breadth, we have a very small number of reporters that know anything about the criminal justice system in particular.

The second initial comment is we have to distinguish between the high profile case from the mundane case. There are a number of cases which have really been pursued and broken by the media. When the story broke on the Donald Marshall case in 1982, the media was literally one day behind the police as the reinvestigation was ongoing. But for the media, the story never would have taken on the legion proportions that it did, let alone the public inquiry never would have happened without ongoing media attention.

Similarly, the Starr scandal in Ontario was also broken as a media event. The initial disclosures about what she had allegedly done came out of the work of reporters, and it was the police that followed up and did the same thing. The ultimate charges in Mount Cashel also resulted from the work of reporters. The original police investigation in 1976 led to nothing, but Cashel broke in the late 1980s as a result of disclosure through the media, and public pressure resulted in a public inquiry and charges being laid.

So in the high profile cases, media concentration can produce very positive results. There's a down side to that because the media often are quick to use names inappropriately and throw around allegations that are not well founded. The libel and defamation laws don't provide a lot of protection because that emphasizes the public's attention on the issue, rather than really acquitting the person who may not have been properly charged in the media.

My third opening comment is, I was reading a public relations report that was done for another law society in Canada and I was struck by the comment, "There is value to a suspicious media chasing after the secrets of people and organizations in a position of trust." In Nova Scotia, the events of the last several weeks, in terms of our former premier, have really heightened the role of the media in doing the digging. Four weeks ago the former premier said there were no trust funds, and all of a sudden, through both disclosures from the party and from disclosures in the media from the public record, the situation has reversed. Those of us that work in the justice system have to be willing to accept that the media is there, and we have to have an open attitude toward them.

To wrap up the paradox that I started off with, though the media has been reduced in number, the response of the system has been to create people to deal with the media. The attorney general's department has created a media relations person, and the police have done it as well. In the courts there is an executive assistant to the chief justices, a person that the media can contact. Even in the bar society, when I took over my job one of the things I did was to be available to the media.

The justice system lived for years behind a barricade and gave no information to anybody, and the media had to probe and push and poke to get any information. Now the system is attempting to open up, and the question is whether this is really opening up in a way that is going to satisfy the public. The media really is the funnel for the public. What we say, what we do, is screened to the public through the media.

If I issue a media release today, I have no guarantee it will be given to the public in the way that I produce it, because it goes through editors and producers and reporters. I had a recent experience where, rather than putting out a short media release, I gave a fairly detailed report to the media about a certain thing that had taken place, and the media got it absolutely wrong. They referred to numbers that in no way were reflected in the report, they referred to what was between the lines. Our effort to be open backfired colossally because people said, you're not being honest, there must be something that is subtle there that you're not telling us and therefore they speculated and got it wrong.

So one of the crucial factors here, is the knowledge of the people in the media. Are reporters knowledgeable about what they're reporting on? For example, three weeks ago, when Thornhill appeared before the courts, everyone went in and said Thornhill pleaded not guilty. Well, it was an arraignment, and he elected to be tried by judge and jury, but he didn't enter a plea. He'll enter a plea before the court when he's tried. You can tell the media that, you can repeat it six times, but they will continually get it wrong.

So the attempt to simplify the system can sometimes lead to misinformation. Although we who are in the system sometimes rely upon the media to describe, to interpret and to make understandable what we're doing, we often do so at our own peril because that information will often be changed and inaccurately reported. The issue of accuracy is very important. And when they get it wrong, not because of ignorance but they just make a mistake, how can misimpressions left with the public as a result of the story be corrected?

I read the newspapers and watch the electronic media regularly, but I feel that I'm absolutely unable to objectively respond to what is there, especially if I'm involved in it. I can no longer say what does the public, or what does my mother, think about that?

We have become slaves of the thirty-second clip. There is a belief among the electronic media that things have to be digested in such a way that they can have a sound bite for radio or a video clip for television, and it's got to be short and crisp. Now if I as a spokesperson have to make statements from time to time, if I really want to abuse the system, then I will perfect that thirty-second clip. I'll find the right comment that will summarize what I want to say. It's of no relevance, if it's catchy they'll use it, if it's provocative it will get used. Unfortunately much of what we're dealing with in terms of crime, justice, policing and legal issues don't easily allow for that thirty-second clip.

I am convinced there is a disservice done when the big case of the week is reported in a total of five minutes over five days. That doesn't apply just to justice issues, of course, that applies to all major issues. The media has forced us to break up our thinking into little bites, to deal with it that way.

Another issue that concerns me is sensationalism. With crime, if there's no blood and gore, or there's no sex, it's not newsworthy. And if it falls into the category of being newsworthy, then they have to show the dead body. They've got to show the corpse. One of the issues that has been dealt with recently in terms of access to the courts is, how does the media get hold of exhibits? Can they see the pictures that the police have produced of the crime scene? Can they see the bodies? Can they put the body on TV? Well, the jury sees the body, why can't the public see the body? Well, the effect of that in my view is that we are increasingly desensitizing the public to crime. Secondly, crime such as break and enter are no longer significant, even though the violation of your space is a very serious matter for the victims. But no blood, no guts, no sex, the media don't cover it.

The final thing is what role should lawyers, law professors and criminologists, the larger group of people who can act as resources to the media, play in interpreting the system to the public? I find the media is not willing, because they don't have the time or the resources, to really go and get good background help. They've got to deal with this story because their deadline is two o'clock this afternoon to get on the evening news.

A secondary concern is whether lawyers involved in cases can ever provide an objective opinion. Ethically, lawyers are quite limited in terms of the comments they can make to the media while a case is ongoing. Some lawyers have an approach that they will talk to the media, and they do it appropriately, while other lawyers can abuse the media. They use the media to their advantage, but to the disservice of the public, because the lawyer is using the media to get certain information out there. And sometimes they want cases argued through the court of public opinion, rather than before the court or tribunal.

Finally, I was involved in the Donald Marshall inquiry, and we would often sit back and chuckle at how some reporters, in the break in the morning proceedings, would form a scrum around particular lawyers. After a while, many of the people in the media realized that they were being used by the lawyers who were conducting the scrum, because the lawyer was trying to get something out through them that they may not have been able to get out otherwise. That is a real risk for the media. When the media get too close to lawyers, they can lose their sense of objectivity.

Reading the News

Darrel Pink makes many comments about the relationship between lawyers and the media. He mentions the important role the media has in exposing crime and yet the difficulty reporters often have in understanding criminal justice procedures. He points out how lawyers run the risk of being misunderstood and misinterpreted by reporters, while at the same time some lawyers use the media to their own advantage. Many organizations rely on the media to inform the public, but the media's focus on the sound-bite makes it difficult to cover complicated issues properly. These are all important topics related to the relationship between the legal profession and the media, and the structural reasons for how distortions can enter into news reports.

Sensationalism is another feature of reporting that can distort stories on criminal cases. Although much crime reporting is innocuous and exhibits the problems pointed out above to a fairly low degree, there are also cases where inaccuracies and the wish to capitalize on the gory are obvious. Sensationalism caters to the worst tendencies of sloppy reporting — to get the scoop, to grab attention, to make a big splash without being careful about all the facts. Sensationalism flourishes in an enterprise where Donald Trump's divorce can mean bigger business than Nelson Mandela's release from prison.

The case of serial homicide reveals perhaps the strongest examples of sensational reporting possible. Homicide tends to be a heavily reported crime in the news media in the first place, and serial killers especially so, even though it has only emerged as a topic relatively recently.

1. *Sex and death.* The following article concerns a very highly reported crime. In Article 9.1, the 'House of Horror' story epitomizes the fear of serial killers: they live alongside other people who see them as affable, really nice blokes; they commit horrific crimes; and the neighbours never suspect the evil in their midst, in this case one of the worst serial killers in British history.

Article 9.1 "British police find eighth body in 'House of Horror'"

Britain's House of Horror yielded another body yesterday... and police... are digging for more victims in one of the country's worst suspected serial killings. A grim-faced policeman emerged from the ordinary-looking home... carrying boxes the size of a television set, draped with black cloth to hide the contents from hundreds of prying eyes. The latest remains [were] dug out of the foundations... [while] three other bodies were dug out of the garden... [The] neighbours, many of them young single people in an area full of cheap apartments whose transient population has little sense of community, remember an affable man who chatted little. "He was a really nice bloke." (*Daily News*, March 9, 1994: 17, Gloucester, England [Reuter])

It is instructive that the article dramatically recounts "grim-faced" policemen carrying remains out of the House of Horror in shrouded boxes while hundreds of people look on. The investigation and gathering of evidence is a media spectacle. The bodies, many of them unidentified and decades old, were dug out of the basement and bathroom. Families of missing women are reported to fear that their daughters were killed and buried in the house.

The perpetrator of the crime is likened to other infamous serial murderers who preyed on harmless women and homeless men, but Frederick and Rosemary West's pattern was to pick up young women from bus stops and assault them. In the article the neighbourhood in which the offender lived is lower class, with little sense of community, where young single people and transients live. This description increases the moral repulsion of the crime because it is linked to depravity and poverty. That purported lack of community is curious but persists as part of the media's depiction of the problem, despite the fact that people knew the murderer. The most unsettling fact, however, is that he was known, but that nothing was known about the crimes. Both Rosemary and Frederick West were ultimately convicted of murder and incarcerated.

There is nothing in the article about the law or the legal procedures Frederick West faced; there is nothing to explain the motivation for the crimes, just the horror of the killings and their discovery; there is nothing about the sexual abuse Rosemary suffered at the hands of her father or the abuse then carried out against Fred's own daughter.

The dead bodies allegedly killed by the accused over the years retrospectively enable the label "serial killer," even though he has been charged with only one death. The linking of this case to other infamous cases, one more than forty years old, grounds the claim that this crime is one of the worst. All these features are embedded in a text that replays the unexamined proposition "you just never know."

In comparison to the previous news story, Article 9.2 is more prurient in its treatment. The House of Horror article simply said there had been a series of slayings and is notably reticent with details: whether, for example, torture was involved or whether these were sex slayings, although we now know that the women were tortured and assaulted before being killed.

Article 9.2 is about a serial killer reportedly terrorizing London's gay community. It speculates that the victims may have been strangled or suffocated after involvement in sadomasochistic sex, explicitly portraying the victims as having been involved in immoral behaviour in a way the victims in the first article were not. Furthermore, the victims' sexual orientation is made a topic, whereas sexual orientation does not seem to be important in the first article. The police are pursuing leads, but there is no indication of why the murders could have continued on for so long.

Article 9.2 "U.K. pathologist to compare bodies of 4 murdered gays"
A top British pathologist plans to re-examine the bodies of four of the five victims of a killer terrorizing London's gay community... Victims frequented bars and clubs in London's gay scene and are thought to have been strangled or suffocated... The killer has vowed in telephone calls to police to kill one gay man a week. (*Toronto Star*, June 21, 1993: A12, London [Reuter])

Whereas the House of Horror article plays more on the traditional aspect of serial murder, the second article topicalizes a (supposedly) deviant sexual angle. This is part of the media's sensationalism, layering the illicit over the explicit. In the minds of some, it might make the victims less innocent but the assailant no less evil. The next section takes this theme further.

2. *Barbie and Ken*. Article 9.3 (from the tabloid *Globe*) deals with one of the most sensationalized cases in Canada, the trials of Paul Bernardo and Karla Homolka. The murders were originally reported in a series of unconnected articles on unexplained deaths in southern Ontario, typical of serial murder coverage. Initially, there is no serial murder pattern because it has yet to be (retrospectively) constructed. As is well known now, the cases involve the sex slayings of three young women and a series of sexual assaults. What

is interesting here as a topic within the story is that the trial of Homolka was subject to a sweeping court-ordered ban, although information was still widely published in newspapers and magazines, on television shows and on the internet.

Article 9.3 "The Ghoul Next Door: Choirgirl's crimes are so savage judge keeps details secret as cops target her yuppie hubby"

They were the picture-perfect pair. Karla Homolka Bernardo, a stunning 23-year-old veterinarian's assistant... long blonde hair and blue eyes... peaches and cream complexion... wouldn't hurt a fly. Hubby Paul Bernardo, 26... accountant... tall... charming... handsome enough to melt a young girl's heart. But behind the Ken and Barbie masks lurked the face of grotesque evil. Karla is now serving two 12-year manslaughter sentences for her part in the grizzly sex slayings of two young girls... Paul Bernardo now stands accused of two charges of first-degree murder and 43 separate counts of sexual assault... The facts of Canada's most sensational sex-murder case are so sickeningly gruesome that Ontario judge Francis Kovacs wrapped them in a cloak of total secrecy. To ensure that Paul gets a fair trial, his stifling gag order even forbids revealing whether Karla pleaded guilty! (*Globe*, September 28, 1993: 24–25)

The cover caption for the story read "Canada's Most Shocking Killings. The untold story of an unspeakable crime." The original article is long, but it combines many of the aspects of serial murder sensationalism: 1) seriality; 2) a connection to other crimes of that type; 3) evil hidden underneath a conventional exterior; and 4) perversion and sexuality. First it details some information about the crimes. For example, it is reported that one victim, Leslie Mahaffy was in the ninth grade, and parts of her body were found encased in concrete in a reservoir lake outside St. Catharines. Ten months later Kristen French was snatched while she was walking home from school, and she was found two weeks later on a remote country road. The article reports that police were also reopening the investigation into the "bizarre" death of Karla's fifteen-year-old sister Tammy, who choked on her own vomit during a family gathering. It is now known of course that she was drugged and assaulted by the pair and died during the course of the crime.

The article was accompanied by pictures of Leslie, Kristen and of course Karla with the caption: "She had breeding, beauty, the best schools — and a taste for sex that ended in the brutal death of 2 young girls"; and "Karla sat stone-faced as the prosecutor detailed her role in the gruesome deaths."

What is interesting is that the article goes out of its way to comment on how out of character the crimes were. This echoes a theme in the House of Horrors article above. The crimes are grisly but the offenders seemed so nice. Friends of the model yuppie couple were reportedly in shock, unable to accept that they could commit such unspeakable acts. Karla would reportedly get mad if someone even tried to kill a fly, and the "striking blonde" had attended the best schools, sang in the choir and had been well-mannered and well-brought up.

Another contrast in the story was that while they seemed the ideal couple, their marriage suddenly came crashing down when Karla went to police claiming that Paul had assaulted her with a flashlight. Then he was charged with a string of sexual assaults and with murdering Leslie and Kristen.

The article plays a lot with the media ban used in Karla's trial in order to protect Paul's right to a fair trial. For example, it stated that as the prosecutor read a "chilling statement" revealing Karla's role in gory detail, horrified gasps filled the courtroom. Paul's attorney was reported to have said that the prosecution may have "made a deal with the devil" in return for Karla's testimony. The paper disingenuously reported that "rumors swirled and were denied," that there were "tales of torture and sex snuff," that police had seized a homemade video showing Karla engaged in a sex act with another woman and that there were reputedly dozens of other tapes.

The media ban caused newspapers as respected as the *Washington Post* to be barred from Canada, although that didn't necessarily stop people from obtaining copies in public libraries. People brought Buffalo news across the border, stories reported in England were faxed in. Articles circulated on the Internet and were reproduced in alt.fan.homolka. By the time the "Ghoul Next Door" article was published, the situation had spun out of control.

The text of the court ruling by Justice Kovacs in the Homolka case was issued on July 5, 1993, and although it does not ban specific media stories, it bans several details of the case from publication: the circumstances of the deaths of any persons referred to during the trial; the plea by the accused; and the transcript of the trial proceedings. Newspapers and magazines were stopped at the border, confiscated from store shelves and in some cases shredded. The article used here, however, was sold openly in Canada and is not known to have been subject to any legal enforcement.

The ban was challenged by various media outlets, including the *Globe* and the CBC, on the basis that it infringed on the public's right to know. A legal decision was eventually released that better clarified the "right to know" and the limits of the courts to impose media bans. But the idea of a right to know the details of horrific crimes is important to separate from the right to openness of criminal proceedings.

3. *Themes.* In the serial killer articles, various themes and images are created. One is that "you just never know" and that there can be "evil in our midst." This is a prominent theme in serial homicide, and in news reports, and the two are difficult to separate. Throughout the last article, the theme

of the "picture-perfect pair" is played, but there is also hidden from first sight that "behind the Ken and Barbie masks lurked the face of grotesque evil." They committed a series of gruesome sex crimes and slayings while appearing to be the perfect couple. While Frederick and Rosemary may or may not have appeared to be a perfect couple they at least seemed ordinary.

Other themes are played out as well, such as the reconstruction of seriality through the link to other cases. This is evident in all three articles. In the "you just never know" theme, anchored by the Barbie and Ken mythology, the construction of seriality and the sexual element that recurs again and again in the texts with melodramatic terms such as "grizzly sex slayings," "sado-masochistic sex" and "sex snuff videos," the twinned themes of perversion and twisted attraction are also anchored. Many other contemporary cases illustrate the theme that although the articles describe facts of the crimes that might be newsworthy, they are also arguably pornographic and cater to the prurient interests of the reader, as in the "gay serial killer" article above.

The reason certain elements of Karla's story were banned in Canada was that details from Karla's case might influence Paul's right to a fair trial. But reporting that Karla had "made a deal with the devil" made the story even more sensationalistic. The ban only served to restrict "quality" publications from publishing details of the case, while the field was left open for underground speculation.

Read as literal descriptions of events, the accounts are gruesome, describing mutilation, sexual assault, torture and murder. Read as metaphor, however, the language takes on a different character: Can one have sex with an unwilling or unconscious person? Are these crimes of lust and sexual urges or violence? and What does it mean to say that there was a "pact with the devil"? This can't be literal, so what is it meant to convey — the evil of the act? As such the articles become dramas, morality plays about danger not only in the city or in the modern world, but within the community, within our midst without our even knowing. Is such sensationalist reporting bizarre, extreme and irresponsible?

Cases of serial killers are by nature sensational, but the media hypes them beyond recognition, distorts the immorality of the killers and often plays upon the innocence of the victims. Serial murder sensationalism has a discursive structure that can be reconstructed by looking for the specific textual devices that convey the features of seriality, danger and sexuality. The articles have several common features: the killers exist unrecognized amidst ordinary people; they prey on innocent or deviant victims; the language used melodramatizes the crimes; and there is little or no account of law and legal procedures.

Sample Study

Serial murder is a modern topic. Even though the behaviour is not new, it strikes at the heart of a modern urban fear in a way no other crime does. It is a crime committed by predators in our midst. As well, serial murder is a topic that borders on fantasy and fiction in a way in which perhaps no other crime does. There is not much that is either romantic or mysterious about robbery, bike theft or vandalism. There is much that is hidden and confused about domestic violence, sexual assault and child abuse. Yet serial murder is mysterious, threatening and yet part of the urban folklore, made for courtroom and theatre alike.

For this sample study, articles on "serial killer" were selected from the *Globe and Mail* for the 1980s. In 1984, "serial killer" appears for the first time in the paper. The article is a comprehensive half-page feature discussing the "peculiar public fascination with multiple murder." It discusses how serial murderers usually work close to home but some roam, are sexually sadistic, are psychotic but not insane and are more often male, older and white.

Interestingly, 1984 seems to be the first time that the phrase appears anywhere in the news media in Canada. It does not get used in *The [London] Times* until 1985 and is referred to as "California speak." It does appear earlier (1981) in the *New York Times*, as explanations are sought (and interpretations develop) in the case of twenty-eight children who go missing and are found dead in Atlanta. For example, Exhibit 9.1 excerpts an early U.S. article to use the phrase and says:

Exhibit 9.1 Early U.S. Article Using the Term "Serial Killer"

Many of those searching for deeper social explanations agree with criminology professor Marc Riedel, who said "the greater degree of randomness entering violent crimes" implies "a social order that is coming unglued," at least in inner cities. Zimring added, "There's an implicit message of urban disintegration and terror which should be quite disquieting... many of the random, hard-to-catch killers — whether serial or more conventional — have been spawned by the tumultuous changes in American values and institutions over the last 20 years. (*Washington Post*, February 20, 1984)

Authorities cited in that article speculated that serial killers were responsible for the increase in the unsolved murder rate from 6 percent in 1966 to 20 percent in 1982.

The second appearance in the *Globe and Mail* is in 1985, a notice about *The Mean Season*, with Kurt Russell and Mariel Hemingway, a thriller about a reporter tracking a serial killer, a movie that sounds like an investigative documentary. The third is a news item about Henry Lee Lucas, who said that the only person he killed was his mother, and that he only confessed to 600 other murders because of police pressure. This sounds like a made-for-television movie based on real-life wrongful convictions. The fact that suspects in several cases were dismissed after Lucas confessed only adds to the dramatic tension. The year 1985 also saw development of a film called *Red Dragon*, a detective story about a serial killer with film star William Peterson, who portrayed convicted murderer Jack Henry Abbot in a play called *In the Belly of the Beast*.

In 1986, there is a review of *Buried Dreams*, about John Wayne Gacy, next to a review of *The Vampire Lestat*, by Anne Rice. There is a review of *Psycho III*; a notice of Bundy's failed attempts to win stays of his execution, a spectacle Phil Donahue tried to televise; a report of an address given by famed profiler John Douglas at a convention of North American prosecutors; a ruling by the Supreme Court that the family of Clifford Olson could keep $100,000 paid to him to lead police to the bodies of eleven victims; and three separate reviews of *Vengeance Is Mine*, based on an "actual serial killer," Iwao Enokizu (Ken Ogata).

In 1987, another serial killer thriller, *The Stepfather*, was released with two separate reviews; Clifford Olson appealed the conditions of his sentence; and a front-page article claimed that "the majority of psychopaths [are] not in jail" and wrote about nurse's aide Donald Harvey, who killed elderly people in his care.

Then there was a series that began with a note about how a serial killer was suspected in six killings on eastern Ontario farms near Hopetown; which received extensive half-page coverage in September, only to have the body count reduced to three; a piece about how FBI profilers had confirmed the police's sole suspect; a denial by the "suspect," James Wise; a criticism of the police for in effect naming a suspect in the media; an article reporting a rifle found that might be tied to the killings; and lastly, an editorial commentary decrying the public's right to know. The last article for 1987 was the ordering of a new trial for a confessed serial killer whose rights were violated during questioning.

The year 1988 saw about a dozen articles: a review of the film *Off Limits*; a lengthy article on Ted Bundy; a review of the novel *The Crosskiller*; and a review of Rod Steiger's role in the play *The January Man*. There was a front-page article about a possible serial killer working the B.C. Lower Mainland. The prostitutes were saying that the new soliciting law, police crackdowns and court injunctions against working certain areas had made the killer's work easier. The prostitutes seemed to have a better working theory of how the killings were possible than did the authorities. The police and prosecutors, for example, denied that theory with their own defensive myths that prostitutes chose dangerous work, they could leave anytime and so on. The year also saw a review of the novel *The Fine Art of Murder*; a small article about Lovie

195

Riddle who claimed to have killed thirty times, including Nicole Morin in Toronto, a claim the police viewed as fictitious; a letter to the editor; a review of the film *Broken Mirrors*; a review of the performance of James Woods in the film *Cop*; and last, a review of the novel *The Last Draw*.

The year 1989 began with another review of *The January Man*; Florida's governor made the front-page quote of the day for saying "justice has been on hold for a decade and it is time Ted Bundy paid for his crimes"; *The January Man* was reviewed again; and an appeal heard in the extradition of "suspected serial killer" Charles Ng, who faced twelve charges of murder in California; a lengthy analysis of the characteristics of the serial killer; and last, an advertisement for a book called *The Man Who Murdered God*.

What are some reflections on this sample? First, there is as much (if not more) fiction as fact on serial murder, which romanticizes and sensationalizes the crime. And even the so-called fact contains a lot of fiction, for example, the dismissal of the claim that a serial killer is operating around Vancouver. However, how do we differentiate fact from fiction, that one is film and the other is news? This is an important question, and the obvious answer is too simplistic. Ever seen the shower scene in *Psycho*? Second, the "serial killer" is a modern topic, having a lineage of only twenty-five years. And while the way serial murder is discussed points to the modern age *creating the crime* of serial murder, there is probably something even more important going on. The modern age has *created the topic*, and as a product of the modern age. Third, even here there is a hierarchy of victims, with prostitutes at the bottom, random strangers in the middle and respectable people at the top.

Analyzing the News

The previous sections have opened up some interesting issues, such as how cases of serial murder are presented in the media, whether the media is sensationalistic in discussing these issues and whether media bans are effective. First, let us look at the consequence of banning mainstream newspapers from covering a sensationalistic serial killer case and also speculate on the usefulness of sensationalism overall.

1. *Media bans*. Much had been written on the trial of Karla Homolka and the (then) upcoming trial of Paul Bernardo. But it was the ban that proved to be eminently newsworthy. There were probably more newspaper articles, editorials, columns, television shows and other media stories on the ban itself than on the actual crimes.

When the *Buffalo News* published the story, and the *Toronto Star* printed a front-page photograph, the Ontario attorney general investigated to see if there had been a violation of the ban. Libraries debated whether to display copies of newspapers carrying banned information and in some cases actually clipped out the offending pieces until they received legal advice that shelving the papers did not constitute publication. A retired police officer in Guelph, Ontario, was found guilty of contempt of court for mailing copies of stories from the *Sunday Mirror* and the *Washington Post*. A U.S. cable show, *A Current Affair*, was blacked out twice in Canada, despite CRTC regulations. Details of the crimes were posted on the Internet faster than newslists and discussion groups could be shut down, contributing to the spread of rumours. However, an Angus Reid poll reported that despite the media ban, 25 percent of Ontario residents had learned banned details of the trial, but 35 percent weren't even aware of the case at all!

This poses an interesting question of whether the ban was necessary, as well as if it was even effective. The ban was an exercise in locking the barn door after the horse has bolted. While the media was banned from releasing details of the crimes as discussed at trial, initial newspaper accounts of the 1991 and 1992 murders had already detailed evidence of the crimes. Furthermore, in imposing the ban after the short, two-hour trial of Karla Homolka in 1993, the judge was quoted in the newspapers as saying, "No sentence that I could impose would adequately reflect the revulsion of the community against the accused for the death of two completely innocent young girls... The accused did not personally inflict the deaths, although she was responsible in law and in fact."

Given that the ban was apparently to ensure a fair trial for Paul Bernardo slated for 1995, the judge's comments are puzzling because they seem prejudicial. And it is difficult to see why there would be a ban on the details of the presumed plea bargain, unless it would be to relieve the legal process of scrutiny in such a horrific case.

Whether it is ordinary crime stories or cases of serial killers, the charge that reporters often "get it wrong" in their search for a story is a technical complaint. Anyone can complain that what they do is not represented accurately by reporters. Reporters may not be interested in or able to synthesize long-winded, complicated professional, academic and legalistic discourses. To expect that reporters could get it right would assume they were able to just report the facts, like a tape-recorder. It assumes that reporters would not have another agenda.

2. *Sensationalism*. The charge that reporters capitalize on the gory crimes of serial and other killers is more of a moral than a legal issue. However, it is also a curious one because the presumption that reporters blow events out of proportion assumes that there is a proper proportion with which to report events. The media has been heavily criticized for its interest in the Homolka-Bernardo cases and for reporting the violence and shocking details of the crimes. Moreover, the idea that sensationalism is voyeuristic, that reporters are just interested in getting a picture of a corpse implies something sleazy about the profession. Maybe there is, but maybe that's more than just a failing.

Both the technical and the moral complaints presume that reporters get it wrong. The first is that reporting is exaggerated, while the second is that reporting is voyeuristic. Both complaints rely on a privileged viewpoint that the reportage could be better, in proportion, moderate. Both complaints presume that the lawyer or other professional has it right but is misquoted, misunderstood or misrepresented in the media. (This does describe the daily lives of professionals who work with the media, but that's another issue). And the moral complaint, especially, implies that the reporter should rise above the commonplace.

Alternately, instead of simply seeing ignorance and sensationalism as inherently wrong, let us question the purpose they play in the larger social order. Does sensationalism have a role to play in our daily lives? Maybe it's a vicarious thrill in an otherwise boring life, or maybe it's simply the tone an article has to have to get noticed. The story found in Article 9.3 above, "The Ghoul Next Door," was not banned in Canada. Some of the headlines, articles and ads in that issue of the (tabloid) *Globe* that give a sense of the context of the story are shown in Exhibit 9.2.

Exhibit 9.2 Tabloid News of Unusual Events, Famous People and Lucky Charms

"Seaquest Stephanie: Housework keeps me slim and sexy at 46."
"Powerful Pygmy potion ends drug addiction!"
"Miracle Boy Learns to Walk — after years in a wheelchair!"
"Oprah's heart is solid gold!"
"Webster runs for cover in Jacko video shocker."
"Secret heartache Raymond Burr took to his grave."
"3 Wishes Voo Doo Doll with Magic Wand."
"Loans by Mail."
"Know Your Future. Live Personal Psychic."
"Love, Money, Success."

These are not stories about ordinary people but about people who have overcome incredible odds, discovered unusual things or are famous and exceptional stars. The advertisements promise the reader wealth, success, love and knowledge of future events. Do you want unlimited credit, do you want to know the direction of your life, do you want to know secrets to get the sex partner of your dreams? These are all available through the ads of the tabloid news. The overall tone of the tabloid is of incredible events and special people who live in a mysterious world where luck and fortune play a role in determining their future.

It is not a question of who reads the tabloids, that lower-class, unedu-cated people do not exercise enough discretion in what they read. Rather, what is important is what they are reading. What messages are people getting when they read tabloids, when they read sensationalism anywhere? When tabloids cover serial killers, they of course do it in a very sensationalistic and melodramatic way, only different by degree from how the mainstream newspapers cover the story. The murder case becomes part of the incredible universe peopled by stars, lucky people and lucky charms. The point is that this tabloid newspaper, because of its context, was able to report on the Homolka-Bernardo case in a far more sensationalistic way than newspapers that were banned.

Reporters do not simply get it wrong, the distortion of events is a part of our reality. The media is part of the institutional process through which we do or do not learn about crime. By imposing a court ban on such stories, the field is left open to the sensationalistic. But the story is going to have an effect whether it is reported well or not. That is the trick: the consequence of misreporting a story can be the creation of a myth, a falsehood. But myths have an effect on the practices people engage in and the lives they live. I argue that sensationalism is not mis-reporting, but reporting of extraordinary events that reflects how they just don't make sense.

Sensationalism in itself is not a problem, but being misinformed about crime and the criminal justice system is. That is the deep complaint. If the mainstream press had been free to report on the trial and its outcome, readers would have had access to more responsible reporting than they were otherwise able to receive.

As a footnote to the Bernardo case, the media took the ban to court, appealing it. Lawyers representing the *Toronto Star*, the *Globe and Mail*, the *Toronto Sun* and the CBC sought a formal order outlining reasons for the ban from Judge Kovacs in October 1993, prior to an appeal heard before the Ontario Court of Appeal in January 1994. Paul Bernardo initially appealed the ban too but eventually dropped his claim.

Meanwhile, the Supreme Court of Canada heard appeals of court-ordered media bans over the airing of the film *The Boys of St. Vincent* and in the sexual abuse trial in Martensville, Saskatchewan. The Ontario Court of Appeal eventually reserved judgement in the case but was eclipsed by future events. On December 8, 1994, the Supreme Court of Canada ruled that the right of the news media to inform readers of the proceedings of jury trials is as important as the right of an accused to a fair trial. It was expected that this decision would encourage more responsible journalism, quell rumours and enable the media to inform the public about the proceedings of criminal trials.

3. *The history of serial killer news.* One researcher pegs the beginning of the use of the term serial in relation to violent crime in the 1960s. However, as we've seen above, it didn't come into common parlance until the 1980s. Testimony before a U.S. Senate committee in 1983 described a new taxonomy

of criminal behaviour. Key in this new discourse was FBI testimony, and in 1983 an article in *Psychology Today* quoted the FBI as saying that 25 percent of murders committed in the U.S. were by serial killers.

The first article in the national news in Canada on serial murder (not "serial killer") was cited by officials at the U.S. Justice Department, the office of Juvenile Justice and Delinquency Prevention and the behavioural science section of the FBI at Quantico. These experts are quoted as saying that now 28 percent of the 20,000 murders in the U.S. every year go unsolved (see Article 9.4).

Article 9.4 "Agency estimates 35 mass killers at large in U.S."
These crimes are often committed in many different jurisdictions by persons without a connection to the community and thus present unusual problems to the police. It is our belief that many missing children are, in fact the victims of serial murderers. The phenomenon of serial murders often involves torture, sexual assault and mutilation, occurs in widely scattered areas, and more often than not, victimizes children. Because the bodies of the victims are not always found, we have no idea what the real number is. (*Globe and Mail*, October 27, 1983: 21)

In 1984, news reports were published of an investigation into twenty killings in the Seattle area in what would come to be known as the Green River killer case. In 1987, articles were published in the *Vancouver Sun* saying there was no link between those crimes and the murders of women in Vancouver. Interestingly, the idea of a killer who committed crimes of a violent, sexual nature over a period of time against seemingly random victims was not new. Articles on Clifford Olson, for example, were first published in the *Globe* in 1982, but he was not called a "serial killer." It took the U.S. news media to export that term into Canada.

For example, in 1984, the first article on "serial killer" was published in Canada's national news. It was reproduced from the *New York Times Service*. Among other facts it said multiple murderers are almost exclusively men, white and in their thirties; some of them roam from state to state looking for victims, but most find them near home; they are not insane; and they are sexual sadists and exhibit no visible signs of derangement. It was said to be a new personality type, exemplified by Ted Bundy and Henry Lee Lucas, who was alleged to have killed 360 victims.

So whether it is 1922 or 1984, this was not news about a person who killed but of a new killing category. The problem was that there was a lot of misconstruction in the idea of the serial killer, perpetuated by the media perhaps, but issued from law enforcement and psychiatric experts. The extent of serial murder is at most 2 percent of all homicides, with a wide diversity of killers in terms of gender, race and age. And what is missing from the typology are medical murders, whose killings are much more likely to go unnoticed.

The FBI had a bureaucratic interest in promoting its scope of enforcement, aided by the social ideology of the time. Lucas, a serial confessor not killer, and a reactionary conservatism against permissiveness, combined with the FBI's interest in expansion, created a serial killer crime wave.

The construction of the stereotype illustrates the attraction of the unknown in the language that is accessible in the day, the "criminal sexual psychopath." Similarly, an article in the *London Times*, in 1922, talks about how "Jack the Ripper" crimes are difficult to solve (see Article 9.5).

Article 9.2 "Double lives"

There is no motive for them — that is to say, nothing to connect the crime with the perpetrator of it. His behaviour is completely abnormal, which means that he has no sane reason for it, and therefore it is hard for sane persons to identify him... the madness may be confined to this one particular external symptom, and may make the lunatic more, not less, cunning than ordinary sane men... A case in point, though only in fiction, is Iago. His crime was really purposeless, though he invented reasons for it; it was the expression and the vent of enormous vanity in a malignant exercise of power... the lunatic wishes to cause as much damage as possible... There he would like to be an anarchist... the difference between real life and dreams has vanished and they act those fantasies which to the rest of us are unconscious. (*The Times*, February 4, 1922: 11, editorial)

The language of the day is political (the anarchist) and psychological (the unconscious). Both are realms un/known, charted and yet dangerous. Similarly, the category of the serial killer was a powerful romantic stereotype constructed in the 1980s. The picture of the rootless, irrational, lustful and obsessive violent killer was attractive because of the times. It was a reaction against modernism, permissiveness and the failure of traditional social controls. While not wanting to stress the functional use of this stereotype, it served to exteriorize contemporary concerns and anxieties.

The serial killer was able to blend into the crowd, he operated at night and he was sexually violent. This was a modern vampire. States drafted laws against predators. Films and movies were made about the monsters and the heroes who tracked and caught them.

3. *The vampire.* If Ted Bundy epitomized the slick charm of the vampire Dracula, Robert Pickton is Nosferatu. Male serial murderers are often characterized as having vampire-like qualities, perhaps best typified in Ted Bundy. Both are compelled and consumed by their lust to sexually violate and

murder. Both kill periodically, at random, both appear superhuman, and both are sensationalized and romanticized in popular culture. If real crime news sensationalizes serial murder, it only approaches what we accept in popular cultural fiction. And if this was a traditional criminological analysis, I would compare cultural representations with reality. However, just as fiction has to seem authentic, so does fact enter into fiction.

We don't talk of monsters, vampires or werewolves anymore. But maybe our serial killers today are the vampires and werewolves of the past. Some have gone so far as to propose that in a "gothic criminology," academic and aesthetic accounts be seen as complementary. If gothic fiction is about the horrors of an imagined world, gothic criminology is about the actual horrors of the modern world.

Article 9.6 "Pickton charged with 6th murder as remains found: Police say human remains have been found at Port Coquitlam pig farm"

For the first time Tuesday, police admitted they have found human remains that led to some of the six first-degree murder charges against Port Coquitlam pig farmer Robert (Willy) Pickton. Families of 29-year-old Sereena Abotsway and Andrea Joesbury, 23, were notified in the last two days that the remains of their loved ones were located on the property last week.

The *Vancouver Sun* has confirmed that other remains... have still not been identified... All of the six women Pickton is charged with murdering are among the 54 who've disappeared from the streets of Vancouver's Downtown Eastside in recent years. In all six cases, the women went missing after July 1998 when Vancouver city police first received information about the Port Coquitlam property from worried relatives... [So and so] said he has known Pickton and his brother David since elementary school and has worked for them at different times over the years. He described them both as kind and generous. "If Willy did this, he deserves to be stopped. But I don't know what to believe," [he] said. (*Vancouver Sun*, April 10, 2002: A1, by Kim Bolan and Jeff Lee)

The vampire commits senseless murders, just as does the serial killer. The two merge as a rhetoric of modern life, one a traditional myth, the other a modern reality. But the reality is a category, a personality type who doesn't show remorse as he kills to satisfy his lust. The myth is also a category, created to collect those bodies savaged by werewolves and monsters.

In the classic case, the vampire is the active terror, but he also lives within a passive landscape. The modern landscape is a metaphorical and yet familiar terrain for a crime scene, with the drug-addicted prostitute the victim of a predator stalking the downtown. And it is Pickton's landscape that is scoured to yield clues as to his nocturnal rampages. The vampire is missing at first as

"Vancouver prostitutes frightened by slayings... peer into slow-cruising cars in the city's several red-light districts, trying to tell the difference between a customer, a plainsclothes cop and a killer" (*Globe and Mail*, September 6, 1988). The fact that it is difficult to tell the difference is telling: you can't tell the good guys from the bad guys without a script, as the saying goes, and there is no script for this new killer.

When "pig farm" first comes into play as a news category in the *Globe and Mail* on February 8, 2002, the landscape is the topic of reporting and investigation. "Police hunt for bodies on B.C. pig farm," the headline reads, as the "probe into missing sex-trade workers zeroes in on Port Coquitlam property." Forensic investigators began excavating on the property, which one victim's mother described as "really creepy." By February 14, the investigation zeroed in on a trailer, embodying the monstrous horrors that had happened within.

There were also published pictures of Pickton, aerial views of the property and photos of the missing women. A map of the "seedy side of town" was displayed alongside a photo of an alley with a woman smoking crack. No trespassing signs barred entrance to the pig farm property, but next door, in one of the housing developments residents worried about property values. After all, it's all about appearances.

Summary

In this chapter, a lawyer concerned with the relationship between the legal profession and the media commented on the difficulty of dealing with reporters. His concerns involve reporters, who are commonly not well versed in the procedures of the criminal justice system, a complaint we've heard before, and lawyers, who ab/use the media in pursuit of advantage for their own clients.

These are common complaints, and anyone who deals with the media in a professional capacity probably has dealt with the problem of the ten-minute interview at two o'clock in the afternoon that has to make it to the evening news. I heard a colleague so often on the news that I joked his name must have been written on the wall of the bathroom down at the CBC.

One specific complaint is that the media is oriented towards the thirty-second clip, to the most sensational story. And in a highly competitive market this is a way to grab the attention of the reader. The topic of serial killers was taken up as perhaps the most outstanding example of sensationalism, in order to reconstruct what sensationalism actually looks like. These accounts of serial murder were found to emphasize certain distinctive themes: violence, sexuality and seriality; as well as that these crimes go hidden, they could happen anywhere and they often involve innocent victims. There is, then, a deeply moral element to these articles.

Through reading the news we can get a detailed understanding of sensationalism and what it looks like. However it would be a mistake to see it as merely exaggeration. The subsequent analysis shows how sensationalistic accounts act as tabloids do, reinforcing ignorance about the world and perpetuating the view that the world is a mysterious place where weird and unusual events occur. The world is full of monsters, some imagined and some real, some fictional and others factual, and sometimes it is difficult to tell the difference.

Regarding the Karla Homolka trial in Ontario, we examined the consequences of leaving the field to tabloids while imposing a ban on responsible reporting. Details of the crime leaked out despite the best efforts of the court to contain them. Though the analysis ends up a long way from where the speaker starts, the point is made that sensationalism is not simply an exaggeration, a mistake, but that it does a disservice by misinforming readers about the world in which they live.

This is not simply bad reporting; some would say that keeping people misinformed about how the world works serves a purpose. And that is perhaps the irony about court-ordered media bans that people are kept in the dark about legal processes. However there is an even deeper theme in this chapter, that the serial killer is a constructed category, stalking Whitechapel's streets in the 1880s, reinvented in 1980s America and imported into Canada, but echoing older themes of vampirism and werewolves. Stalking these monsters takes us into unfamiliar territory, both real and imagined, and it is a dark and dangerous world.

10

The Westray Mine Explosion
Covering a Disaster and a Failed Inquiry

Pack journalism describes a process whereby the media takes a uniform convergent line on a story, a line from which the stories seldom deviate. In her talk, Deborah Woolway recounts how the media covered the Donald Marshall inquiry in Nova Scotia, a wrongful conviction case where an aboriginal person was jailed for eleven years for a murder he didn't commit. Through her talk we are exposed to the idea that journalists are not always as critical as they should be and often unwittingly take the line lawyers and politicians want them to.

In Reading the News, we look at a tragedy and the inquiry that followed — the Westray mine disaster at Plymouth, Nova Scotia, where a methane explosion occurred deep in a mine, killing twenty-six men. The media initially covered the explosion as a human tragedy story, and the coverage was an overwhelming example of pack journalism. Many of the critical issues Deborah Woolway identifies from the Marshall inquiry are similar: how to get a story and get it right, covering the legal issues while also reporting a human tragedy.

What subsequently came to light was that there had been warning signs that an explosion at Westray was likely to occur, that safety standards were not adhered to at the mine and that the provincial department of labour had issued warnings about safety that were ignored. The Sample Study shows how coverage of the disaster was massive and declined over time once the legal ins and outs of a very complex case were being discussed in the courts. The disaster is contrasted with media coverage of listeriosis and the danger that poses to the public in the next section.

In Analyzing the News, the adequacy of media coverage of the explosion, the subsequent criminal investigation and the inquiry is examined. What were the consequences of the line the media took on the tragedy? Did the media coverage itself become part of the story of the Westray disaster? It also extends the analysis of risk by looking at news coverage of listeriosis using the Google News Archive.

The theme the chapter deals with is the ideology of danger, and the emotion is anxiety and its naïve opposite, assurance. Studies I have found useful in thinking about corporate crime are Burns and Orrick (2002), Fitzgerald (2009), Lynch, Stretesky and Hammond (2000), McMullan and McClung (2006) and Maguire (2002).

Deborah Woolway's Talk

It seems a long time ago now when the news director of the day came into the station and said, "Does anyone want to cover this Marshall inquiry thing? It's probably going to last about three weeks." No one had any idea what we were getting ourselves in for, but I leapt at the chance. I could see, even then, that it was going to be probably the biggest story to hit these parts in many, many years, and I wanted in, I was excited by it. So that's how I got involved.

And from the very beginning, CBC Radio news did this in a very calculated way. They decided there would be one person who would stay with the inquiry for the duration and that person would handle both the local and national requirements. That person would also do documentary work and debriefs with *Information Morning* or wherever they were required. What was stressed over and over, and my editors kept telling me over and over, and I strived to do it over and over, was to provide context.

However, my problems were different from other media outlets. There were a number of private stations covering the story that I used to call sausage machines because they'd just churn out the stories. It was unbelievable: thirty-second hits every hour on the hour, where they'd synthesize what they'd just heard into a succinct little package. But it offered nothing beyond a headline. And that's clearly what I was not to do. I was to provide context. I strived to do that within the limitations of my one minute and thirty, plus my debriefs and so forth and the other work that I did.

But all the media was different. There was also the drop-in approach of the Sunday morning team, which would come in and do the big hit, the big splash, and do a pretty good job picking the brains of everybody who'd been involved in the thing, and then get out. They'd parachute in and parachute out. And then there were the colour commentators and the columnists who were there to provide context and flavour. And then there was TV. This was an especially difficult thing for TV to cover, I think, because TV is pictures. I don't deal with TV, I don't actually know a lot about TV, and I think TV really had a lot of problems covering this inquiry.

Needless to say it was a demanding assignment, and I'm giving you a personal look at what I was doing at the time, so what I say is purely anecdotal. It was pretty demanding filing stories all day, every day: 12:30 news, 1:00 news, *Canada at Five*, the afternoon regional run, *World at Six*. And then turning around, rewriting the whole thing again for the morning for *World Report* and for the local stations and so forth. So like a lot of people, we all worked very long hours and became quite obsessed, quite frankly, with this whole thing.

You can well imagine, some very interesting and possibly very unhealthy relationships developed between the media and the people they were covering, specifically the lawyers. While as journalists we talk about objectivity, it is a myth. There is no objectivity, but what you strive to do is to be fair. I mean, of course you have a perspective and a point of view. You try and control it, and assess it, and clear it in your own head, so when you're dealing with controversial information you can assess it as coolly as you can and try and be fair. And that, I think, is what we're striving for, not to be objective but to be fair. That's the best you can hope for.

In the inquiry hall what was required was stamina. There was an enormous amount of reading to do, and I had a problem of synthesis: I had to compile everything I'd heard into a minute-thirty, two-minutes-max news story, using clips and so forth. There was always the temptation to go for the juicy clip, and we almost always did. There were very few days when the clip did not match, or that I felt I was taking anything out of context. Nobody's perfect, of course, but I think what I was trying to do was convey the sense and the context of what was happening, using the voices that were available.

Often I'd get up in the morning and look at the *Globe and Mail's* reams of stuff, and I'd think "Oh God, if only I had that time and space," you know. But then they'd say to me, "Oh, Debbie, you know, I wish we had the immediacy and the power to put the voices on the air and to convey the sense." We all had different problems is my point.

Some days my biggest challenge was just writing a lead that did not contain the phrase "Donald Marshall, the Micmac who spent eleven years in prison for a murder he did not commit." That became his name, and it was difficult. That was part of the job, part of the problem. It was a struggle to remain objective as it became so overwhelmingly obvious that the wave of the system had crushed an innocent person.

But to get back to the relationships that developed. It became pretty obvious that certain reporters and lawyers felt at ease with each other and would be sharing information. Some journalists would have their pet lawyers, and maybe some lawyers had their pet journalists. I don't know but it seemed to work that way. And at every break you'd often find the same couple of journalists caucused around a lawyer and saying what did this mean and what did you think of that, and speculating and becoming almost part of the story. I didn't think that was a terribly healthful sort of pattern to get into, and for the most part I tried to distance myself from that and to rely more heavily on commission counsel, which created another set of problems, because their version of what they were hearing was of course an interpretation.

It was an interesting time. To give you an illustration of the cozy and somewhat unhealthy relationship that can develop, I'll tell you this story. We'd finished a very grim day at the inquiry, I forget the testimony now, it was something to do with Marshall's suffering at Dorchester and the lousy compensation package that he got the first time out. And a journalist who shall remain nameless went over to a couple of Donald Marshall's lawyers at the end of the day and was kind of chewing the fat with them, and they were sort of laughing grimly about the evidence they'd heard, and they said to him, "Yeah, and that money didn't include the $30,000 payback Marshall had to give Dorchester for room and board." The journalist, who in every other respect is a very astute person, had a deadline and was probably past it and had to do a live debrief. He turned around and walked out of the room, walked straight onto the air and talked about a $30,000 payback.

First thing I heard about it is when I get a screaming phone call from my editor the next morning saying, "Debbie what's this about a $30,000 payback?" I said, "I don't know. What are you talking about? I don't think that's right." So I went down to the inquiry and I walked straight up to commission council and I said, "What's all this about this payback?" I drew blanks there, so turned around and walked down to Donald Marshall's lawyers and said, "What is this all about, this payback?" Her face turned as white as this sheet, and she said "Debbie, he said that on the air?" I said, "Yeah." She said, "We were just joking."

Well, I didn't know lawyers actually joked. My point is he had no reason to doubt these lawyers, they'd dealt with him in the past. And the lawyers hadn't done anything wrong, you know, it was just because of the relationship that had developed, the sort of informal chatter that went on, and they assumed that he realized they were joking, and he didn't, and he went straight to air with that.

Anyway, we all had problems, and I'll tell this one on myself. There was a day when in a live debrief I referred to a judge, live on the air, as deceased. Well, the gentleman wasn't deceased, and the switchboard lit up. I honestly thought that the judge was dead. He has subsequently died, and without being crass, I was right eventually. Anyway, there were a lot of facts, figures, names, personalities, and we all made mistakes. I spent a weekend in hell twitching nervously from that one, but we all recovered. The joke was I happened to have lunch with a lawyer on the following Monday and told her my tale of woe, and she said, "It's okay, Debbie, I thought he was dead too." So I felt a little better about that.

To get back to a couple of comments about pack journalism, because it's the thing that journalists are always afraid of, and often get accused of, whether it's a group of journalists covering the legislature or doing anything intensely for a long period of time. I was busy doing what I was doing, we watched and read and talked to each other and read each other's work and listened to each other, but there was a fair degree of cooperation that happened among the journalists that I wouldn't characterize as pack journalism at all.

Now maybe I'm a Pollyana here, but I didn't see it at play the way I've seen it at other places, especially the legislature, where there are certain rules to play by, and if you don't play by them, you get left out in the cold. Generally there was a fair degree of cooperation. I recall one day a private radio guy filing a story, and in the midst of all the chaos of the media room, the working conditions were abominable, he made an error in his report, and there was a chorus around him saying, "No John, Sandy Seal was sixteen years old. You said he was twenty years old," or something, helping him out.

In wrapping up, there are a couple of other points, in no particular order. I disagree from my own perspective about the role of the media being to get the sexiest, juiciest clip or lead right off the top. I saw my goal as personally quite different. I don't know if I succeeded, but that's what I worked toward, to do a more interpretive explaining kind of thing within the confines. And some of us didn't go home. I did a documentary piece and news stories one year to date, trying to analyze where the recommendations have gone. In our defence, a lot of it has been largely forgotten, but I've done some stuff, and I know some other people have too.

Reading the News

On May 9, 1992, at 4:47 a.m. Saturday morning, methane alarm warnings sounded in the Westray mine at Plymouth, Nova Scotia, and then twenty-five seconds later another alarm went off. These proved to be false alarms, although the *Globe and Mail* published an allegation that the alarms had been ignored, a story it later retracted under threat of lawsuit. Thirty-three minutes later, at 5:20 in the morning, an explosion occurred.

Article 10.1 "The Westray Mine explosion"

The most likely causes appear to have been either a methane gas explosion or a collapse... a resident of nearby Stellarton and a former miner and mine rescue worker for more than 20 years, said he believed methane, perhaps ignited by a spark from equipment, had caused the blast. [He] said the seam of coal worked in this mine — known as the Foord Seam — is "a very gassy seam of coal and a very dangerous seam of coal. It's considered the most dangerous in Nova Scotia... The Foord Seam in my lifetime has never been more than a graveyard... If there's been a gas explosion there's not much hope for the men." (*CanWestNews*, May 9, 1992, by Elaine Flaherty, Southam News)

The reaction to the disaster was swift and massive: police and rescue teams left for the scene immediately and hordes of media descended on the mine. Despite an intense rescue effort no one was found alive and many of the bodies were not recovered. It was eventually determined that twenty-six men had been killed underground. While there was initial speculation that the cause of the explosion was methane combustion, it would take some time to establish that fact.

Article 10.2 "Company denies allegations of unsafety"

[The company spokesperson] responded Monday to allegations that the Westray mine was unsafe despite recently winning an award for its low accident rate. Some miners have suggested men were paid not to report accidents. And one newspaper story said two Alberta miners quit Westray, disgusted and frightened by the lack of safety procedures. [He] flatly denied the allegations. "We consider these rumors to be an affront to our people," he told reporters. "These allegations are most defeating in this time of sorrow and anguish." "CanWestNews, May 12, 1992, by Elaine Flaherty, Julian Beltrame, Southam News)

The marathon news coverage of the Westray mine disaster was extensive, yet not necessarily intensive. Speculation was rampant as reporters worked to bring themselves up to speed on the issues. The explosion happened on a Saturday morning, and most stories first appeared in print on Monday, May 11. Then, between Monday and Saturday, more than a hundred stories were published by the *Halifax Herald*. Article 10.3 details the extensive effort on the part of the media to cover the disaster.

Many of the stories focused on the families of the fallen miners and the meaning of the tragedy to the community. More than half of the 503 "Westray disaster" stories published in 1992 came out in the first month after the explosion, between May 11 and June 12. In 1992 more than seven hundred newspaper articles were published in the *Halifax Chronicle-Herald* and *Mail-Star* alone under the topic of "Westray."

Article 10.3 "Explosion triggers media marathon"

Plymouth — A media marathon was in place early Saturday morning as a shocked community struggled to grasp a disaster which trapped 26 of their neighbors deep in the bowels of the Westray mine... hordes of media and their support crews converged on the mine area... reporters from provincial news agencies and across Canada drifted in. They were immediately directed to a community centre, located just up the road from the mine site. (*Halifax-Herald*, May 11, 1992: A14, A16, by Paul MacNeill)

Many of the articles, especially in the early stages, just detailed what had happened in the explosion and what was involved in the rescue effort, and provided updates. Any chronology of events would begin with the explosion, recount the actions of the police, firefighters and rescue teams, and note the presence of the media. Explanations were offered to account for what happened in regular briefings, and these became part of the textual reconstruction of events.

The first press briefing was conducted on Saturday by the Stellarton RCMP detachment. At that time it was believed that twenty-three miners were trapped 1.5 kilometres underground. On Sunday there were several press briefing by RCMP and Westray officials, and the number trapped was revised to 26. Mine officials declined to speculate on how long it would take to reach miners and said gas was the probable cause of the explosion. On Sunday, Westray officials defended the gas monitoring program at a press briefing and said rescue workers were within 600 metres of the goal. Later that day eleven miners were announced dead. The premier said it would be a long time, if ever, before Westray mine would reopen.

This chronology is not simply a listing of the progression of events but a recursive display of the organizational work of the media: its presence at the disaster as a witness, setting up camp, taking photos, attending press briefings and interpreting explanations for what happened. The disaster is defined here prominently in terms of the presence of the media. But the presence of the media was not without issue.

Exhibit 10.1 The Media Becomes the Story

All week, there was one story above all the reporters huddled in the community centre here wanted dearly to write. "Trapped miners found alive," it would say... Many people here and in the surrounding Pictou County area, would greet this story with skepticism or surprise. To them, we were ghouls, intruding on their privacy and feasting on their sorrow... We brought too many cars and too many cameras. We took too many liberties and asked too many questions...

But the tensions that developed... illustrate a dilemma reporters always face when covering an incident such as this: How do you convey tragedy and sorrow without exploiting it? Coverage of this mine disaster was a far cry from the Springhill incidents of 1956 and '58 when reporters mingled with families and rescue workers at the pithead. This time, we were down the road, separated from the families by police and far enough away to prevent us seeing any of the explosion's victims... [Those] who directed their wrath at us weren't family members at all but people who felt they were protecting the bereaved by warning us off... we were an easy, convenient and hard-to-miss target.

For officials of Westray... the fact that people chose to take their anger out on us was to their advantage... [they] were able to deflect questions about safety at the mine. Other than issuing a blanket denial of allegations of safety violations, mine officials simply told us this was not the "appropriate time" to discuss it. When it is the "appropriate time" to discuss it, let's hope they're as available to the media as they have been this week. (*CanWestNews*, May 15, 1992, by Elaine Flaherty, Southam News)

Newspapers across the country ran stories on the disaster. For example, the *Toronto Star* placed its stories on page one for the first week. The first day of reporting, Sunday, the day after the explosion, was about tragedy, as were most of the stories. But by Tuesday, in a story filed in Ottawa, the angle took a more political turn. It was pointed out that in 1987 the federal regional development minister, Robert de Cotrêt, responsible for the Cape Breton Development Corporation (Devco), had said the Plymouth mine was neither economic nor safe because of methane deposits. Another article pointed out that the mine was located in the former federal riding of Brian Mulroney and in the provincial riding of Premier Don Cameron. It was made to seem as if politics had played a hand in where the mine was built.

Cameron was industry minister when the project was announced and former Tory MP Elmer MacKay, who gave up his seat for Mulroney, helped put together the project before becoming the federal public works minister and head of the Atlantic Canadian Opportunities Agency (ACOA). Cameron endorsed the mine and lobbied Mulroney to approve a financing deal that saw Curragh get a $12 million loan from the province and a federal loan guarantee of $85 million. Curragh was also able to negotiate a fifteen-year contract with Nova Scotia Power Corporation to buy $200 million worth of coal over fifteen years. It seemed like a deal too good to be true, especially given the volatile nature of the coal seam.

Stories like this that stressed the economic and political side of the disaster were few and far between, perhaps because the emotional, family angle was so obvious, but also because it is so difficult to research and document (what was not yet known to be) corporate crime.

Much coverage comprised stories on the draegermen who risked their lives to help those trapped underground and stories on the explosion, safety and other disasters. There were updates on the tragedy and the progress made in trying to reach the underground miners, if any were still alive. The premier announced calls for an inquiry quite early. However, only a few of the stories listed attempted to offer explanations of what had occurred, such as Exhibit 10.2.

Exhibit 10.2 An Inquiry Is Set

An inquiry headed by Justice Kenneth Peter Richard of the Nova Scotia Supreme Court's trial division is to start as soon as possible and will be wide-sweeping. Its terms of reference include an examination of the May 9 blast and whether it was preventable, including whether negligence was a factor;

THE WESTRAY MINE EXPLOSION

whether there were problems in the mine's operations, including if its structure took into account the geological formations in the area and whether all rules were followed; and, perhaps the most important question for the futures of all the politicians whose fingerprints are on the Westray coal mine project — anything else relating to the mine's establishment and operations.

There have been serious allegations of safety violations in the Westray mine and while officials have issued a blanket denial, the inquiry is certain to closely investigate these potentially damning stories. It will also be looking at what could be the crucial question: Should a mine ever have been opened in an area known to be one of the most dangerous in the world for coal mining? (*CanWestNews*, May 18, 1992, by Elaine Flaherty, Southam News)

The initial articles on Westray overwhelmingly focused on the tragedy of the explosion, the attempt to rescue the miners and the effect on the families. A few articles compared the explosion to other mining disasters in the province, such as the one at Springhill on October 23, 1958, and made references to the 244 miners who had died in the history of mining coal in Pictou County.

Although most of these articles simply tried to come to grips with what had happened and to portray the tragedy affecting the families, only a few articles raised claims that the mine was unsafe. Inspection records from the provincial department of labour were said to reveal that the mine's owners were cautioned about the unstable structure of the coal seam, high methane gas levels, improper storage of flammable materials and the use of unauthorized equipment. Equipment was said either to have no gas-monitoring component or to have one that had been turned off, an allegation more fully explored at the inquiry. Two miners on the last crew to work before the explosion said methane levels had exceeded 3.5 percent even though the law required evacuation after it reached 2.5 percent.

When the premier announced that there would be an inquiry into the explosion, he said that "no one would escape scrutiny." A fourteen-year veteran of the Nova Scotia Supreme Court trial division was appointed to lead the inquiry. The terms of reference for the inquiry are important for they set the limits and boundaries of what could be investigated. As we see above in Exhibit 10.2, the commissioner was to inquire into and make recommendations respecting whether "the occurrence" was or was not preventable; whether there was any neglect or defect in the working of the mine; whether the mine and its operations were in keeping with the known geological structures in the area and whether there was compliance with applicable statutes, regulations, orders, rules and directions. These terms of reference were broad and seemed to give the inquiry authority to establish criminal responsibility, something in fact it could not do, which became a problem later.

On September 17, four months after the explosion, the RCMP took control of the mine and seized documents and equipment to determine if there was a basis for charges of criminal negligence causing death. A separate trial, subject to a media ban, heard whether the inquiry or the RCMP could view seized documents that Curragh maintained were privileged communication between the firm and its lawyers. Eighty-five of the 125 documents in question were subsequently ruled confidential. In both September and December, the RCMP also seized documents from the inquiry itself.

Initially, it seemed that the provincial labour department had no knowledge of safety problems or of the risk of methane buildup in the mine, and at the end of May inspectors in the mine found evidence of a second explosion and cave-in that had not been reported. However, although the province could not find federal reports that cautioned against mining the Foord seam, provincial labour department inspectors had issued four different orders to clean up dangerous working conditions between December 1990 and April 29, 1992, a week before the explosion. And the province's department of natural resources had retroactively approved unauthorized changes to the mine even though it was apparent that worker safety was at risk.

Exhibit 10.3 The Focus Turns to the Labour Department

One day after the Nova Scotia labor department laid a raft of charges against the owners of the Westray mine and four of its managers, the department itself came under fire. Opposition politicians complained the 52 charges — dealing with 15 safety issues at the mine where 26 men died in an explosion May 9 — were too long in coming and that the department failed to examine its own role in detecting and dealing with potential safety problems.

Reporters complained that a statement about the charges was delayed until just before 5 p.m. Monday, so court offices would be closed and documents and officials unavailable... [The Labour Minister] refused to comment on whether inspectors working for his department might have overlooked safety concerns at the mine or neglected to take forceful action against Westray if it failed to comply with safety orders. Just 10 days before the mine blew up in what is believed to be a methane gas explosion and fire fuelled by coal dust, the company was ordered to lay down stone dust to control excessive levels of coal dust. [He] has been unable to say if the mine ever complied with that order. (CanWestNews, October 6, 1992, by Elaine Flaherty, Southam News)

In October, Curragh and four of its managers were charged with fifty-two violations of the provincial *Occupational Health and Safety Act*, charges that had to be laid within six months of the infractions. The charges included failure to prevent the accumulation of coal dust, improper use and storage of flammable materials and tampering with monitoring devices for methane detection. The maximum penalty for any of these offences was $10,000 and a year in jail.

As Exhibit 10.3 points out, it also came to light that previous warnings had been given by inspectors to the mine managers, a fact that caused the labour minister some embarrassment. Three weeks before the safety violations charges, the provincial cabinet had finally formally transferred responsibility for enforcing the *Coal Mines Regulation Act* from the Department of Natural Resources to the Department of Labour, six years after that responsibility had been transferred in practice.

Meanwhile, the Supreme Court of Nova Scotia heard arguments late in September 1992 for an injunction against the public inquiry on the grounds that it was delving into criminal matters. The inquiry's mandate was under provincial jurisdiction but appeared also to involve questions of criminal responsibility, a federal matter. The provincial attorney general said the mandate of the inquiry could be changed so it would not conflict with the criminal investigation, but that would require Cabinet approval and the head of the inquiry was himself reluctant to request such a change.

In October, the Supreme Court of Nova Scotia ruled that the Inquiry should be postponed until a formal legal challenge could be heard, in order to protect the constitutional rights of the managers to a fair trial. In November the inquiry was struck down on the basis that its terms of reference involved assigning criminal responsibility. This could have been foreseen, as it had been an issue in the inquiries into baby deaths at Toronto's Hospital for Sick Children in 1984 and into the fund-raising activities of Patricia Starr in 1990.

In June 1993, the United Steelworkers of America appealed the Nova Scotia decision to the Supreme Court of Canada. A decision was expected in late 1994, and the trial of Curragh and the mine managers began in February 1995.

In December 1992, thirty-four of the fifty-two charges under the *Occupational Health and Safety Act* were stayed by the director of public prosecutions to avoid interfering with criminal charges that were anticipated to be laid by the RCMP. In March 1993 the remaining eighteen charges were stayed as well, a decision that led to questions about the competence of the director of public prosecutions. But it wasn't until April 1993, almost a year after the explosion, that criminal charges were laid. The charges read that Curragh Inc. and two mine managers had committed criminal negligence causing death and manslaughter, both carrying a maximum penalty of life imprisonment.

The charges were quickly criticized as flawed because they did not specify exactly what unlawful acts or omissions on the part of Curragh or the mine managers had led to the deaths of the miners. The first charges were thrown out, and charges were refiled. These were then criticized on the basis that the prosecutors had not specified how failing to comply with provincial statutes was connected to the criminal charges of negligence and manslaughter. There were also allegations that insufficient staff and funds were allocated for the Crown investigation and that officials from government departments possibly implicated in the disaster attended meetings with government prosecutors.

Spreading blame around, in April 1993, the new labour minister (the minister at the time of the explosion had been removed) revealed the results of a report that showed the Department of Labour was disorganized and had failed to follow up on safety orders. The independent report criticized the department for unplanned and reactive inspections, incomplete file documentation, inadequate identification of violations in order to ensure compliance and lack of follow-up to see if orders had been carried out.

While the inquiry was barred from holding public sessions until the criminal charges were heard, it requested federal documents on Westray. The Mulroney government initially refused to hand over thousands of pages of documents. This withholding pointed to further questions about the involvement of the federal and provincial governments in the financing and sponsorship of the Westray mine.

It was reported that the danger of explosive methane in the Foord seam had been known in 1986, and in 1988 Clifford Frame, the chair of Westray, had pointed out the hazards of mining the seam in a letter to the government requesting funds. The politics of the disaster were further evidenced by the fact that the contract for coal negotiated with the Nova Scotia Power Corporation attached to the loan agreement was better than that held with the Cape Breton Development Corporation.

In 1989, the vice-president of mining for Curragh had met with then-premier John Buchanan and then local MLA Don Cameron, after previous meetings between Clifford Frame and former defence minister Robert Coates, advisers from the Prime Minister's Office, local MP and future head of ACOA Elmer MacKay, and Robert de Cotrêt, the minister responsible for the Department of Regional Industrial Expansion (DRIA). The next year, in May 1990, more than $100 million in loans and guarantees were extended to the mine.

Between 1989 and 1992, there had been eight cave-ins and numerous safety violations, but no charges were ever laid. In 1992, three weeks after the explosion, a Cape Breton MLA made the allegation that the premier had called him in 1990 and threatened him after he was critical of the government sponsorship of the mine, an allegation the premier denied. After the explosion, the U.S. expert brought in to advise on the disaster was alleged to have participated in a cover-up of government responsibility in a mine explosion in Kentucky.

Two days after the explosion, the federal government set up a Westray task force at the federal industry department, and $400,000 was allocated to explain the federal role at Westray. At the provincial level, it passed unremarked that the media relations officer for the Department of Justice was moved to the Labour Department.

The facts on the politics of the disaster received little attention in the press, even though Dean Jobb, one of the staff reporters at the *Herald*, eventually was nominated for several awards for his investigative reporting on Westray, which later appeared in book form.

While the chronology of facts recounted here is gleaned from the media, which is to its credit, the way in which those facts appear is detailed in the next section.

Sample Study

The topic of analysis is Westray coverage. That is summarized here, and then its implications are discussed in the next section alongside a different type of disaster.

To conduct the study, complete coverage of the Westray disaster in the *Halifax Herald* was obtained for two years. Every article was read in order to construct an analytic timeline of how the disaster was discussed. Fourteen percent of the total citations indexed under "Westray disaster" for two years were published in the first week. In the first month, 36 percent of the total citations for the next two years were published. This massive coverage provided smothering detail of the tragedy: the explosion, the attempt to rescue the trapped miners, discovering the bodies, flooding the mine and the suffering of the families. It was the human interest story next door, a tragedy in a primary industry in a traditional economy.

Much of the reporting was not critical or informative but emotional, containing phrases such as "the price of mining coal has been measured in human lives." Emotional coverage is not bad coverage, but the following editorial full of sentimental phrases unfortunately comes across as an apologetic for the disaster.

Exhibit 10.4 Tragedy at Westray

Underground coal mining in Nova Scotia... has long been a story of great human courage pitted against great natural hazards... too often, it has also been a history of hope and fortitude and heartbreak in the face of unbearable tragedies. So it was again in Plymouth, Pictou County, this weekend, when a methane bump early Saturday buried 26 miners underground. The scene was the Westray mine... sunk last year into one of [the] most treacherous troves of coal... The dimension of the tragedy... was truly heartrending... all of Nova Scotia is now waiting and praying... we share the pain and grief of the families and friends of the men who have perished... [This] is a terrible reminder of the enormous sacrifice made by generation after generation of brave men to mine Nova Scotia's deep coal seams... [This is] an awesome testament to the courage of those who go down to the deeps. It's a reminder, too, that advanced technology... hasn't changed the equation. It is still brave men toiling in the face of unseen danger in the dark. The risks are still there; the men still go knowingly to meet them. And our hearts still mourn when the danger claims these finest of men. ("Tragedy at Westray," *Halifax Herald,* May 11, 1992: C1)

The phrases that are apologetic include: "testament to courage," "technology hasn't changed the equation," "toiling in the face of unseen danger," "the risks are still there," and "the men go knowingly to meet them." The elision accomplished by such a characterization misconstrues the event as human tragedy rather than workplace homicide.

Similar misconceptions, which mystify the disaster, are found in the quotations in Exhibit 10.5. In an article entitled "Call of the coal," an academic expert who was a former provincial deputy minister of development said that coal mining is engrained in the culture of Nova Scotia. In another excerpt, an academic expert attributed the acceptance of the disaster to fatalism.

Exhibit 10.5 Misconceptions and Distortions

There's always that thing in the back of every Nova Scotian's mind — I think they grew up with it in their mother's milk — that coal once paid for everything and maybe someday it'll do it again... When people die in an accident like this, it just reinforces that this is the price we've got to pay and just keep pluggin' on. (*Halifax Herald,* May 16, 1992)

We really are a region of the country where there are horrendous disasters, whether it's people lost at sea or in a mine. You just accept it because it's there. That may be the reason we accept coal mining, because it's just part of the culture... Yeah, coal mines are dangerous. You could lose your life doing it. But you could lose your life fishing, too. We just accept it. (*Toronto Star,* May 16, 1992)

In the first edition of this book, the type and progression of coverage of the Westray explosion in the *Halifax Herald* was charted. Seven hundred articles were collected and read. The amount of coverage was linked to major events as the story unfolded, showing both the extent of coverage and also the change in subject matter. During 1992–93, about seven hundred articles were indexed under "Westray disaster" in the *Halifax Herald.* This includes articles, editorials, commentaries and letters to the editor. The sample was not just limited to news coverage because it is in those other features that the topic gets debate, discussed and critiqued. The articles were broken into fifty-unit blocks, with the average number of articles per day represented on the line. So, for example, the first fifty citations were published in the first two days and represent an average of about twenty-five per day. During the first month, 250 articles were published, 36 percent of the total coverage for two years.

In that first month, certain topics were paramount. For example, during the first week when coverage was highest, the explosion was paramount and the promise to establish an inquiry was announced. The focus was on tragedy and the need to do something to get to the bottom of what happened. The number of citations published per day quickly dropped to about an average of seven at the end of the first month.

During June, one month after the explosion, the coverage increased slightly over the discussion about whether to flood the mine. This decision was emotional and controversial. The evidence and any remaining bodies would be lost to the sea water flooding in underground.

By the time safety charges were laid in October, the number of citations had dropped to an average of about one and a half a day. The inquiry was (temporarily) quashed in November, and in April criminal charges were finally laid by the RCMP.

An estimated two hundred journalists descended on Plymouth with the modern technology of communication at their disposal. However, they were quickly separated from the families and told the latter did not wish to speak to them. Instead of seeing this as information control, the media focused on the rescue effort and the explosion. It was patronizing to say that all most viewers really needed or wanted was to know whether the miners had survived.

However, the media missed the story about safety concerns at the mine before the explosion occurred. The extreme danger had become routine. Safety regulations were not observed or were flagrantly violated, and miners were often ordered to work in unsafe conditions and verbally abused when they protested. Day after day the danger became almost banal, as the workers anticipated they could be killed at any time. Miners even told their relatives that if there was an explosion to make sure that somebody got to the bottom of what happened.

The fact that Curragh was going to operate Westray was certainly no secret; safety had also been known to be a concern at its Yukon mine; and the political manoeuvring to establish the mine at Plymouth merited more investigation. Investment in mining is a risky business, and companies are going to go where the red tape is minimal. One columnist wrote how he had learned that a miner had called a local paper to complain about rockfalls in the mine, suggesting they contact the mine inspector, but the newspaper had failed to follow up on the lead. Overall, by the time the safety issues and the legal debates were being reported, coverage had dropped. When the story was the human tragedy coverage was at its highest, but when the story became legal, coverage was at its lowest.

Analyzing the News

As we can see from Reading the News, not only was the coverage on Westray massive, coverage was a separate story in itself.

1. *Romanticizing the disaster.* As shown above, coverage was intense in the early days after the explosion. The event was framed as a disaster, not a crime but a tragedy. It was a disaster and an accident, but only quietly was it called an accident waiting to happen. This "framing" of the issue as a tragedy made it less likely to be seen as a criminal matter. The use of emotion, moreover, brought us closer to the victims and their families and at the same time distanced us from seeing it as a crime.

The sentiments expressed in Exhibit 10.4, for example, are admirable. However, "brave men courageously working underground" ignores the fact the work is done out of necessity. Saying that the men knew the risks says that they knew what they were getting into and accepted it. To state that they sacrificed themselves to mine coal, which can then turn on them capriciously despite the best of technology, mystifies the relations of production that allowed those men to work in conditions that precipitated the explosion.

In such a depiction we do not get a sense that people most often work because they have to work to live, that occupational safety standards might not have been followed, that workers often have no choice about working in unsafe conditions. There is no analysis of the politics involved in establishing Westray or acknowledgement that it was not run perfectly. Where are the inspector, the owner, the manager and the politician?

The image readers get from such coverage is individualistic and romantic, of courageous men working on the frontier, pitted against capricious nature. Such a portrayal gives us no way to understand the disaster as anything other than an accident. This explosion was about as much an accident as the grounding of the Exxon Valdez in Alaska, the release of isocyanate gas from the Union Carbide plant in Bhopal, India, the collapse of the Ocean Ranger and many other examples of corporate crime. The media frame that individualizes responsibility and romanticizes causes reinforces dominant ideological definitions of corporate deviance as accident.

The problem with these explanations is that they romanticize and justify the disaster, offering no critical insight into why the tragedy occurred and how it might have been prevented. But it would be a mistake to see this frame as a mistake. Framing the issue as inevitable or as an accident or as personal sacrifice and tragedy obscures the relations of power that make occupational risk inevitable. It was not an accident, but an accident waiting to happen. It was, as the inquiry judge would later frame it, both predictable and preventable. For the media to say otherwise placed it on the side of power not on the side of the workers, but in all fairness it would take time to uncover that other story. There were voices criticizing the corporation, the politics and the lack of safety, but these voices were overwhelmed by the dominant ideology of danger.

2. *Documenting the coverage.* The Sample Study looked at the amount of coverage and its changing subject over time. The consequence of massive coverage at the beginning and its subsequent drop as time progresses is that the amount of information published declined as the legal and criminal issues came to the fore. Initially, when the topic was the "Westray disaster," the coverage of human suffering and tragedy was massive and overwhelming. When the topic became the "Westray case," the coverage was minimal in comparison. There are, of course, several possible reasons for this: after saturation coverage, interest in the case declined; reporters lacked the ability to understand and communicate the legal technicalities; or new topics captured public attention and the Westray story's shelf life had expired.

Whatever the explanation, the consequence in terms of the textual construction of the disaster is that readers were exposed to information on tragedy but not to information that would increase their understanding of the legal, criminal, economic and political issues involved in the case. Reporting that emphasizes the emotional side of the disaster, instead of the crime, ignores or mystifies the conditions that led to the explosion in the first place, making it likely that in the long run these conditions will be reproduced.

3. *Convergence in framing.* The tendency of reporters to cover a story in the same way has been called pack journalism. This term has often been used to describe how different media converge in their news content. Pack journalism results in part from the organization of the news media, their need to maximize resources and the reliance of reporters on the work of others to gain a sense of the newsworthiness of stories. The ideological consequence of pack journalism is a uniform, homogeneous, lowest-common-denominator type of coverage where orthodoxy rules. Instead of a heterodoxy of opinion, readers are exposed to a uniform world view.

The convergence in the news about Westray meant that not many media stories were critical in how they covered the explosion. The journalists seemed overwhelmed by the disaster and struggled to put it into context, but they seemed unsure about the technology and terminology of mining, and there was both complaint and praise for their role. Furthermore, the media missed the story about safety concerns at the mine before the explosion occurred. The extreme danger had become routine.

Mining is a risky business. In general, the risk of being killed at work is higher than that of being murdered. In the primary industries of forestry and mining, the risk is greatest. The Law Reform Commission said the occupational fatality rate around mines, quarries and oil wells is the second highest in Canada, at 83.6 deaths per 100,000 people, surpassed only by the rate for work in forestry. Between 1989 and 1991, the number of injuries in mining in Canada went down by 25 percent and was down 16 percent in all occupations. In Nova Scotia, however, the number of time-loss injuries in mining went up by 28 percent, even though the overall provincial occupational injury rate went down 9 percent. Mining was certainly not getting safer in Nova Scotia.

The Workers' Compensation Board routinely collects information on the number of people killed by occupation in Canada and passes it on to Statistics Canada, but the last year that survey was published was 1986. Injuries and fatalities are highest in the primary occupations, and, because these industries are located in certain regions, it can be argued that occupational danger is part and parcel of regional economic inequality in Canada. This danger is part of Maritime history, whether on the water or in the mines, but this is not a natural fact but an organizational feature of capitalism. This story is all the more shocking because of its familiarity.

The Westray disaster could be a story about political interference in the way grants are given to the mining business. It could also be a story of laxity and ineffectiveness in the provincial Department of Labour. While the inspectors have been cleared, we still do not know enough about why safety standards were not in place or not enforced. It could also be a story about the political economy of death and how risk is part of the calculation of profit. It could also be a story about how the media contributed to a climate where the explosion was able to happen in the first place. The media was certainly part of the story, but how was it part of the crime?

4. *Constructing danger*. Let's return to the phrase "The risks are still there; the men still go knowingly to meet them," and instead of criticizing this as emotional obfuscation designed to secure the ideological compliance of the public in the face of corporate crime, let's ask a different question.

It is not that miners *knew* the danger they were going to face underground. Rather it is that we all think we know where danger lies. Parachuting, wrestling crocodiles and fistfights all seem to contain obvious risks. On the other hand, there are other activities that we undertake without any thought of risk: gardening, eating supper, a walk in the park. These activities seem safe, innocent. However, this is as much a matter of ideology as the obfuscation of risk.

When we go into a grocery store to buy a can of soup for supper, we take it home, open it, heat it up and eat it, all with never the thought that it might kill us. What do you do when consuming food made by a corporation can result in illness or death? And, how does the corporation maintain its legitimacy and contain the symbolic threat posed by its food if it is revealed that there are problems with its product. This is a similar problem that faced Westray in the months after the mine explosion.

The following information was found using Google News Archive. In 1985 the Jalisco cheese factory near Los Angeles produced cheese linked to at least sixty-two deaths and illness in at least 150 people. The pasteurization equipment had failed, allowing listeria to propagate in the milk, which then remained in the food product, killing mostly children and pregnant women. Allegations at the time were that the company could not have pasteurized all the milk it had purchased and thus knowingly processed untreated milk. When concern developed in 1987 about the presence of listeria bacteria on the rind of soft-surface ripened cheese, it was disclosed that since 1983, over 111 cases of listeriosis had been documented in Switzerland, resulting in thirty-one deaths.

In 1988 listeria was also found in frozen, canned lobster in Halifax. A Health Department spokesman was quoted as saying that "everything is under control. The product is contained we are getting samples in and we are testing." By 1989, the threat of listeriosis had passed to paté, chicken salad and turkey dogs. The bacteria was said to pose no risk for healthy people but could cause flu-like symptoms in children and the elderly. In 1992, an outbreak in France killed sixty-two people and caused miscarriages. Almost three hundred people were infected. By 1995 it had been found in sliced meats, potato salad and smoked salmon. A health survey in Britain found high levels of campylobacter, salmonella, listeria and escherichia coli in both prepared and homemade school sandwiches. In 1997, concern had spread to hummus, ice cream and some seafood products. In 1999, a bacterial outbreak linked to hot dogs produced by a Michigan meat-processing plant killed 8 people. In 2001, Sara Lee, one of the largest producers of deli meats in the U.S., pled guilty to a misdemeanour charge that it produced and distributed tainted meat that killed about fifteen people and sickened dozens of others. The company recalled fifteen million pounds of meat and spent millions on renovating facilities.

By 2002, it was apparent that legislation to require comprehensive and thorough testing was inadequate. The Centres for Disease Control was reporting that up to five hundred deaths a year in the U.S. were attributable to listeriosis.

In 2008, an outbreak of listeriosis in Canada killed twenty-two people who ate contaminated Maple Leaf deli meat. A shortage of food inspectors was cited as the problem; however, investigation revealed that contamination had been found in slicers in 2007 and sanitation had been improved to try to correct the problem. That issue was not reported because legislation did not require it. The company faced recalls and major public confidence issues. However, messages delivered by the company's president on measures taken by the company to restore safety probably did much to restore legitimacy.

A review conducted in 2009 pointed to problems regarding federal-provincial jurisdictional issues and the need for a better response to emergencies and clearer communication with the public. However, critics faulted the review as inferior to those charged with investigating Canada's tainted blood scandal, the Walkerton tainted water crisis and the SARS epidemic. The review showed that changes to legislation in 2008 did not require companies to report problems to government under the "compliance verification system." The move to self-inspection relied on companies to conduct their own investigations into product safety. The company was very proactive in discussing compliance in public advertisements, but the underlying problems were related to the organization of health safety in the food industry, which is poorly regulated by government.

The point of this section on listeriosis is that perhaps the miners did know the danger they were heading into, but the reasoning that they went willingly or were somehow responsible for shouldering that risk is not equally true. Similarly, we know what we are doing when we go into grocery stores to buy food, but that does not make us aware of, let alone responsible for illnesses that may result. We fear the alley but not the supermarket, and we don't own or create that anxiety or its attendant cousin, assurance.

5. *The criminaloid.* I find it disappointing that criminology has lost the word "evil" in its interest in being secular and scientific. It has suffered a loss of moral compulsion in its analysis as a result. In the early twentieth century, sociologists had not yet lost sight of the conjoining of morality and crime and in fact coined the term "criminaloid" because of the perceived immunity enjoyed by a certain class of perpetrators. The deviant practices they identified, which we would call white collar and corporate crime, had not yet come under the ban of public opinion or even guilt in the eyes of the law. Because their actions didn't fit the stereotype of those of the street criminal and because they were not censored by the public, their own attitude was not that of the criminal. They escaped both punishment and ignominy with little opposition while ordinary criminals could not escape public attention. The so-called criminaloids encountered feeble opposition and committed crimes of far greater consequence in terms of both injury and cost.

Criminology on the cusp of the twenty-first century has had to search for the connection between morality and crime anew, and it was not until 2003 that we had a law against workplace homicide passed in Canada. Is every company responsible for harm that may come to the public, workers or the environment because of actions it takes or fails to take? Of course not. But in some cases, companies, with the lack of oversight by government, can wreak far more extensive harm than individuals ever could. Compensation was eventually paid in the Westray case, and class action lawsuits were settled to the tune of $25 million dollars in the 2008 listeriosis outbreak, but the preconditions for such a tragedy happening again when there is a lack of oversight is obvious.

Summary

To conduct the research for this chapter, hundreds of articles on the Westray explosion were looked at. The Westray explosion has been called a tragedy and a disaster, and it led to an inquiry and a failed court case. The Westray case is a story about safety, politics, economics and the media.

In Reading the News, we looked beneath the surface of an incredible drama of life and death, of families coping with the loss of brothers, sons, fathers and husbands. In the Sample Study, we stood back from the tragedy and looked at the overall pattern of reporting. In this way we can see how, when it came time to cover the legal issues of the Westray case, news coverage dwindled to a trickle.

We could use a similar methodology to unpack many other cases in the news. Two were alluded to above: the grounding of an oil tanker, the Exxon Valdez, off the coast of Alaska on March 24, 1989, which released 41 million litres of crude oil into Prince William Sound and polluted more than two thousand kilometres of coastline; and the release of forty tons of methyl isocyanate gas from the Union Carbide factory in Bhopal, India, which killed 2,000 to 5,000 people and injured 200,000 more.

A more recent example is the outbreak of disease-related illnesses in ordinary factory-produced food products. The advantage of examining listeriosis in the news is that it does not fit the stereotype of crime we should fear. Was it a crime, perhaps not, but it was a threat that momentarily rocked the naïve assurance that danger only exists in the dark.

The initial approach taken in the media to such events is to treat them simply as disasters and then, at some point when emotions have been rubbed raw, to begin to see the political and economic conditions that underlay these tragedies. The trick is to see how the textual construction of the event in the news overlays the event and conditions our understanding, creating the risk of a reproduction of the very conditions that make disasters possible in the first place, whether food-borne contamination or workplace injury.

Conclusion

Conclusions are always hard to write because it is difficult to summarize all the work that has gone before. However, understanding some things about conclusions makes it easier. A conclusion is often read first because the reader wants to get a quick synopsis of where the writer ends up. A smart writer puts the ending in the preface so as to help both of them. A conclusion is also often written first because usually it's not only where the writer ended up but where they wanted to arrive in the first place. A smart writer sees the beginning in the end. A smart reader knows how a smart writer writes. A smart writer knows how a smart reader reads.

Sometimes, individual topics can take on a life of their own, and the writer must then face the task of summing up underlying themes and issues that have revealed themselves in the process of discovery that is writing.

The method used in this book was eclectic, drawing techniques and analytic ideas from many sources. The media was used as a resource and topic — as a source of materials and a site of analysis. The sampling was systematic, but the point was to focus on some key issues, to use the strongest examples possible and then reconstruct an analysis to interpret the issues. For that reason, my conclusions here are ultimately the result of analysis, not simply the result of method.

The analysis developed here is built upon the idea that crime in society is as much a matter of a general attitude as any person's individual actions. Crime is not simply an act of violence, for example, as people have to react to that act and define it as a problem in the first place. The law itself sets the context for how people react to crime, and combined with the (apparent) commission of a crime, the reaction of others (through the medium of public discourse) creates an interwoven moral drama. Some of these dramas are easier to de/construct than others, such as the myths reproduced in sexual assault discourse; in some the emotional investment is too high, as in the case of child abuse; in others the ideological obfuscation is too difficult, as in the case of corporate crime. But it is in the reading of stories that document our reactions to an individual's behaviour that we can see that crime is discursively re/constructed. People rely upon and create a web of meanings for understanding action, and

226

it is this active sense-making that is the condition for taking crime for granted in the first place.

The news media is an integral part of this process because it affirms and confirms the meaning of crime in public discourse. The media does not simply create a consensus but participates in debating the dissensus over the significance of crime in modern society to our communities. Witness the debate over prostitution in Vancouver, for example. In this way the media is not as uniformly monolithic as stricter analysis has thought. There are fissures and fractures within which issues are debated.

So, crime is not found simply in the act, or even in the label, but in its social construction in public debate. And of course in modern society the media has become an inextricable part of this construction. To accuse the media of sensationalism is to create a red herring because the media both exaggerates and silences certain realities. And to simply accuse the media of making us excited is also not the problem. There are a wide range of emotions that are predicated in the reading of news stories: fear, disgust, apathy and so on.

To accuse the media of doing a bad job of informing us about the reality of crime in society is also to miss the point. It is not that the media misses some issues and sensationalizes others; to think it could do a better job is to wish it would do the job as we would want it. But what privileges one discourse over another? It seems that to improve crime reporting, we need to improve both reading and writing.

What follow are comments and suggestions on how news read/writ/ing on crime could be improved. These comments are general because the issues are quite different in the reporting of sexual assault from those in the reporting on arson, for example. However, some major points can be made, based on the idea that there is a "typical crime narrative" which mis/constructs crime.

Issues and Recommendations

1. *Moralism*: Writing and reading about crime tends to be reactionary. Although the news media has often been on the forefront in breaking scandals and exposing political corruption, when it comes to street crime especially the critical edge seems lost. News articles often adopt a moral point of view when reporting on crime, trading upon easy stereotypes and reproducing off-the-shelf labels, whether writing about prostitution, sexual assault or infanticide. This moralism can result in blaming the victims, misunderstanding the act and failing to see the deeper reasons behind the commission of the crime in the first place. To overcome this, editors, reporters and columnists need to become schooled in the various myths our society perpetuates about crime and deviance. This seems especially important in crimes dealing with

gender and sexuality, where it is very easy to project morality into legislation. The result will be a better informed public, itself less inclined to look for and reproduce moralistic judgments in their daily lives.

2. *Independence*: The news media needs to be more critical of the role of the police and the workings of the criminal justice system. It is difficult for reporters to be critical of the police when they are a main source of information on crime. However, the tendency to be dependent on the police is linked to reporters' general ignorance of the criminal justice system; as reporters learn more about the nature of the criminal justice process, they will be better able to form independent interpretations. This also requires being less dependent on lawyers, government and other authorities, who are not above trying to manipulate the press in favour of their own interests. It may mean being more patient and avoiding the compulsion to beat out the competition by publishing the quick story first or by using anonymous sources. Readers do not switch papers easily, and they are motivated by the desire for more information. Taking the time to develop a better story ultimately leads to more control of the story. For their part readers should use the alternative media more to balance accounts in the mainstream media.

3. *Interpretation*: Reporting still trades on the idea that the only thing important is to "get the facts." But what do we mean when we use the word "fact"? Do we mean indisputable, not a matter of opinion, reputable, authorized by expert advice? When seeking balance, experts are often used to show opposing points of view, which simply shows just how contestable facts are. A fact is a very malleable thing; it depends on whose point of view is represented, on what sources are consulted, on what slant is taken, on what is left out and what is left in. Reporters need to trust less in this naive dictum and more in the idea of investigative reporting, digging deeper and going for the more difficult story. A reporter doesn't want to become part of the story, of course, but needs to be more critical of the easy story, for the easy story often reflects a dominant point of view that simply reproduces the status quo, particularly when reporters rely on authorities rather than advocates, victims and victims' families. Readers also need to learn how to identify slant, interpretation and misdirection and to be critical of how interpretations are couched.

4. *Fragmentation*: The news media tends to report on crime in fragments, as incidents, reflecting how crime is treated institutionally. Focusing on the initial crime and the subsequent arrest, readers get a sense of isolated bizarre incidents committed by individuals. Such treatment, paradoxically, leads to a feeling of alienation on the part of readers. The more crimes reported and the more random and unconnected they seem, the more people feel crime is out of control. This individualistic treatment of crime ironically feeds into the conservative point of view that there is a need to return to a law-and-

order agenda, with stronger laws and stricter punishments. The media needs to focus more on the larger picture and to be more responsible in reporting trends. Stories should follow cases through to the end, so readers can develop a more realistic sense of the reality of crime, how the system works and that criminals are punished. Readers can also exploit the new social media to better control the news that is routed to them.

5. *Sensationalism*: The tendency to sensationalize the unusual creates illusions and delusions about the nature of social life. Horrific crimes do occur in society, but to focus on them contributes to an overwhelming fear of others among the public and caters to the worst instincts of gossip and voyeurism. The media can actually contribute to an escalation of problems by drawing attention to and exaggerating them. It is not simply a matter of avoiding the sensational but of balance and proportion because, in the process of sensationalization, much more mundane yet serious crime goes unreported. Domestic violence is largely invisible in the media, as is corporate crime — yet both affect society far more than armed robberies do. Celebrity crime is part of this phenomenon as well, for example, as stalking only became an issue when famous people began to be stalked and the media covered the stories.

6. *Context*: Discussing legislative changes is dry stuff and portraying the larger context is hard. Going for the sensational and the quick soundbite is just too easy. The feeding frenzy that accompanies violent crime or a whiff of conspiracy in the upper echelons can lead all too easily to creating a story where there is none or to losing perspective and missing the real crime. From Airbus and Watergate to BCCI and Bernie Madoff, it is easy to resort to pack journalism in the drive for ratings and to miss the more mundane crimes that happen every day. In covering court trials, it is easy to take the point of view of the prosecution — for after all, if a person has been charged with a crime, they must be guilty, right? It is also easy to downplay some crimes out of a sense of political correctness or embarrassment, forgetting that the community the media serves is a complex and diverse one. Readers want a sense of context but also need a critical frisson in the context that is presented to them. When it came to covering Mount Cashel and Cornwall, for example, it was too easy to focus on the deviance rather than the crime.

7. *Weight*: In relation to context, giving a crime the proper weight also helps readers to keep things in perspective. Statistics are dry, numbers are boring, eyes glaze over when viewing percentages, but knowing how infrequent murder is makes it both unusual and less alarming. The best source for such information, of course, is police statistics collected from monthly reports generated from the public. However, it can also be supplemented by victimization surveys and self-report surveys. The resultant body of information is not only an important corrective to

sensationalistic accounts but also helps create information about topics hidden and not discussed.

8. *Integrity*: Public confidence in the media sags when reporters and journalists are perceived as opportunistic and willing to do anything for a story. Exaggeration and sensationalism are just some of the most obvious faults in a business where there is a lot of pressure to get the story and beat out the competition. The seamier side involves doctoring photographs, exploiting tragedy, staging crime and faking events. It need not be anything spectacular; spinning the truth can be as simple as selecting an expert for their willingness to support a particular point of view.

9. *Rationality*: Many of the preceding comments are based on the idea that crime can be accurately measured against some objective rule. We used to think that crime statistics collected by the police were the best measure of crime, but that fails to take into account all those crimes not reported to police. Vandalism, theft from cars, these might be considered minor offences, but imagine the surprise when the first victimization survey showed that less than 10 percent of all sexual assault cases were reported to the police! For crimes involving intimacy, shame, embarrassment or power, such as in child abuse, silence is the norm, and police statistics are compromised. We can seek better information, and should, but in a world where information is political and multiple viewpoints contribute to a heterodoxy, point of view is relative.

10. *Emotions*: Many of the preceding comments are based on the idea that if we just keep our heads and count correctly that the world will be better and more fairly represented. To argue that biases enter in and prevent the media doing a good job presumes that we know what doing a good job would look like, but it also presumes that it is a matter of rationality. Both reading and writing are more than rational activities. We enter into both fearful when there is a predator in the community, outraged when the victims are weak, dismayed at the depths that people can descend to and shocked when presented with the crime. Reading and writing need to be done in a way that will change our lives. The traditional approach to dealing with emotions is to exorcise them, and there are ways to make the news more emotionally responsible, but not at the cost of forgetting that emotions are a resource we come with to a reading of crime in the news and a topic for its public discussion.

Increasingly, the old media will be replaced by the new. However, in a world made increasingly small because the media has the ability to show us how large it is, we risk alienation and a feeling of a lack of control. To counter the in/effective distance we experience from reading, watching and hearing the news from places we'll never see of events we can't control written by and of people we'll never meet, we need tools to re/place ourselves back within the public discourse.

When all is said and done, I still enjoy reading the news. And now I write it too, through a column on crime and criminal justice that aims to bring the work of criminology to the media. It has been going six years now, and I have written on stalking, media bans, bike theft, wrongful convictions, corporate environmental crime, and all manners of deviance and criminal behaviour. My purpose has been to use the venue of a column to be educational and to take the discussion of crime and justice to the public arena because, after all, crime matters.

Select Crime and Media Reading List

Altheide, David. (1997). "The News Media, the Problem Frame, and the Production of Fear." *The Sociological Quarterly* 38, 4.

_____. (2009). "Moral Panic: From Sociological Concept to Public Discourse." *Crime Media Culture* 5, 79.

Ardovini-Brooker, Joanne, and Susan Caringella-MacDonald. (2002). "Media Attributions of Blame and Sympathy in Ten Rape Cases." *The Justice Professional* 15, 1: 3–18.

Ash, Amin. (2003). "Unruly Strangers? The 2001 Urban Riots in Britain." *International Journal of Urban and Regional Research* 27, 2: 460–63.

Banks, Mark. (2005). "Spaces of (In)security: Media and Fear of Crime in a Local Context." *Crime Media Culture* 1, 2: 169–87.

Barak, Gregg. (1995). *Media, Process, and the Social Construction of Crime: Studies in Newsmaking Criminology*. New York: Routledge.

Bazhaw, Melissa. (2008). "For Better or for Worse: Media Coverage of Marital Rape in the 1978 Rideout Trial." MA thesis, Georgia State.

Benedict, Helen. (1992). *Virgin or Vamp: How the Press Covers Sex Crimes*. New York: Oxford University Press.

Benett, Lance. (1988). *News: The Politics of Illusion*. New York: Longman.

Berger, Arthur Asa. (1988). *Media U.S.A.: Process and Effect*. New York: Longman.

Best, Joel. (1987). "Rhetoric in Claims-Making: Constructing the Missing Children Problem." *Social Problems* 34, 2: 101–21.

_____. (1990). *Threatened Children: Rhetoric and Concern about Child-Victims*. Chicago: University of Chicago Press.

Best, Joel, and Gerald Horiuchi. (1985). "The Razor Blade in the Apple: The Social Construction of Urban Legends." *Social Problems* 32, 5: 488–99.

Blendon, Robert, John Benson, Catherine DesRoches, Elizabeth Raleigh, and Kalahn Taylor-Clark. (2004). "The Public's Response to Severe Acute Respiratory Syndrome in Toronto and the United States." *Clinical Infectious Diseases* 38: 925–31.

Brodie, Mollyann, Elizabeth Hamel, Lee Ann Brady, Jennifer Kates, and Drew Altman. (2004). "AIDS at 21: Media Coverage of the HIV Epidemic 1981–2002." Supplement to the March/April 2004 issue of *Columbia Journalism Review*.

Bullock, Cathy Ferrand, and Jason Cubert. (2002) "Coverage of Domestic Violence Fatalities by Newspapers in Washington State." *Journal of Interpersonal Violence* 17, 5: 475–99.

Burns, Ronald, and Lindsey Orrick. (2002). "Assessing Newspaper Coverage of Corporate Violence: The Dance Hall Fire in Qoteborg, Sweden." *Critical Criminology* 11, 2.

Carll, Elizabeth. (2003). "News Portrayal of Violence and Women: Implications for Public Policy." *American Behavioral Scientist* 16, 12.

Carriere, Kevin, and Richard Ericson. (1989). *Crime Stoppers: A Study in the Organization of Community Policing.* University of Toronto: Centre of Criminology.

Chadee, Derek, and Jason Dixon. (2005.) "Fear of Crime and the Media: Assessing the Lack of Relationship." *Crime Media Culture* 1, 3: 322–32.

Cheit, Ross. (2003). "What Hysteria? A Systematic Study of Newspaper Coverage of Accused Child Molesters." *Child Abuse & Neglect* 27: 607–23.

Chiricos, Ted, and Sarah Escholz. (2002). "The Racial and Ethnic Typification of Crime and the Criminal Typification of Race and Ethnicity in Local Television News." *Journal of Research in Crime and Delinquency* 39, 4: 400–20.

Chiricos, Ted, Sarah Eschholz and Marc Gertz. (1997). "Crime, News and Fear of Crime: Toward an Identification of Audience Effects." *Social Problems* 44, 3: 342–57.

Chomsky, Noam. (1989). *Necessary Illusions: Thought Control in Democratic Societies.* Toronto: CBC.

Cohen, Stanley. (1972). *Folk Devils and Moral Panics: The Creation of the Mods and Rockers.* St. Albans, UK: Paladin.

Commentary. (2001). "From Oldham to Bradford: The Violence of the Violated." *Race & Class* 43, 2: 105–31.

D'Arcy, Stephen. (2007). "The 'Jamaican Criminal' in Toronto, 1994: A Critical Ontology." *Canadian Journal of Communication* 32, 2.

Davis, F. James. (1973). "Crime News in Colorado Newspapers." In S. Cohen and J. Young (eds.), *The Manufacture of News: Social Problems, Deviance and the Mass Media.* London: Constable.

Ditton, Jason. (2005). "Crime and the Fear of Media." *Criminal Justice Matters* 59, 1: 4–5.

Dixon, Travis. (2008a). "Crime News and Racialized Beliefs: Understanding the Relationship Between Local News Viewing and Perceptions of African Americans and Crime." *Journal of Communication* 58: 106–25.

———. (2008b). "Who Is the Victim Here? The Psychological Effects of Overrepresenting White Victims and Black Perpetrators on Television News." *Journalism* 9, 5: 582–605.

Doob, Anthony, and Glenn Macdonald. (1979). "Television Viewing and Fear of Victimization: Is the Relationship Causal?" *Journal of Personality and Social Psychology* 37, 2: 170–79.

Dor, Daniel. (2003). "On Newspaper Headlines as Relevance Optimizers." *Journal of Pragmatics* 35: 695–721.

Dowler, Kenneth. (2003). "Media Consumption and Public Attitudes Toward Crime and Justice: The Relationship Between Fear of Crime, Punitive Attitudes, and Perceived Police Effectiveness." *Journal of Criminal Justice and Popular Culture* 10, 2: 109–26.

Dowler, Ken, Thomas Fleming, Stephen Muzzatti. (2006). "Constructing Crime: Media, Crime, and Popular Culture." *Canadian Journal of Criminology and Criminal Justice* 48, 6.

Doyle, Vincent. (2000). "Lead Us Not Into Temptation: The London, Ontario 'Kiddie-Porn Ring' and the Construction of a Moral Panic." *International Journal of Canadian Studies* 21.

Eagleton, Jennifer. (2004). "SARS: 'It's as Bad as We Feared but Dared Not Say':

Naming, Managing and Dramatizing the SARS Crisis in Hong Kong." *English Today* 77, 20, 1.

Eichelberger, Laura. (2007). "SARS and New York's Chinatown: The Politics of Risk and Blame During an Epidemic of Fear." *Social Science & Medicine* 65: 1284–95.

Entman, Robert. (1993). "Framing: Toward Clarification of a Fractured Paradigm." *Journal of Communication* 43, 4: 51–58.

_____. (1994). "Representation and Reality in the Portrayal of Blacks on Network Television News." *Journalism Quarterly* 71: 509–20.

Ericson, Richard. (1991). "Mass Media, Crime, Law, and Justice: An Institutional Approach." *British Journal of Criminology* 31, 3: 219–49.

Ericson, Richard V., Patricia M. Baranek and Janet B.L. Chan. (1987). *Visualizing Deviance: A Study of News Organization.* Toronto: UTP.

_____. (1989). *Negotiating Control: A Study of News Sources.* Toronto: UTP.

_____. (1991). *Representing Order: Crime, Law, and Justice in the News Media.* Toronto: UTP.

Escholz, Darah, Ted Chiricos, and Nark Gertz. (2003). "Television and Fear of Crime: Program Types, Audience Traits, and the Mediating Effect of Perceived Neighborhood Racial Composition." *Social Problems* 50, 3: 395–415.

Escholz, Sarah. (2002). "Racial Composition of Television Offenders and Viewers' Fear of Crime." *Critical Criminology* 11: 41–60.

Eyres, John, and David Altheide. (1999). "News Themes and Ethnic Identity: Los Angeles Times News Reports of Vietamese, Black, and Hispanic Gangs." *Perspectives on Social Problems* 11: 85–103.

Fasiolo, Raffaele, and Steven Leckie. (1993). *Canadian Media Coverage of Gangs: A Content Analysis.* No. 1993—14. Ottawa: Solicitor General.

Fawcett, Brian. (1986). *Cambodia: A Book forPpeople who Find Television too Slow.* Vancouver: Talonbooks.

Ferrell, Jeff. (1993). *Crimes of Style: Urban Graffiti and the Politics of Criminality.* New York: Garland.

Fishman, Mark. (1978). "Crime Waves as Ideology." *Social Problems* 25, 5: 531–43.

Fitzgerald, Amy. (2009). "'It's a Horrible Coincidence': Corporate Responsibility and the 2007 Pet Food Recall." *Critical Criminology* 17, 3.

Fleming, Thomas. (2007). "The History of Violence: Mega Cases of Serial Murder, Self-Propelling Narratives, and Reader Engagement." *Journal of Criminal Justice and Popular Culture* 14, 3.

Fritz, Noah, and David Altheide. (1987). "The Mass Media and the Social Construction of the Missing Children Problem." *The Sociological Quarterly* 28, 4: 473–92.

Garland, David. (2008). "On the Concept of Moral Panic." *Crime Media Culture* 4, 1: 9–30.

Gaver, Martha. (1987). "Pictures of Sickness: Stuart Marshall's 'Bright Eyes.'" *October* 43: 108–26. AIDS: Cultural Analysis/Cultural Activism.

Gebotys, Robert, Julian Roberts and Bikram DasGupta. (1988). "News Media Use and Public Perceptions of Crime Seriousness." *Canadian Journal of Criminology* 30, 1: 3–16.

Gilliam, Franklin, Nicholas Valentino, and Matthew Beckmann. (2002). "Where You Live and What You Watch: The Impact of Racial Proximity and Local Television News on Attitudes about Race and Crime." *Political Research Quarterly* 55, 4: 755–80.

Gilman, Sander. (1987). "AIDS and Syphilis: The Iconography of Disease." *AIDS: Cultural Analysis/Cultural Activism* 43, October: 87–107.

Glassner, Barry. (1999). "The Construction of Fear." *Qualitative Sociology* 22, 4.

Greer, Chris. (2004). "Crime, Media and Community: Grief and Virtual Engagement in Late Modernity." In Jeff Ferrell et al., (eds.), *Cultural Criminology Unleashed*. London: Glasshouse.

Grenier, Marc (ed.). (1992). *Critical Studies of Canadian Mass Media*. Toronto: Butterworths.

Gross, Kimberly, and Sean Aday. (2003). "The Scary World in Your Living Room and Neighborhood: Using Local Broadcast News, Neighborhood Crime Rates, and Personal Experience to Test Agenda Setting and Cultivation." *Journal of Communication* September.

Guillen, Thomas. (2002). "Serial Killer Communiques: Helpful or Hurtful." *Journal of Criminal Justice and Popular Culture* 9, 2: 55–68.

Haggerty, Kevin. (2009). "Modern Serial Killers." *Crime Media Culture* 5: 168.

Hailey, Arthur. (1990). *The Evening News*. New York: Doubleday.

Hall, Stuart, Chas Critcher, Tony Jefferson, John Clarke and Brian Roberts. (1978). *Policing the Crisis: Mugging, the State, and Law and Order*. London: Macmillan.

Hallgrimsdottir, Helga Kristin, Rachel Phillips, and Cecilia Benoit. (2006). "Fallen Women and Rescued Girls: Social Stigma and Media Narratives of the Sex." *Canadian Review of Sociology and Anthropology* 43, 3.

Harcup, Tony. (2003). "'The Unspoken—Said': The Journalism of Alternative Media." *Journalism* 4: 356.

Hayward, Keith, and Yar Majid. (2006). "The 'Chav' Phenomenon: Consumption, Media and the Construction of a New Underclass." *Crime Media Culture* 2, 1: 9–28.

Herman, Edward, and Noam Chomsky. (1988). *Manufacturing Consent: The Political Economy of the Mass Media*. New York: Pantheon.

Herman, Edward, and Gerry O'Sullivan. (1989). *The 'Terrorism Industry': The Experts and Institutions that Shape Our View of Terror*. New York: Pantheon.

Herrmann, Robert, and Rex Warland, (2000). "Awareness of an Unfamiliar Food Safety Hazard: Listeria 1999." *Consumer Interests* 46.

Hier, Sean. (2003). "Risk and Panic in Late Modernity: Implications of the Converging Sites of Social Anxiety." *British Journal of Sociology* 54, 1: 3–20.

Holmes, Helen, and David Taras (eds.). (1992). *Seeing Ourselves: Media Power and Policy in Canada*. Toronto: Harcourt Brace.

Jarvis, Brian. (2007). "Monsters Inc.: Serial Killers and Consumer Culture." *Crime Media Culture* 3: 326.

Jefferson, Tony. (2008). "Policing the Crisis Revisited: The State, Masculinity, Fear of Crime and Racism." *Crime Media Culture* 4, 1: 113–21.

Jenkins, Philip. (1992). *Intimate Enemies: Moral Panics in Contemporary Great Britain*. London: Aldine de Gruyter.

Jiwani, Yasmin, and Mary Lynn Young. (2006). "Missing and Murdered Women: Reproducing Marginality in News Discourse." *Canadian Journal of Communication* 31.

Kinsella, James. (1989). *Covering the Plague: AIDS and the American Media*. New Brunswick: Rutgers University Press.

Klein, Roger, and Stacy Naccarato. (2003). "Broadcast News Portrayal of Minorities: Accuracy in Reporting." *American Behavioral Scientist* 46, 12: 1611–16.

end

Kurtz, Howard. (1994). *Media Circus: The Trouble with America's Newspapers*. New York: Random.

Lamb, Sharon, and Susan Keon. (1995). "Blaming the Perpetrator: Language that Distorts Reality in Newspaper Articles on Men Battering Women." *Psychology of Women Quarterly* 19: 209–20.

Lee, Martin, and Norman Solomon. (1990). *Unreliable Sources: A Guide to Detecting Bias in News Media.* New York: Lyle Stuart.

Lippert, Randy. (1990). "The Social Construction of Satanism as a Social Problem in Canada." *Canadian Journal of Sociology* 15, 4: 417–39.

_____. (2002). "Policing Property and Moral Risk through Promotions, Anonymization and Rewards: Crime Stoppers Revisited." *Social and Legal Studies* 11, 4: 475–502.

Lofquist, William. (1997). "Constructing 'Crime': Media Coverage of Individual and Organizational Wrongdoing." *Justice Quarterly* 14, 2: 243–63.

Lowman, John. (2000). "Violence and the Outlaw Status of (Street) Prostitution in Canada." *Violence Against Women* 6, 9: 987–1011.

Lowry, Dennis T., T.C.J. Nio and D.W. Leitner. (2003). "Setting the Public Fear Agenda: A Longitudinal Analysis of Network TV Crime Reporting, Public Perceptions of Crime, and FBI Crime Statistics." *Journal of Communications* 53, 1: 61–73.

Lubbers, Marcel, Peer Scheepers, and Maurice Vergeer. (2000). "Exposure to Newspapers and Attitudes toward Ethnic Minorities: A Longitudinal Analysis." *The Howard Journal of Communications* 11: 127–43.

Lupton, Deborah. (1993). "AIDS Risk and Heterosexuality in the Australian Press." *Discourse and Society* 4, 3: 307–28.

Lupton, Deborah, and John Tulloch. (1999). "Theorizing Fear of Crime: Beyond the Rational/Irrational Opposition." *British Journal of Sociology* 50, 3: 507–23.

Lynch, Michael, Paul Stretesky, and Paul Hammond. (2000). "Media Coverage of Chemical Crimes, Hillsborough County, Florida, 1987–97." *British Journal of Criminology* 40: 112–26.

Macmillan, Barry. (2002). "Scapegoating in a Time of Crisis." *The Furrow* May.

Maguire, Brendan. (2002). "Television Network News Coverage of Corporate Crime From 1970–2000." *Western Criminology Review* 3, 2.

Maguire, Brendan, Georgie Weatherby, and Richard Mathers. (2002). "Network News Coverage of School Shootings." *The Social Science Journal* 39, 3: 465–70.

Manoff, Robert Karl, and Michael Schudson (eds.). (1986). *Reading the News: A Pantheon Guide to Popular Culture*. New York: Pantheon.

Mastroa, Dana, and Amanda Robertson. (2000). "Cops and Crooks. Images of Minorities on Prime Time Television." *Journal of Criminal Justice* 28: 385–96.

McKibben, Bill. (1992). *The Age of Missing Information*. New York: Random House.

McLuhan, Marshall. (1964). *Understanding Media: The Extensions of Man*. New York: Signet.

McLuhan, Marshall, and Quentin Fiore. (1967). *The Medium Is the Massage: An Inventory of Effects*. Toronto: Bantam.

McMullan, John, and Melissa McClung. (2006). "The Media, the Politics of Truth, and the Coverage of Corporate Violence: the Westray Disaster and the Public Inquiry." *Critical Criminology* 14: 67–86.

Messner, Michael, and William Solomon. (1993). Outside the Frame: Newspaper Coverage of the Sugar Ray Leonard Wife Abuse Story." *Sociology of Sport Journal* 10: 119–34.

Mills, Kay. (1990). *A Place in the News: From the Women's Pages to the Front Page*. New York: Columbia.

Myers, Daniel. (2000). "The Diffusion of Collective Violence: Infectiousness, Susceptibility, and Mass Media Networks." *American Journal of Sociology* 106, 1: 173–208.

Navarre, Max. (1987). "Fighting the Victim Label." *October* 43: 143–46. AIDS: Cultural Analysis/Cultural Activism.

Pitman, Beverly. (2002). "Re-mediating the Spaces of Reality Television: America's Most Wanted and the Case of Vancouver's Missing Women." *Environment and Planning A* 34.

Postman, Neil, and Steve Powers. (1992). *How to Watch TV News*. New York: Penguin.

Poynting, Scott. (2007). "What Caused the Cronulla riot?" *Race & Class* 48, 1.

Raimondo, Meredith. (2003). "'Corralling the Virus': Migratory Sexualities and the 'Spread of AIDS' in the US Media." *Environment and Planning D: Society and Space* 21: 389–407.

Richardson, John. (2001). "'Now Is the Time to Put an End to all This': Argumentative Discourse Theory and 'Letters to the Editor'." *Discourse & Society* 12, 2: 143–68.

Roche, John. (2002). "Print Media Coverage of Risk–Risk Tradeoffs Associated with West Nile Encephalitis and Pesticide Spraying." *Journal of Urban Health* 79, 4.

Romanow, Walter I., and Walter C. Soderlund. (1992). *Media Canada: An Introductory Analysis*. Toronto: Copp Clark Pitman.

Romer, Daniel, Katheen Hal Jamieson, and Sean Aday. (2003). "Television News and the Cultivation of Fear of Crime." *Journal of Communication* 53, 1: 88–104.

Russell, Adrienne. (2007). "Digital Communication Networks and the Journalistic Field: The 2005 French Riots." *Critical Studies in Media Communication* 24, 4: 285–302.

Ryan, Charlotte, Mike Anastario, and Alfredo DaCunha. (2006). "Changing Coverage of Domestic Violence Murders: A Longitudinal Experiment in Participatory Communication." *Journal of Interpersonal Violence* 21, 2: 209–28.

Sabato, Larry J. (1991). *Feeding Frenzy: How Attack Journalism has Transformed American Politics*. New York: Free Press.

Saxton, Alison. (2003). "'I Certainly Don't Want People Like That Here': The Discursive Construction of 'Asylum Seekers'." *Media International Australia, Incorporating Culture & Policy* 109.

Shih, Tsung-Jen, Rosalyna Wijaya, and Dominique Brossard. (2008). "Media Coverage of Public Health Epidemics: Linking Framing and Issue Attention Cycle Toward an Integrated Theory of Print News Coverage of Epidemics." *Mass Communication & Society* 11: 141–60.

Shilts, Randy. (1987). *And the Band Played On: Politics, People, and the AIDS Epidemic*. New York: Penguin.

Shutt, Eagle, Mitchell Miller, Christopher Schreck, and Nancy Brown. (2004). "Reconsidering the Leading Myths of Stranger Child Abduction." *Criminal Justice Studies* 17, 1: 127–34.

Silveirinha, Maria João. (2007). "Displacing the 'Political': The 'Personal' in the Media Public Sphere." *Feminist Media Studies* 7, 1.

Simmons, Katie, and Amanda LeCouteur. (2008). «Modern Racism in the Media: Constructions of 'the Possibility of Change' in Accounts of two Australian 'Riots'." *Discourse & Society* 19, 5: 667–87.

Slingerland, Wade, Heith Copes, and John Sloan. (2006). "Media Construction of White-Collar Violence Revisited: An Examination of Two Nightclub Tragedies." *Deviant Behavior* 27, 4: 423–55.

Sontag, Susan. (1990). *Illness as Metaphor: AIDS and its Metaphors*. New York: Anchor.

Soothill, Keith. (1991). "The Changing Face of Rape." *British Journal of Criminology* 31, 4.

Soothill, Keith, and Sylvia Walby. (1991). *Sex Crime in the News*. London: Routledge.

Stephens, Mitchell. (1988). *A History of News: From the Drum to the Satellite.* Harmondsworth: Penguin.

Stillman, Sarah. (2007). "'The Missing White Girl Syndrome': Disappeared Women and Media Activism." *Gender & Development* 15, 3: 491–502.

Surette, Ray. (1990). *The Media and Criminal Justice Policy: Recent Research and Social Effects.* Springfield, IL: C.C. Thomas.

_____. (1992). *Media, Crime and Criminal Justice: Images and Realities*. Pacific Grove: Brooks/Cole.

Taylor, Rae. (2009). "Slain and Slandered: A Content Analysis of the Portrayal of Femicide in Crime News." *Homicide Studies* 13, 1: 21–49.

Treichler, Paula. (1987). "AIDS, Homophobia, and Biomedical Discourse: An Epidemic of Signification." In Douglas Crimp (ed.), *AIDS: Cultural Analysis/ Cultural Activism*. Cambridge: MIT.

Walby, Sylvia, Alex Hill, and Keith Soothill. (1983). "The Social Construction of Rape." *Theory, Culture and Society* 2, 1.

Wallis, Patrick, and Brigitte Nerlich. (2005). "Disease Metaphors in New Epidemics: The UK Media Framing of the 2003 SARS Epidemic." *Social Science & Medicine* 60: 2629–39

Warner, Kate. (2004). "Gang Rape in Sydney: Crime, the Media, Politics, Race and Sentencing." *Australian and New Zealand Journal of Criminology* 37, 3: 344–61.

Warwick, Alexandra. (2006). "The Scene of the Crime: Inventing the Serial Killer." *Social and Legal Studies* 15, 4: 552–69.

Washer, Peter. (2004). "Representations of SARS in the British Newspapers." *Social Science and Medicine* 59: 2561–71.

Watney, Simon. (1987). "The Spectacle of AIDS." *October* 43: 71-86. AIDS: Cultural Analysis/Cultural Activism.

Weitzer, Ronald, and Steven Tuch. (2004). "Race and Perceptions of Police Misconduct." *Social Problems* 51, 3: 305–25.

Welch, Michael, Eric Price, and Nana Yankey. (2002). "Moral Panic over Youth Violence: Wilding and the Manufacture of Menace in the Media." *Youth and Society* 34 1: 3–30.

Wortley, Scot, John Hagan, and Ross Macmillan. (1997). "Just Des(s)erts? The Racial Polarization of Perceptions of Criminal Injustice." *Law & Society Review* 31, 4: 637–76.

Wright, John, Francis Cullen, and Michael Blankenship. (1995). "The Social Construction of Corporate Violence: Media Coverage of the Imperial Food Products Fire." *Crime and Delinqency* 41, 1: 20–36.

Young, Jason. (2003). "The Role of Fear in Agenda Setting by Television News." *American Behavioral Scientist* 46, 12: 1673–95.

Zgoba, Kristen. (2004). "Spin Doctors and Moral Crusaders: The Moral Panic behind Child Safety Legislation." *Criminal Justice Studies* 17, 4: 385–404.

Contributors

Anne Derrick, formerly with Buchan, Derrick and Ring in Halifax, was appointed a provincial/family court judge in 2005. Admitted to the bar in 1981, her practice involved public interest and equality litigation, criminal law and social justice advocacy. She represented women working as prostitutes against a civil injunction brought by the Attorney General in 1984, Donald Marshall Jr. before two royal commissions, Dr. Henry Morgentaler before the Supreme Court and *Pandora Magazine*, whose policy to publish material only by women made it the subject of a human rights hearing.

Debi Forsyth-Smith was president of the Nova Scotia Advisory Council on the Status of Women from 1987 to 1993 and served as chief of staff for the Leader of the Official Opposition in Nova Scotia. She has served on the Dalhousie University's Medical School task force on violence against women, children and the elderly, and on the boards of MediaWatch and the Service for Sexual Assault Victims.

Sharon Fraser is a former editor of rabble.ca who worked for a number of years as a freelance journalist and broadcaster. She contributed to regional and national media outlets, including *This Magazine*, CBC Radio and Television, *Canadian Forum* and *Catholic New Times* on political, social and cultural issues. She contributed publications on current affairs, women's issues, the fishery, culture and politics. She has taught university classes in women's studies and journalism, and wrote a column on women's issues for the *Halifax Daily News*.

Gary Kinsman studied at the Ontario Institute for Studies in Education, at the University of Toronto. He teaches sociology at Laurentian University and previously taught at Memorial and Acadia. He is the author of *The Regulation of Desire* and is also a gay, AIDS and socialist activist.

Paul MacDonald was a constable (now retired) in the Halifax Police Department, and worked as the media relations officer and also as the community policing officer.

Joy Mannette is a professor at York University in Toronto, where she teaches in the Education Department. She is perhaps best known for her work on the Marshall Inquiry and working on treaty issues with the Mi'kmaq First Nation. She is the author of *Elusive Justice*, a book on the Marshall Inquiry.

Chris McCormick is a professor in the Department of Criminology and Criminal Justice at St. Thomas University. He has published books on the history of criminal justice, criminological theory and corporate crime. He teaches courses on crime and media, wrongful convictions, cultural criminology and visual studies of deviance.

Darrel Pink studied at Acadia, Dalhousie and the London School of Economics. He has been a lecturer at the Dalhousie Law School, on the board of directors of the Metro United Way, president of the Children's Aid Society of Halifax and executive director of the Nova Scotia Barrister's Society and has served on several committees of the Canadian Jewish Congress.

Eric Smith fought a long but ultimately unsuccessful battle to regain his post as a teacher after his confidentiality as an HIV-positive person was violated. He often represented the Persons Living with AIDS Coalition.

Tony Thomson is a professor in the Department of Sociology at Acadia University. He has done research on policing, young offenders and child abuse.

Deborah Woolway was the executive producer for news and current affairs at CBC Radio in Halifax and now co-hosts *Maritime Noon*. She has an undergraduate degree from the University of Toronto and a bachelor's in journalism from Carleton University. In 1988, she won a Canadian Bar Association Scales of Justice Award for her work on the Donald Marshall Inquiry.